FUNDAMENTALS OF

Track and Field

Gerry A. Carr, PhD
University of Victoria

Leisure Press
Champaign, Illinois

Library of Congress Cataloging-in-Publication Data

Carr, Gerald A., 1936-
    Fundamentals of track and field / by Gerry A. Carr.
        p.   cm.
    Includes bibliographical references (p.   ).
    ISBN 0-88011-388-X
    1. Track-athletics.   I. Title.
    GV1060.5.C368   1991
    796.42--dc20   90-34880
                                                       CIP

ISBN: 0-88011-388-X

Acquisitions Editor: Brian Holding
Developmental Editor: June I. Decker, PhD
Managing Editor: Dawn Levy
Assistant Editors: Valerie Hall and Robert King
Copyeditor: Julie Anderson
Proofreader: Linda Siegel
Production Director: Ernie Noa
Typesetters: Angela K. Snyder and Brad Colson
Text Design: Keith Blomberg
Text Layout: Denise Lowry
Cover Design: Jack Davis
Cover Photos: Dave Black
Interior Art: Sandra Dailey, Karen Ostrom, and Beth Tarasuk
Printer: Versa Press

Leisure Press books are available at special discounts for bulk purchase. Special editions or book excerpts can also be created to specification. For details, contact the Special Sales Manager at Human Kinetics.

Printed in the United States of America   10 9 8 7

Leisure Press
A Division of Human Kinetics
Web site: http://www.humankinetics.com

United States: Human Kinetics, P.O. Box 5076, Champaign, IL 61825-5076
1-800-747-4457
e-mail: humank@hkusa.com

Canada: Human Kinetics, Box 24040, Windsor, ON N8Y 4Y9
1-800-465-7301 (in Canada only)
e-mail: humank@hkcanada.com

Europe: Human Kinetics, P.O. Box IW14, Leeds LS16 6TR, United Kingdom
(44) 1132 781708
e-mail: humank@hkeurope.com

Australia: Human Kinetics, 57A Price Avenue, Lower Mitcham, South Australia 5062
(08) 277 1555
e-mail: humank@hkaustralia.com

New Zealand: Human Kinetics, P.O. Box 105-231, Auckland 1
(09) 523 3462
e-mail: humank@hknewz.com

CONTENTS

FOREWORD

There are numerous books on the technique of track and field, but few are devoted exclusively to teaching the various events. *Fundamentals of Track and Field* is the most in-depth and meticulous treatment of grass roots teaching of the sport to raw beginners that I have read. Gerry Carr is eminently qualified to author this book by reason of his personal athletic career, academic background, and long and successful teaching and coaching career.

Dr. Carr was an Olympic finalist representing Great Britain in the discus, participated in the same event while representing UCLA during his undergraduate days, and engaged in top-level European competition over an extended period. He has taught track and field and coached at the University of Victoria for more than 20 years.

Teaching track and field to beginners is difficult business. Dr. Carr has wisely divided the various skills into parts that lead the learner in sequential steps to the performance of each event as a whole. Unique features of his book include coaching tips, performance standards according to age and sex, and error corrections where applicable to individual events.

This book is not for elite champion athletes. It was written strictly for beginners. Coaches and teachers of youngsters just learning the skills of track and field will agree that the focus of its contents is directly on target.

Fred Wilt
Coordinator of Coaches Education
The Athletics Congress

PREFACE

The idea for writing this text developed from discussions with a number of physical educators and teachers. All were faced with the difficult task of teaching track and field to novices using limited equipment and with severe time restrictions. These educators indicated that material containing the following items was needed:

- a large number of well-illustrated lead-up activities from which to make selections;
- a series of highly illustrated drills and coaching tips;
- suggestions for planning the track and field program as well as individual instructional sessions;
- methods for improving the level of safety during instructional sessions, particularly when teaching jumping and throwing events;
- descriptions of major errors that youngsters are likely to commit and advice on how to eliminate such errors;
- ideas for graded competitions that can be used at different stages in the learning process;
- suggestions for assessing performance; and
- standards which can be used as a guide for awarding grades.

These physical educators and teachers also felt that information dealing with the intricacies of track and field rules and regulations was less important, particularly because this information is available in related literature. Consequently, *Fundamentals of Track and Field* concentrates on teaching progressions, drills, and problems of organization and assessment.

This material is written for the instructor working at the grass roots level, and the book covers not only popular events but also events frequently omitted from many track and field manuals. You will find excellent teaching progressions for the 400-meter hurdles, hammer, triple jump, pole vault, and steeplechase. These events have been included because they are becoming increasingly popular at all age levels and with both genders. The trend in track and field is to make more events available to females rather than continue to limit competition in certain events to males. Also, these events have been included to demonstrate that the basic skills that these events require can be safely taught to young students by using modified equipment and substitutes for competitive implements.

Fundamentals of Track and Field offers a wealth of information to help solve organizational and teaching problems that you will face. The book emphasizes the use of teaching techniques that will make track and field a pleasurable experience. While enjoying the challenge and diversity that is offered in the lead-ups and drills, your young athletes will improve in performance and at the same time experience great satisfaction.

Please note that unless otherwise indicated material in this book describes the actions of a right-handed performer.

ACKNOWLEDGMENTS

My thanks are due to Sandra Dailey, Beth Tarasuk, and Karen Ostrom for their assistance with the illustrations and diagrams used in this text.

I am also indebted to William H. Freeman for reviewing the manuscript and for his invaluable advice and suggestions.

PLANNING AND ORGANIZING TRACK AND FIELD PROGRAMS

The block of time allocated to a track and field program must be carefully organized. You must define the overall intent (or goal) of the program and decide which particular events you will teach. When time is limited, you may decide to lead the whole class for the entire class period and only teach the basics of one or two events. In a more favorable setting, you may start out with the whole class as a unit and then move to a station approach after teaching certain events. With this arrangement, different events are practiced at each station and you move freely from station to station.

DETERMINING WHAT TO TEACH

The number of events taught in a block of time allocated to track and field will depend upon the following.

- The time available
- The ages, abilities, and maturity levels of the students
- Your knowledge and experience

- Your ability to establish a level of control and discipline such that group activities can operate safely and successfully
- The class size in relation to available equipment and space
- The availability of assistants and the possibility of team teaching.

Which event should be introduced first, second, or third in the program? Here are some questions to consider.

- Will available equipment allow large numbers of students to be actively involved?
- Does an event provide a foundation or background for another event and so provide a teaching sequence that you can follow?
- Does the event allow coed participation?

Events that are fundamental, require the minimum of equipment, and allow a large mixed group to be actively involved (such as sprints, distance running, and relays) should be introduced early in the track and field program. Begin with these events and thereafter work toward events that are best taught at stations.

The following list outlines the major characteristics of each event and will help you plan and organize a track and field program.

Running Events

Some running events (such as hurdles and steeplechase) require considerable equipment. Other running events (such as sprinting, relays, and distance running) do not. Begin with those that require little or no equipment and move to those which require equipment.

Sprinting and Sprint Starts

Sprinting is a basic locomotor skill and is fundamental to track and field. Sprinting requires little more than a good running surface; maximum activity can be achieved without the use of equipment. As such, sprinting forms an excellent introduction to the track and field program. Although sprinting is a pleasurable activity, repetition can quickly make the activity tedious; it is advisable to make sprinting part of other activities and events such as minor games, relays, hurdles, long jump, and triple jump.

Relays

Relay racing is one of the most enjoyable activities in track and field. This activity demands little equipment and can be practiced both indoors and outdoors. Relays add the excitement of team competition to sprinting. They are frequently used as a means of adding spice to warm-ups and to a workout's culminating activities.

Hurdles

You can introduce hurdles early in the track and field program by using substitutes for competitive equipment. Bamboo canes laid across traffic cones give added organizational flexibility in that novices can hurdle in both directions. Foam-rubber practice hurdles are excellent for reducing the fear of hitting the hurdle, and scissor-style practice hurdles can be lowered to accommodate the smallest class member. Sprint starts and shuttle relays (which require runners to sprint back and forth) combine well with hurdling, particularly if the practice hurdle is designed to be approached from either direction.

The rhythm and pacing taught in hurdling are important lead-up skills for long jump and triple jump. For this reason, it is excellent planning to teach hurdling prior to these events. Hurdling also serves as preparation for steeplechase. The 400-meter hurdles is best introduced to mature athletes who have backgrounds in sprint hurdling (100/110-meter hurdles) and sprint endurance training.

Distance Running and Steeplechase

Distance running is an all-year activity and like sprinting and relays requires only a good running surface. Variations in pace, distance, and terrain (e.g., track or trails) make this activity more enjoyable. Because of its cardiovascular benefits, distance running should be introduced early to young athletes and made a regular part of their physical education programs. Many of the elements of steeplechase are taught in distance running, especially in cross country running, which requires the athlete to cross ditches, water jumps, and other obstacles.

Throwing Events

One of the best ways to teach the complex technique of throwing events and still maintain a high level of safety is through the use of safe, easy-to-handle substitutes for the competitive implements. Besides increasing safety, substitutes help to simplify difficult techniques and allow the novice to concentrate on 1 technical element at a time. Substituting rubber rings for discuses, or balls for shots and javelins, you can teach the fundamentals of the throws to the whole class at the same time.

Introducing Throwing Events

Begin by using lightweight, safe substitutes for competitive implements. If there is enough of this kind of equipment, introduce the event as a whole-class activity. If you don't have enough equipment, introduce the event as a station activity with instructor supervision.

If you have enough competitive implements, the entire class can use these after learning the event with substitute equipment. If not, teach first with substitute equipment and then use competitive equipment when the class is split in groups and practicing at stations. If both substitute and competitive equipment are limited, teach first using substitute equipment in stations, then refine the skill with stations utilizing competitive equipment. Provide instruction and supervision at the station where students are using the competitive equipment.

Javelin

Of all the throwing events, the javelin throw most closely resembles the normal throwing action. Using balls instead of the javelin, you can easily teach the required technique as a whole-class activity. Because the basic throwing action is less complex than other throwing events, javelin throwing (using balls) is one of the first throwing events introduced.

Shot Put

Modern shot put features both the glide and the rotational technique. The glide technique is more popular and is considered the easier technique; for this reason, the glide technique is introduced first. The rotational technique is based on the movement pattern used in the discus throw. This technique should be taught after the glide technique has been mastered, after the rotational discus throw has been taught, and only as an experimental technique for mature athletes practicing under instructor supervision.

The basic elements of shot put using the glide are easy to learn, and as with javelin, students can quickly achieve moderate levels of success. You can teach fundamentals as a whole-class activity, using tennis balls filled with lead shot and bound in tape, medicine balls, softballs, or baseballs. If these are not available and you have only a small selection of competitive shot, divide the class into groups and teach the shot put as a station activity.

Discus

The discus throw is a rotational event, and difficulties with footwork and handhold make it more complex than shot put or javelin. You should teach this event after introducing nonrotational events (e.g., javelin and shot put). Rubber rings (quoits) and small ''hula hoops'' are good substitutes for the discus and eliminate problems of handhold while footwork is taught. Using this equipment, you can teach the fundamentals to a whole class. Discus throwing using the competitive implement then follows as a station event.

Hammer

The hammer is seldom taught in schools, and at the club level it generally has fewer devotees than other throwing events. This is unfortunate, because many consider the hammer to be one of the most satisfying and pleasurable of all throwing events. It also can be dangerous, and safety is obviously of paramount im-portance. The event requires a large area of land; this land can be used for other throwing events, but damage to the turf makes it unfit for other activities. Usually the hammer is last of all throwing events to be taught (if it is taught at all). Many instructors avoid this event because problems of safety (and turf damage) are simply too great.

You can safely teach the basic technique of hammer throw using substitutes for the competitive implement, such as a medicine ball in a net (see chapter 14). There is every indication that in the future this event will be open to both males and females, rather than to males only.

Jumping Events

The high jump, long jump, and triple jump are closely related in that their introductory and lead-up activities are very similar. However, these events differ in an organizational sense; it is far easier to keep a large group active in long jump and triple jump than in high jump.

The pole vault demands gymnastic ability and a certain degree of fearlessness. Because of its specific physical demands, the pole vault is normally taught as a station activity to a select group.

High Jump

Lead-up activities for high jump using no crossbar or using elastic surgical tubing as a crossbar can occur as whole-class activities. However, a single high jump used by a large class means wasted time and minimal activity for each individual.

Once you have some idea of each individual's high-jumping ability, you can group students of similar abilities together and position the high jump as a station event. When each group rotates to the high jump, the amount of time lost in altering heights is reduced. Using elastic surgical tubing in place of a metal crossbar not only eliminates the time taken in replacing the crossbar after a foul jump but also eliminates the discomfort of falling on top of a crossbar.

Because the flop technique of high jumping requires a deep, well-cushioned landing area, you should use large regulation-size landing pads, irrespective of the height jumped. The substitution of gymnastic crash pads for regulation pads is not recommended.

Long Jump

The construction of large jumping pits is one of the simplest and cheapest improvements you can make to assist instruction in track and field. Run-ups can approach from both ends, and a wide pit allows several participants to jump simultaneously from the side rather than waiting in line at the end of a run-up. Long jump should be one of the first jumping events you introduce in the program. You can teach this event in combination with triple jump, or the event can even follow the triple jump in the teaching sequence. You can teach these 2 jumping events immediately after sprinting, sprint starts, and relays.

Triple Jump

Although predominantly an event for males, triple jump is becoming more popular in women's track and field, and you should consider it an event for both sexes. Many instructors will teach the long jump after the triple jump, for several reasons. Rates of improvement in triple jump are much higher than for long jump, and this boosts enthusiasm. Also, most youngsters consider the triple jump a lot more fun than the long jump. Finally, the third jump in triple jump is an elementary long jump, and methods of teaching the run-up are similar for both events.

One factor to remember, though, is that the repetitive bounding of triple jump is particularly stressful for young athletes, and fatigue occurs very quickly. With this in mind, be ready to provide a tired group with alternative activities that are less demanding.

Pole Vault

Pole vault is seldom a class activity. It is usually taught as a station activity with the instructor assisting. You need short, light, flexible training poles and if possible an elevated ramp from which athletes can ride a pole down into sand. Irrespective of the students' levels of performance, large regulation-size landing pads are essential.

For even moderate levels of success, performers must be able to hang on the poles and have sufficient abdominal strength to elevate their legs to horizontal. In any instructional group, there will be those who cannot perform these actions. You should give these students the option of working at other events when their groups rotate to the pole-vault station.

MOVING FROM WHOLE-CLASS ACTIVITIES TO GROUP ACTIVITIES

You can organize groups when you want the class to practice more than 1 event at the same time. Start the class period teaching the class as a single unit,

and then after a series of lessons divide the class into two large groups. Then work with one group while the other practices activities previously taught. Increase the number of groups as you introduce more activities.

There are many ways to organize groups, and all methods have advantages and disadvantages. Whichever method you decide to use, set up the groups to assure maximum activity and trouble-free rotation from 1 activity to the next (i.e., from 1 station to the next).

The following suggestions will help you achieve smooth rotations.

- Begin by arranging students in groups according to height and weight.
- After you have introduced high jumping, consider a reorganization of groups based on high-jumping ability.
- Provide a large number of substitutes for competitive equipment, particularly in the throwing events. The cheapness of these items, in addition to their safety, means that events like the discus, shot, and javelin can be introduced as whole-class activities.
- Provide as wide a variation as possible of competitive equipment (e.g., discuses, javelins, shot, pole-vault poles, and practice hurdles). These will help you accommodate the huge ranges in body size and strength that will exist in any class.
- To satisfy differing levels of ability, place takeoffs at varying distances from jumping pits. If possible, build two large practice pits, one for the long jump and the other for the triple jump. If these pits are both long and wide, position takeoffs using short run-ups on grass and from the sides of the pits. Use takeoff areas rather than takeoff boards for long jump and triple jump; this not only speeds up the rate of jumping but boosts enthusiasm, because foul jumps are virtually eliminated.
- Measure throws with methods that are safe, fast, and easy to employ.
- Make pole vault an optional event for those whose strength–weight ratios prevent the students from hanging or swinging on a pole. These participants should have the option of working on other events.

PLANNING THE INDIVIDUAL INSTRUCTIONAL PERIOD

Individual instructional periods require you to make the same series of decisions made in planning a track and field program. Each period must have a series of objectives that are carefully planned and organized prior to instruction. Each objective should be followed systematically by the next, not only within individual instructional periods, but from one instruction period to the next.

Divide each instructional period into sections, each of which has its own specific objectives.

Introductory Section

The objectives of the introductory section are the physical and mental preparation of the participants for what will follow in the main section of the instructional period. The introductory section will contain warm-ups and stretching activities performed by the whole class as a unit and should last about 1/4 of the class period. During this section, you will explain the tasks that are to follow.

Some activities you might use in the introductory section include stretching and flexibility exercises specific to the event to be taught in the main section of the instructional period, or jogging and striding with progressive increases in speed. During the introductory section you can lead the class as a unit, or individuals can warm up according to their choices of event.

Main Section

The main section of the instructional period should last for about 1/2 the total time. The choice of objectives for the main section will depend on what progress has been made in previous classes. These objectives can be to learn an activity for an event not yet taught; to learn an activity that is designed to improve a technique or movement pattern in an event previously taught; or to assess performance in an activity you have already taught.

You can use the main section to introduce a new event. For example, to teach the basic movement patterns for the javelin event, give each participant a ball and teach the javelin-throw technique.

You can also use this time to refine and polish the technique of an event (e.g., eliminate minor errors and increase speed of movement in the javelin event using the competitive implement). A small group would practice this activity under instructor supervision.

A performance assessment might include a subjective assessment of an individual's technical performance with no assessment given for distance thrown, height jumped, or time run. (This might be an assess-

ment of a discus throw in which you check the athlete's ability to perform a standing throw with the discus.) Or, a performance assessment could be strictly based on distance, height, or time.

The organizational format will vary depending on the progress that the class has made. One format is to lead the class as a unit. Or, you can set up stations and spend time teaching at each station, moving from one station to the next. Groups may rotate from station to station and so practice different events. You can also allow students to work at their choices of event, while you move freely from 1 station to the other to give assistance where needed. You can even appoint some of your most skilled students to assist you in working with groups.

Closing Section

This section will occupy approximately 1/4 of the total class time. Objectives for this section will vary according to what occurred in the main section of the lesson.

The final section can include an activity that brings the class together as a unit (e.g., a warm-down during which you comment on the tasks that were completed and those that will occur in subsequent instructional periods). Or, this section can include an activity that is competitive and/or has aerobic value (e.g., a relay competition or a timed distance run). Follow this activity with a light warm-down coupled with wrap-up comments.

SUGGESTIONS FOR TEACHING TRACK AND FIELD SKILLS

Break each event down into a series of major components, each of which builds upon the prior component. This text refers to these components as *steps*. (For example, to put the shot using a glide, the student must first learn to put the shot from a standing position. The standing put is the first of a series of steps.) This text contains drills for each step, and each drill draws on the skills learned in the previous drill. You can view the refined technique of an event as a wall that has to be built. Each drill is an individual brick, each step a line of bricks. All bricks have to be in place for the wall to be complete. Likewise, the basic movement patterns must be learned thoroughly if the complex technique of the event is to be performed correctly. Teach these basic movement patterns first, and correct errors before students attempt the more complex movement patterns of the event.

Track and Field Skills as Movement Patterns

The drills used to teach a complex movement pattern must be taught in a particular sequence. This sequence is as follows:

1. Teach the basic movement pattern of the skill first. If necessary, break the movement pattern down into parts, and teach each part separately. Reducing the speed of movement when possible will assist in the learning process. In many track and field events (particularly the throws), teachers use substitutes for the competitive equipment because they simplify the learning process and allow the learner to move slowly through the required actions. With this method, you can eliminate errors before progressing to the next stage in the learning sequence.

2. Once you have taught and polished the basic movement pattern, add finer and more discrete movements. Again, correct errors before progressing further.

3. When students reach the final technique, instruct them to repeat it frequently so that it becomes as familiar as possible. Then, have students progressively increase their speeds of movement.

Correcting Errors in Performance

Errors in the performance of a complex physical skill vary in type and intensity. Beginners tend to commit fundamental errors that involve mistiming and incorrect movement of major body parts. Experienced performers, on the other hand, tend to commit two types of errors. The first includes variations and idiosyncracies that minimally affect performance. The second includes major faults in technique that are learned early and become ingrained during repetitions of the skill; these are particularly difficult to correct.

To correct errors of any type, you must have a reasonable biomechanical understanding of the skill and an ability to give instructions that the performer can easily understand.

First, watch the skill being performed, and carefully observe the sequence of actions and the timing that is used. As you watch a young athlete putting the shot, for example, ask yourself these questions.

1. Are the initial stance and the subsequent movement of the body as a whole technically correct? Or is the athlete staying in the same spot instead of moving toward the direction of the throw?

2. Are individual actions performed correctly by the feet, legs, and hips? Is there a powerful extension from the legs in the final throwing stance, or are the legs hardly used at all?

3. What is the athlete doing with the torso, the arms, and the head? Are these actions technically correct? Is the chest pushed upward, or are the chest and head allowed to drop downward?

4. Is the *sequence* of actions performed correctly? Or does the athlete push the shot with the arm before using the legs and muscles of the back?

5. Is the *rate of acceleration* correct? Or does the athlete start fast and finish slowly?

Once you identify errors, use the following sequence to eliminate them.

1. Pick out major errors and select the most fundamental error; correct this lst. Then correct the next most important error, and so on.

2. Correct errors one at a time. Frequently when fundamental errors are corrected, many lesser errors disappear.

3. Decide on the activity and conditions that can be used to correct each error. This may mean reworking a certain aspect of technique at reduced speed and from a totally different approach than used previously. The method of correction should be relatively easy to perform and, if possible, novel and interesting to the performer.

4. Always use instructions that are easy to understand and that are meaningful for the performer (i.e., don't befuddle a young athlete with needless technical jargon).

5. Insert the corrected aspect of technique into the movement pattern, and have the student repeat the complete skill at reduced speed and effort.

6. Progressively increase speed and effort.

SAFETY IN TRACK AND FIELD

For each event, this text provides suggestions for improving the level of safety when teaching or coaching. Many of the major problems that you will face are considered here, but unfortunately this text cannot cover all the circumstances that may arise during an instructional session. You must use your own judgment to ensure that the teaching environment is safe and that the material taught is adequate for the age, maturity, and experience of the class.

The following comments are intended as a general introduction to the issue of safety in track and field. Specific comments relating to each event are found in their respective chapters.

Responsibility for Safety

Safety in track and field begins with the planning and layout of the facilities, followed by the manner in which events are conducted or taught. Ground staff, officials, teachers, coaches, and the participants themselves all play a part in maintaining a high level of safety.

In the United States and Canada, your legal obligation is to provide a reasonable, prudent, and professional standard of care during an instructional session. The word *professional* gives you the responsibilities of checking that equipment and facilities are in good order and using the best available methods and practices in teaching and supervising the class.

When you conduct an activity, plan to do the following.

- Use adequate teaching techniques, teaching progressions, and drills that take into consideration the ages, genders, maturity levels, and fitness levels of the participants.
- Ensure that the equipment, apparatuses, and throwing implements are in good order and are appropriate in weight and size for the ages and physical maturity of the participants.
- Teach good safety habits as an integral part of each instructional period, and make participants aware of specific dangers that may occur in an activity.
- Use repetition as the key to learning. This applies not only to the learning and subsequent performance of an athletic skill but also to its associated safety regulations. This means that the fundamental rules controlling the conduct of an event, together with good safety habits, are reinforced during each instructional session.

All of these points are closely interrelated. You must select the best teaching progressions relative to the ages, genders, and maturity and fitness levels of the participants; what is adequate for a fit adult will be inadequate for an immature youngster. This means that you must not only know how to teach a skill but also understand how to modify this skill to fit an individual's physiological and psychological maturity. The same consideration must be exercised when warning of dangerous conditions that could develop. Adequate warning to adults may be inadequate for

children. Track and field events themselves are not dangerous, but the way they are conducted can be dangerous; thus, you must know the specific characteristics of each event and activity. A verbal explanation outlining these characteristics is not enough. You must instruct, demonstrate what is required, and supervise in such a way that dangerous conditions are eliminated and that good safety habits are developed by each member of the group.

Discipline and Control

Always establish a high level of control, beginning from the first instructional period. Control does not mean removing fun and pleasure from track and field or turning every instructional period into the equivalent of boot camp. Good organization coupled with good leadership will not only improve the teaching environment but will also enhance safety. This is important particularly if you wish students to practice independently at stations. However, you may have immature and unreliable students who simply cannot be expected to practice without supervision. If this is the case and you do not have additional assistance, you will not be able to progress to group activities but must remain in charge of the whole class until students have developed the required levels of reliability and self-discipline. Any decision to allow young athletes to practice on their own must be based on a careful assessment of their maturity, self-discipline, levels of responsibility, and knowledge of the event and its safety requirements.

When you set up stations, stay at the station where competitive implements are being thrown and position yourself so that other events are also in view. The possibility of moving freely from one station to the other will depend on what events are being practiced, whether safe substitutes for competitive implements are being used, and whether you are able to vocally and visually control all stations from your position.

One of the difficulties you will face is that in trying to eliminate every possible danger, you can become excessively authoritarian and in doing so remove the challenge from the activity; students may feel they have no rights and can express no individual differences. However difficult it may seem, you must strike a balance between providing a safe environment yet one in which students can learn.

Eliminating dangerous conditions does not mean removing the challenge in physical activity. Part of the pleasure provided by track and field is that the individual strives to run faster, jump higher, and throw farther. The challenge itself should occur in a safe environment, but because a certain degree of risk occurs in all human activity, accidents can happen. Keep this in mind, know the basic principles of first aid, and have a procedure well established for accident emergencies.

A FINAL NOTE

Knowledgeable personnel using excellent planning and carefully selected teaching progressions make track and field a safe and enjoyable sport. Whether teaching a large class or coaching a small group of advanced athletes, aim for the highest standard of organization and instruction and at no time allow this standard to be compromised.

CHAPTER

2

SPRINTS AND SPRINT STARTS

Sprinting as a race category includes all distances up to 400 meters, with the 400 meters classified as a long sprint. Races beyond 400 meters usually fall into the category of middle distance, though elite athletes may sprint much of the distance.

The act of sprinting occurs in every race, including the marathon. As the competitive distance increases from the very short sprints (50-and 60-meter dashes) to longer distances, so the demands on the athlete change. In short sprints, the athlete races on stored energy supplies (anaerobic capacity). As the race distance increases, so does the demand on the athlete's anaerobic capacity, and the aerobic capacity begins to be taxed as well. Long distance races require tremendous aerobic capacity and place less demand on the athlete's stored (anaerobic) energy supplies. Thus, the balance of anaerobic-aerobic training must change according to the competitive distance raced.

[Good sprinting requires fast reactions, good acceleration, and an efficient style of running. The sprinter must also develop an excellent sprint start and maintain top speed for as long as possible.] A season's training usually begins with drills to develop power, technique, and sprint endurance. As the competitive season approaches, reduce power and sprint endurance training and emphasize ''quality'' high-speed sprinting: The athlete attempts to sprint at top speed with as much relaxation and lack of tension as possible. Most technique training will be completed in the preseason and never fully forgotten during the competitive period. For a beginner faced with a short season and little time to prepare, training should concentrate

on improving basic sprinting technique and the ability to relax while sprinting at top speed.

SAFETY SUGGESTIONS

Because of their simplicity, sprinting events require fewer safety regulations than throwing or jumping events. However, you should consider several points.

Sprinting is a highly explosive event, and it is essential that the sprinter warm up thoroughly prior to all training sessions and competitions; this reduces the likelihood of muscle tears and pulls. The warm up should begin with light, easy running and flexibility exercises. Intensity is increased with fast striding, short sprints, and practice starts.

The athlete must be particularly careful with some of the special activities used for developing sprinting technique, such as high-knee running and high-knee skipping, which can produce hamstring pulls and other muscle injuries unless preceded by a careful warm-up. This problem can affect even a well-conditioned athlete who fails to warm up adequately. When you work with a group of novices, insist on a good warm-up and avoid cutting the warm-up short because of time restrictions. In cold weather, a complete and thorough warm-up is particularly essential.

Make sure students have sufficient room to turn and to slow down during sprinting activities. This is usually not a problem on open grass areas, but it is particularly important in gymnasiums. In particular, activities in which participants sprint to a line or to an object and back must be organized carefully so that sufficient room is provided for deceleration and turning.

Weight training has become an important element of modern sprinting, but it must always be coupled with stretching and flexibility exercises specifically chosen to complement sprinting. Overuse of weights can be detrimental to sprinting, and weight lifting should always be practiced as a secondary form of training.

Teach young children to stay in designated lanes and not move off the track or to the center of the track until it is safe to do so; this prevents collisions. Also teach young children the use and care of spikes in both training sessions and competition. In hot weather, athletes frequently take off their spikes and run on the infield barefoot, so it is essential that spikes and spike pins are stored properly.

Strictly control starting pistols and their ammunition; lock them in a safe place when they are not in use. In no circumstance leave a loaded starting pistol unattended. Starting pistol ammunition is designed specifically for track competitions, and it should not be used for any other purposes. The loss of starting pistols must be immediately reported to the appropriate authorities.

An excellent substitute for a starting pistol is a pair of starting clappers. This is made of two boards hinged at the base, with 1/2 of a black-and-white disk attached to each board (Figure 2.1). The "crack" of the boards when they are brought together gives an acoustical signal that starts the athletes. The black-and-white halves of disk when brought together give a visual signal for starting stopwatches.

Figure 2.1 Starting clappers

TECHNIQUE

When sprinting at speed, the athlete runs on the balls of the feet with the upper body inclined forward slight-ly. The arms are bent at 90 degrees at the elbow and are swung in the direction of the run. The hands and facial muscles are relaxed. Each leg drives powerfully to full extension, and the thigh of the leading leg is lifted to horizontal. The hips remain at the same height throughout (Figure 2.2).

Officials stop their watches when the sprinter's torso crosses the plane of the finishing line. Immediately prior to the finish the sprinter will lean forward and drive the chest (torso) at the tape (Figure 2.3).

Figure 2.2 Sprinting technique

Figure 2.3 The lean at the finish

TEACHING STEPS

STEP 1.	Lead-Ups
STEP 2.	Sprinting Technique
STEP 3.	Sprint Starts

Step 1: Lead-Ups

Lead-up activities for sprinting emphasize quick reactions, the development of coordination, and acceleration. You must teach participants to react to visual, auditory, and tactile signals. Chase, tag games, and relays are excellent for this purpose and also emphasize the competitive aspect.

Shadow Run

Pairs run freely. Runner A tries to shake off B, who shadows A. B tries to remain in tagging distance of Runner A throughout. On the signal, the runners change roles. Be sure to use sufficient space in this lead-up activity to avoid collisions!

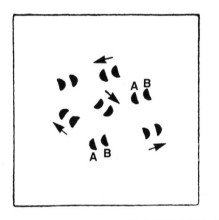

Figure 2.4   Shadow run

Coaching Tips

- Try to shake off your shadow. Suddenly accelerate and change direction! Keep your eye on those around you so there are no collisions.

Reaction and Acceleration Drill

Teams (3 to 4 per team) line up behind a starting line. On the signal, the first member of each team sprints around his or her team's cone, set 20 to 25 meters

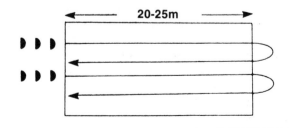

Figure 2.5   Reaction and acceleration drill

away. The runner then turns and sprints back to tag the next runner in the team. (Be sure to allow sufficient space between teams for the turnaround!)

Variation

Athletes use different starting positions (e.g., sitting, lying, kneeling, or the set position in sprint starts).

Shuttle Relay

Split teams into 2 groups (A and B), with 3 to 4 students in each group. On the signal, the 1st member of Group A sprints to cross a line 20 meters away. That runner then tags the 1st member of Group B, who sprints back. The sequence is repeated with the 2nd runner of Group A, and so forth.

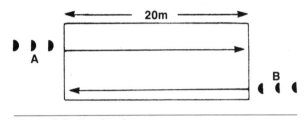

Figure 2.6   Shuttle relay

Variation

Team members exchange a baton or use a hand tag. Students can use different starting positions as listed for the reaction and acceleration drill.

Chase and Tag

Pair off members of Team A with opponents in Team B. All members of Team A run slowly to a line 15 meters ahead. The runners touch the line and then accelerate back to the starting line. Members of Team B, in a ready position 4 to 5 meters behind the line, attempt to tag their opponents in Team A after the

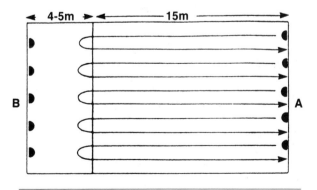

Figure 2.7   Chase and tag

line has been touched and before members of Team A can get back to the safety of their starting line.

Coaching Tips

Team A

- Run slowly to the line; there's no need to sprint.
- When you get near the line, straighten your body for the turn around—you don't want to be leaning forward.
- Pivot quickly and accelerate as fast as you can to safety.

Variation

Cones can be placed on the 15 meter line. Members of Team A run to touch (or circle) the cone and sprint back to the safety of the starting line. Vary the starting positions of Team B (e.g., kneeling, lying, sitting, or the sprint-start set position).

Pendular Relay

Divide students into 2 groups with 3 to 4 in each group. The groups face each other 20 to 25 meters apart. Sprinter 1 sprints the 20- to 25-meter distance, circles around the back of the team, and tags Sprinter 2 from the rear. Sprinter 2 sprints, and Sprinter 3 shifts into Sprinter 1's position to receive the tag from Sprinter 2.

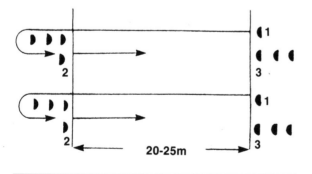

Figure 2.8 Pendular relay

Coaching Tips

- Crouch down and look back over your shoulder for the tag. Be ready to accelerate.

Variation

Runners use a baton, and you determine the type of exchange.

Circle Relay

On the signal, Runner 1 of each team (from 4 to 8 per team) sprints around the outside of the circle and tags the 2nd member of the team who has moved out to the circumference of the circle. Runner 2 repeats and tags Runner 3. (Be sure to make the circumference of the circle large enough so that runners are able to get sufficient traction when running on the curve!)

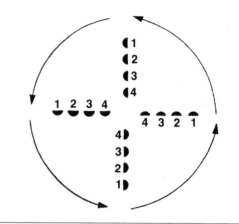

Figure 2.9 Circle relay

Variation

Vary starting positions (e.g., sitting, lying, kneeling, or the sprint-start set position). Runners use a baton, and you determine the type of exchange.

Step 2: Sprinting Technique

The following drills all play a large part in the improvement of sprinting technique. They have been set in groups—drills to improve coordination and sprinting technique, drills to improve leg power and acceleration, and drills to improve sprint endurance—according to the desired effect. Select examples from each group when planning an instructional period.

Drills to Improve Coordination and Sprinting Technique

An acceptable method for developing sprinting technique is to practice the correct elements slowly in a "clockwork," formalized manner. Once beginners learn the correct actions and grasp the necessary rhythm, their speeds of movement are increased. Novices will find these drills quite strenuous. Recommended distances are from 10 to 15 meters with 2 to 3 repetitions. Students can use a loose easy walk as a recovery.

High-Knee Marching

Each participant marches forward slowly, forcefully driving the thigh of the leading leg up to horizontal. The arms are bent at 90 degrees at the elbow. The supporting leg extends fully up onto the toes as the participant lifts the opposing knee.

Figure 2.11 High-knee marching with lower leg extension

Figure 2.10 High-knee marching

Coaching Tips

- Lift each thigh to horizontal.
- Work your arms forward and backward, not across your body.
- Push up vigorously onto your toes with each step.

High-Knee Marching With Extension of the Lower Leg

This differs from the previous practice in that the lower leg is extended after the thigh has been raised to horizontal. The drill is performed in the following sequence.

The performer extends up onto the toes of the left leg, raises the right thigh to horizontal, and extends the lower right leg. The right foot is placed down on

the ground, and the left foot steps forward normally to repeat the sequence.

The performer extends up onto the toes of the right leg, raises the left thigh to horizontal, and extends the lower left leg. The left foot is placed down on the ground, and the right foot steps forward normally to repeat the sequence.

These steps are repeated in sequence; the lower leg is extended with each elevation of the thigh.

Coaching Tips

- Keep your vision directly forward, and relax your shoulders.
- Keep your arms held at 90 degrees at the elbows.
- Lift your thigh as close to horizontal as you can. When your thigh is in the air, kick your lower leg forward and step down to repeat.

High-Knee Skipping With Lower Leg Extension

This drill is quite strenuous; 3 to 4 short individual efforts, each followed by a rest, are sufficient to begin with for novices. The skipping action is similar to that done with a rope. Instead of walking, as with the previous drill, the performer pretends to be skipping

Figure 2.12 High-knee skipping with lower leg extension

a rope. The thighs are raised to horizontal, and the lower leg is kicked out to an extended position. The performer looks straight ahead, holds the arms at 90 degrees at the elbows, and swings them forward and backward vigorously.

Coaching Tips

- Concentrate on your legs; forget about the arm action to begin with.
- Get the action started by skipping in place. Then move forward very slowly and try to keep the skipping action going.
- Think of a rhythm of "up–extend, up–extend."
- Add the arm action once you have the legs working.

High-Knee Running With Lower Leg Extension

This simulates the prancing action of a horse. Movement forward is still slow, but the speed of the legs resembles running in place. The performer can begin with simple high-knee running and then include the lower leg extension once the rhythm of the high-knee lift is established.

Figure 2.13 High-knee running with lower leg extension

Coaching Tips

- Set up the rhythm while running in place, and then try to move forward at a slow jog. Slowly increase the speed of your legs.
- Look forward and keep your arms working hard forward and backward throughout.

Seat Kicks

Each athlete moves slowly forward, kicking up the heels to the rear and attempting to hit the buttocks. This practice helps to establish the pattern of leg movement to the rear of the body and also stretches and loosens the quadriceps.

Figure 2.14 Seat kicks

Coaching Tips

- Start by running in place and kicking your heels up easily to your rear.
- Begin moving slowly forward, kicking your heels up higher as you go.
- Concentrate only on getting your heels up to your rear (there's no need to lift the thighs upward).
- Don't worry if you can't hit your seat with your heels to begin with.
- Work on raising the heels as high as possible.

Sprint Arm Action

In this practice, the athlete concentrates on maintaining the angle of the arms at the elbow (90 degrees) together with a forward and backward swing that must be parallel to the direction of run. This is initially practiced standing still, then walking, and thereafter jogging and sprinting.

Coaching Tips

- Pull your elbows back and upward.
- Relax your hands and the muscles of your face; let your jaw hang.
- Look directly ahead and lean forward slightly.
- Let the legs work on their own; concentrate on the arms.

Figure 2.15 Sprint arm action

High-Knee Running Followed by Acceleration Sprints

Each runner moves forward slowly 5 meters, emphasizing high-knee lift without lower leg extension. On the signal, runners sprint forward for approximately 10 meters, accelerating as vigorously as possible.

Figure 2.16 High-knee running and acceleration sprints

Coaching Tips

- Keep the upper body upright during the high knee lift. On the signal, lean forward and drive powerfully with your legs to accelerate.
- Work your arms forward and backward as vigorously as you can, not across your body.
- Look straight ahead; don't lean back.

Counting Strides Over a Selected Distance

The athlete sprints at medium to high speed over 20 to 25 meters, while you count the number of strides the athlete takes to run the distance. The athlete must try to maintain the same tempo throughout and maintain good technique without overstriding.

Coaching Tips

- Concentrate on drive (supporting leg), lift (leading thigh), and reach (lower leg).
- Look forward; relax and work your arms as powerfully as possible.
- Concentrate on good form; don't turn your sprint into a series of bounding long jumps!

Testing Leg Speed

Athletes run in place while counting how many leg beats (i.e., foot contacts with the ground) they can make in 10 seconds, 15 seconds, and 20 seconds. You call out the time. (A partner can help count the number of beats.)

Coaching Tips

- Lift each foot just clear of the ground each time.
- Concentrate throughout on sheer speed of leg action.
- Use short, fast arm movements.

1/2 and 3/4 Speed Sprints

The emphasis in this practice is on maintaining the sprinting form established in earlier practices while maintaining the required speed without strain or tightening up. The participant uses a sprint start or flying start, and the distance run depends on maturity and fitness. Beginners run 25 to 30 meters, more mature athletes 45 to 50 meters.

Coaching Tips

- Think of good drive, knee lift, and arm action.
- Relax as you run; let the muscles of your face and hands relax.
- Don't drop your head backward or swing your arms across your body.
- Keep the arms and knees swinging directly back and forth.
- Force your elbows back and up with each arm swing.

Flat-Out Sprinting

Using a flying start, the athlete runs a selected distance that is marked by 2 lines. You start the watch when the athlete crosses the first line, and an assistant signals by lowering an arm when the athlete crosses the second line (the finish). For beginners, an acceptable distance is 35 to 40 meters, but mature athletes will sprint farther. The number of repetitions and rest periods will depend upon fitness and maturity (2 to 3 for beginners).

Coaching Tips

- Work on maintaining good sprinting form throughout; don't tighten up in an attempt to sprint faster.
- Look forward; relax your face and hands and run on the balls of your feet.

Drills to Improve Leg Power and Acceleration

These activities are very demanding. Use them sparingly with beginners, and increase intensity and repetitions slowly. Students should practice on a cushioned surface, such as mats or grass. The recommended number of repetitions for beginners is 2 to 3, with walking rests between each effort. (For more examples, see chapters 8 and 9.)

Distance Hopping

Each participant hops 2 to 3 paces with the left leg, then repeats the same action with the right leg. With each hop, athletes swing their arms forward and upward and drive with their legs as powerfully as possible. The thigh of the free leg is lifted to horizontal on each hop.

Figure 2.17 Distance hopping

Coaching Tips

- Swing your arms forward and upward as vigorously as possible to help gain distance.
- Drive powerfully with each jumping leg.
- Make each hop the same size.
- Don't hop for height; drive for distance.
- Try the hopping sequence from standing and then from a 2- to 3-step run-up.

Bounding (Striding) for Distance

This is a favorite drill of triple jumpers. Each bounding stride is long and reaching, and 2 to 3 are performed in sequence.

Coaching Tips

- Lean forward slightly and jump long and low, not upward; keep the momentum going.
- Make each bounding stride about the same size.
- Drive forward and upward with your arms on each stride.
- Try the bounding strides from a standing start and then from a 2- to 3-step run-up.

Rabbit Hops

These are two-legged jumps, 2 to 3 performed in sequence. Students see who can cover the greatest distance after 3 jumps.

Figure 2.19 Rabbit hops

Coaching Tips

- Drive forward as powerfully as possible with each jump.
- Be sure to synchronize the actions of your arms; swing them up and forward as you drive with your legs.

Combinations of Hopping and Bounding Over Low Obstacles

Bamboo canes set across cones (or low elastic high-jump "bars") are combined with mats to form a series of low obstacles. These are set in a sequence that forces the performer to strive for distance on each of 3 to 4 successive jumps. Mats cushion the landings.

Figure 2.18 Distance bounding

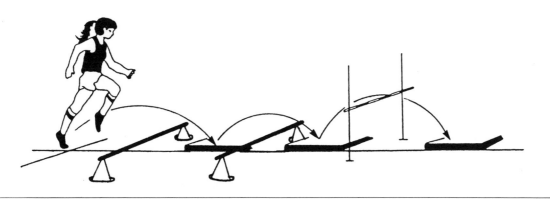

Figure 2.20 Hopping and bounding over obstacles

You make up the sequence of required hops and bounds.

Coaching Tips

- Don't high jump the obstacles.
- Use the drive of your legs and your arm lift to "float" as long as you can with each jump.
- Imagine you are a ball that has been thrown forward and down at the ground. Try to simulate the series of long, low bounces that the ball would make.

High-Knee Running, Moving Backward, Then Forward

The group begins by running in place, emphasizing high-knee lift. On the first signal they shift to slow backward running (with high-knee lift). On the second signal they revert to slow forward running with high-knee lift. Recommended distance for beginners is 5 meters backward, then 5 meters forward.

Coaching Tips

- Keep your knees working high and as fast as possible. Listen to the rhythm of your footfalls and try to keep this rhythm both fast and regular.

Figure 2.21 Forward and backward high-knee running

- Lean your upper body slightly backward when you move backward.
- Tilt your body forward to shift forward.
- Keep your knee lift going as fast as possible.

Sprinting With Partner Resistance

Using a strap or belt, one athlete pulls another along like a horse and cart. The sprinter (horse) wears the strap or belt around the abdomen, with the partner (cart) holding the lines and providing a mobile but gentle resistance. The resistance should be sufficient to make the horse work as vigorously as possible, as though sprinting flat-out. Both horse and cart move forward 10 meters at a speed equivalent to a fast jog. A surface that provides sufficient traction will be necessary. Partners change roles after 2 to 3 repetitions.

Figure 2.22 Sprinting with partner resistance

Coaching Tips

Cart

- Don't stop the horse from moving forward. Give just enough resistance so that the horse can really lean into the action and work the legs and arms as vigorously as possible.
- Lean backward to provide the right amount of resistance.

Horse

- Lean forward and work your legs and arms as hard as you can! See if you can overcome the resistance the cart is giving you.

Drills to Improve the Leg Power and Acceleration of the Mature Athlete

These drills are intended for the mature athlete who has worked beyond elementary sprinting drills and who has developed additional leg power during the off-season through weight training and other complementary activities. A novice attempting the following drills is likely to experience extreme muscle soreness. Don't allow beginners to be hasty. They should progress slowly, working at drills appropriate to their levels of maturity.

Running, Bounding, and Jumping Up Stairs

Running, bounding, hopping, and jumping are performed up stairs; as the athlete's leg power increases, steeper stairs are used. This is a familiar activity for football players who run and bound up stadium steps as part of their training. Introduce this activity on steps that are low (shallow) and wide enough to allow plenty of room for each landing and takeoff. Initially, have students practice one type of jump at a time in order not to disrupt rhythm. Later, use combinations of all types of jumps. Experienced athletes may also bound down shallow stairs using a controlled double leg takeoff and double-leg landing. *Note*: This practice demands excellent control and is particularly stressful on the legs. It is not a drill for beginners.

Coaching Tips

- Keep your eyes on the steps throughout.
- Drive as powerfully as you can and lift your thighs with each jump.

Figure 2.23 Running, bounding, and jumping up stairs

- Remember to swing your arms forward and upward.
- Rest and breath deeply once you have reached the top of the steps.

Depth or Rebound Jumping— "Plyometrics"

Depth or rebound jumping develops explosiveness and elastic rebound in the leg muscles. The performer steps (or jumps) down from the top of a vaulting box onto the floor and immediately rebounds up onto another box. Sprinters and jumpers, particularly the triple jumper, frequently use this activity. For several more examples of this type of training together with coaching tips, see chapter 9.

Figure 2.24 Rebound jumping

These drills are very strenuous and extremely demanding. They demand a specific technique for landing at the end of the jump and are recommended only for physically mature athletes who have already developed power in the legs with considerable bounding, jumping, and strength training (squats). These drills are not intended for novices.

Drills to Improve Sprint Endurance

Rolling Sprints

Teams of four (or more) jog or run slowly around the track. At the signal, Runner D sprints to the front of the team. On the next signal, Runner C sprints to the front and so on. Reducing the time between signals and increasing the size of teams will increase the intensity. One full lap of a 400-meter track is adequate for beginners.

Running Inclines

Athletes run up moderate inclines of 250 to 400 meters at 1/2, 3/4, and full speed. Increase repetitions as ath-

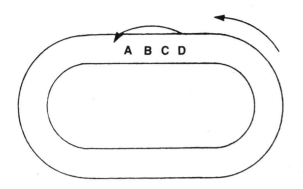

Figure 2.25 Rolling sprints

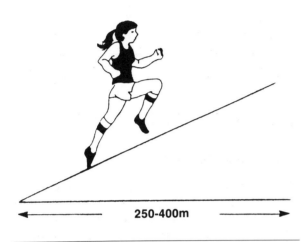

Figure 2.26 Running an incline

letes' stamina and fitness improve. Athletes can use the walk to the base of the incline as the recovery.

Continuous Relays

Form a team of 9 members. Each team member runs 50 meters on a 400-meter track: Number 1 runs 50 meters then passes the baton to or tags Number 2, and waits at Number 2's position for the next round of exchanges. Number 9 moves into Number 1's position to receive the tag (or baton) from Number 8.

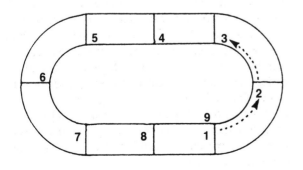

Figure 2.27 Continuous relays

Fartlek

This is a varied cross-country course of 2 to 3 miles. Students alternate short bursts of sprinting with jogging. (See chapter 5 for a more detailed explanation of fartlek.)

Interval Sprints

Participants sprint the curve and jog or walk the straightaway on a 400-meter track; or they sprint 50 meters and jog or walk 200 to 300 meters. They repeat the interval 3 to 4 times.

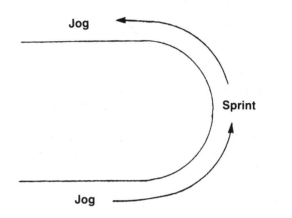

Figure 2.28 Interval sprints

The length and type of rest depends on the fitness and performance ability of the athlete. The pulse rate provides a good measure; if the pulse falls below 120 beats per minute at the end of the rest, the next repetition can begin. If the pulse stays above 120, the intensity of training is too high and should be reduced. (For a discussion of interval training and the difference between anaerobic and aerobic training, see chapter 5.)

Intense Sprint Training for the More Mature Athlete

Repetition Sprint Starts With Maximum Effort Over 40 to 60 Meters

Each athlete works through a complete sprint start sequence of commands; at the sound of the gun, the athlete sprints flat-out over 40 to 60 meters. The selected distance and the number of repetitions will depend on individual fitness and ability. An example is 4 to 6 repetitions with a 2- to 3-minute pause between each. This improves the sprinter's anaerobic endurance and will also improve coordination and sprinting power.

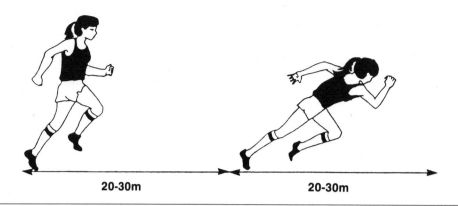

Figure 2.29 Sprints from a flying start

Repetition Sprints From a Flying Start

The athlete accelerates over 30 meters and then sprints with maximum effort for 20 to 30 meters. The distance and the number of repetitions will depend on individual fitness and ability. For example, the athlete can perform 2 to 3 repetitions with rest pauses of 2 to 3 minutes. This helps to improve anaerobic endurance and coordination while the athlete runs at high speed.

Ins and Outs

"Ins and Outs" is a common name given to periods of high-speed sprinting followed by equal distances of loose, relaxed, fast running. For example, the athlete can run 100 to 150 meters in the following manner: out—20 meters of relaxed, fast running; in—20 meters at high speed; out—20 meters of relaxed, fast running. The objective is to improve sprint endurance and coordination.

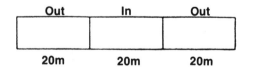

Figure 2.30 Ins and outs

Repetitive Relays

Sprinter A accelerates over 40 meters and passes a baton to or tags Sprinter B. Sprinter A takes the position of Sprinter B, who repeats with Sprinter C. Sprinter C jogs back to the start and tags Sprinter D, who is waiting at the start and who repeats the process. The objective is to improve anaerobic endurance.

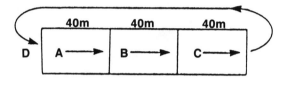

Figure 2.31 Repetitive relays

100-Meter Repeats

These repeats are run at 80 to 90 percent of the individual's 100-meter best performance. The number of repetitions will vary depending on fitness, and the rest period should be long enough to allow for full recovery. (This type of training is often used by 400-meter runners.)

Step 3: Sprint Starts

After the "on your marks" command has been issued, the athlete is positioned in the blocks with the body weight resting equally on the rear knee and the hands. The arms are shoulder-width apart, and the hands are to the rear of the line. The fingers and thumb form a *V*. The shoulders are rotated forward, slightly ahead of the hands (7 to 8 centimeters or 3 to 4 inches).

The stronger leg normally drives from the front block, because contact with this block is longer. The forward foot on the blocks is commonly 1-3/4 to 2 foot lengths from the starting line. The rear foot on the blocks is usually 1-1/2 foot lengths behind the front foot (Figure 2.32). Breathing is steady and regular.

In the "set" position, the athlete is like a coiled spring. The athlete's seat is raised up and forward so that the angle of the leading leg is approximately 80 to 90 degrees at the knee, the rear leg 110 to 130 degrees at the knee. The body weight is equally supported by arms and legs and both feet are well in contact with the blocks.

Figure 2.32 Two views of the "on your marks" position

The back and the head form a straight line, and the athlete looks directly forward at the ground. The athlete holds the shoulders in their position slightly ahead of the vertical plane of the hands (Figure 2.33). On the set command, the athlete holds his or her breath.

Figure 2.33 "Set" position

At the sound of the gun, the forward leg extends vigorously and the knee of the rear leg is driven forward. The arms work vigorously to counterbalance the powerful action of the legs (Figure 2.34). The athlete inclines the body forward for the first 5 to 6 meters of the race. Beyond this distance the sprinter assumes a more upright sprinting position for the rest of the race. By 40 meters, the sprinter is fully upright.

Sprinters use three basic block positions, which vary in the distance between the front and rear block and also in the distance that the blocks are set from the line. These distances will be determined by the body position required following the set command.

The best position for each athlete depends upon the individual sprinter's body length, leg length, leg power, and coordination. Leg length is the most important single characteristic determining block posi-

tions. Figure 2.35, a-c, illustrates the three basic block positions.

Position A shows the greatest distance in foot lengths between the forward foot and the rear foot. This type of starting position is often called an *elongated start* and is frequently used by athletes with long legs. Position C shows the shortest distance between the front and rear blocks. This is often called a *bunched start* or *bullet start* and is used by athletes with short legs. The most commonly used stance is Position B, which is simply called a *medium start*.

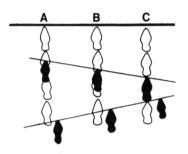

Figure 2.35 Three basic starting block positions: a, enlongated; b, medium; c, bunch

Starting Practice

Each participant walks forward, stops, and places both feet together on a line. On a signal each individual leans forward slowly. Once the body weight is tilted

Figure 2.36 Leaning followed by sprinting

Figure 2.34 Drive from the blocks

sufficiently to require a step forward, the participants sprint forward 15 to 20 meters.

Coaching Tips

- Who can tilt forward the farthest and begin sprinting without stumbling?
- Keep your knees swinging directly forward when you accelerate; try to avoid turning the knees and feet outward.
- Drive with your legs as powerfully as possible as you accelerate.
- Lift your thighs to horizontal.
- Lift your elbows as high as possible to the rear with each arm swing.

Touch the Ground Drill

The group jogs slowly, abreast, and in a line. On a signal each individual touches the ground with both hands, momentarily simulating a set position, and immediately sprints for 10 to 15 meters. Participants then resume the jog, and on the signal they repeat the set position and sprint. Repeat 3 to 4 times.

Coaching Tips

- Don't worry about your body position when you touch the ground.

- Be sure the fingers and thumb of both hands touch the ground simultaneously on each signal.
- Accelerate as fast as you can.

Developing Explosive Drive From the Set Position

The group jogs slowly, abreast, and in a line. On a signal each participant rotates 180 degrees with a small jump, dropping immediately into a momentary set position and sprinting in the opposite direction for 10 to 15 meters. On the next signal, athletes repeat the sequence. Dropping from a small jump into a set position and driving out of the set position helps students develop a feel for the explosive response needed in a sprint start.

Coaching Tips

- Don't jump high in the air as you turn around; otherwise you will collapse into the set position and find it even more difficult to get out of it.
- Only the feet and hands touch the ground in the set position; don't sink all the way down onto your knees.
- Lean forward and work your arms and legs as vigorously as possible as you accelerate.

Figure 2.37 Touch the ground drill

Figure 2.38 A jump rotation into the set position

Variation

Abreast in a line, the group moves slowly backward with high-knee lift until you give a whistle blast. Participants immediately drop into the set position and sprint forward to cross a line that is 10 meters ahead. They re-form the line and repeat the sequence.

Running Lines and Practicing the Set Position

Draw chalk lines on the ground 5 meters apart. From a standing start position, participants run to the farthest line (25 meters), jump turn, drop momentarily into a set position, run back to the start, jump turn, drop into a set position, run to the next nearest line (20 meters), and repeat.

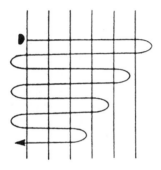

Figure 2.39   Running lines

Coaching Tips

- This is not a race; run at medium speed, and use a low jump for the turnaround.
- Drive with your legs as vigorously as possible out of the set position.

"On Your Marks, Get Set, Go"

Using a standing start, participants lean forward and relax down into the "on your marks" position. On the command, each raises his or her seat into the set position. You move from one runner to the next and correct individual positions. On a signal, the group sprints for 10 to 15 meters.

Coaching Tips

- Make sure your arms are shoulder-width apart.
- Your thumb and fingers should form a *V* to the rear of the starting line.
- Set your shoulders slightly ahead of your hands on the "on your marks" command. Then simply raise your seat with the "get set" command.

- Concentrate on achieving the correct angle at the knees with the "set" position.
- On "go," work your arms and legs as vigorously as possible.
- Don't look up in the air or jump straight up with the "go" command.
- Try to drive down the track so that after 4 to 5 strides you are up in the sprinting position.

Partners as Starting Blocks

Using a partner as blocks, each athlete can work through a complete sprint start sequence, experimenting with various foot positions and distances between the front and rear blocks. You should assist each individual in finding the correct block positions. Students with longer legs will find the correct starting position by setting the blocks further apart and further from the starting line.

Figure 2.40   Using a partner as starting blocks

Coaching Tips

- If you are acting as blocks for your partner, use the flat of your feet as blocks and be ready to resist the leg drive that will occur when the whistle blows.
- Lean backward, straighten your arms, and be sure to turn your fingers to the rear. This makes you more stable and helps you to resist the backward drive of the performer practicing the start.

Sprint Start and Acceleration Practice

At your signal, runners practice starting and accelerating using starting blocks, and other participants act as judges at the finish line, 20 to 30 meters away. A second line is set 2 to 3 meters beyond the finish line. Initially require novices to run through the tape and continue sprinting to the second line. Once the athletes understand that they must sprint through the finish, they can try pushing their chests forward at the tape. With practice they can attempt a partial lean. Avoid having novices attempt excessive lean at the finish, because this will cause stumbling. First practice this drill on 25 to 30 meters of straightaway, then the same distance on a curved segment of track.

Coaching Tips

Starting on the curve

- Line up your starting blocks so that you sprint on a tangent toward the inside edge of the lane.
- Lean inward as you sprint around the curve and swing your right arm more powerfully than the left.

- Keep your feet parallel to the curve; don't turn your feet or knees outward.
- Look forward and swing your arms forward and backward, not across your body.
- Sprint through the tape as though the finish is really at the second line.
- When practicing the lean, drive your chest ahead of your arms and lean toward the tape when you are approximately one full stride away. Don't jump at the tape or lean too early, or you will stumble.

COMMON ERRORS AND CORRECTIONS

SPRINT TECHNIQUE

ERROR	REASONS	CORRECTIONS
The athlete runs in a "sitting" position. The legs never fully extend, and there is no forward body lean.	The driving leg is not extending, and the upper body is leaning backward.	The athlete should practice leg-strengthening activities, sequence hopping with right and left leg, running on inclines, and bounding strides mixed with sprinting.
The arms are not swinging in the direction of the run.	The shoulders and torso twist and rotate during the sprint, and the line of vision is incorrect. The head swings around, and the arms swing across the chest.	The athlete should work to correct the arm action while running in place or sprinting at 1/2 and 3/4 speed. The line of vision should be directly ahead.
The athlete runs with the head tilted back or with the upper body inclined backward.	The torso and head position is incorrect, and vision is not directly ahead. The athlete may have weak abdominal muscles.	The athlete should practice running in place, then change to running backward followed by running forward. Emphasize correct angle of head and torso. Have the athlete practice starts from a crouch and front-lying position, emphasizing correct position of head and torso. The athlete can also do abdominal exercises.
The athlete has poor forward and upward thrust of the thigh of the leading leg.	The athlete may have weak quadriceps, poor flexibility in the hip area, or poor coordination between arms and legs.	The athlete should practice high-knee running, skipping and bounding exercises, and repetitive hopping and jumping.
The athlete does not run in a straight line down the track.	The athlete may be running with the head back, running with the eyes closed, or tightening up during the run.	The athlete should practice running down a line, keeping vision directly ahead. Also helpful are repetition sprints with increasing speed on each sprint; emphasize head and torso position.

<u>**ERROR**</u>	<u>**REASONS**</u>	<u>**CORRECTIONS**</u>
The athlete appears extremely tense. Fists are clenched, shoulders tight, and muscles of the face tense.	Tension is caused by inexperience and lack of training in relaxing while running at speed. The athlete wrongly feels that tension equals maximum effort and speed.	Have the athlete practice running with the jaw relaxed and the fingers loose (as though carrying an egg in the fingers of each hand).

SPRINT START

<u>**ERROR**</u>	<u>**REASONS**</u>	<u>**CORRECTIONS**</u>
In the set position, the athlete's shoulders are behind the hands, and the body weight is back over the legs.	Weight is not equally distributed over arms and legs. The shoulders are not far enough forward, or blocks may be too far back from the starting line.	Correct the positioning of the blocks. Have the athlete practice lifting his or her weight up and shifting the shoulders forward so that they are slightly ahead (i.e., in front) of the hands.
In the set position, the angle of the leading leg is too small (much less than 90 degrees).	The starting blocks are set too close to the line. The seat is not raised high enough in the set position.	Correct the starting position. With the use of a partner, the athlete works at lifting into the correct starting position.
In the set position, the angle of the leading leg is too large (much more than 90 degrees).	The legs are almost fully extended, and the seat is lifted too high in the set position.	Correct as for the previous error.
In the set position, the athlete's back remains parallel to the ground.	The athlete's vision is on the finish line, and the blocks are too far apart.	Correct the line of vision, instructing the athlete to look at a point approximately 1 to 1-1/2 meters ahead of the hand position. Set blocks closer together.
The athlete stands up or jumps up out of the blocks. The initial strides from the blocks are short and weak.	Immediately after the gun is fired, the athlete elevates the upper body and raises the head and the line of vision. The athlete has poor drive from the blocks and during the strides that follow and may have poor leg power.	Correct the angle of the body out of the blocks during the first 2 to 3 strides. Have the athlete practice working the arms and legs vigorously immediately after the gun is fired. Improve the athlete's leg power with jumping, bounding, hopping, and weight training.
The athlete stumbles or staggers from the blocks.	The athlete has poor or incorrect arm action or drive from the legs. The legs are driven out to the sides instead of in the direction of the run. The athlete may have poor leg power.	At the gun, the athlete must drive vigorously from the blocks; arms must work as vigorously as legs. The athlete should also try leg-strengthening activities.

ASSESSMENT

1. Assess the following theoretical elements as taught during instructional sessions.

   a. Fundamental rules governing sprinting and sprint starts.
   b. Good safety habits for use in sprinting and sprint starts.
   c. Basic elements of sprinting and sprint start technique.
   d. Basic elements of sprinting and sprint start training.

2. Assess the performance of technique during the following stages of skill development.

   a. Sprinting over varying distances (e.g., 50 to 200 meters) using a flying start.
   b. Sprint start and acceleration from the blocks.
   c. Sprint start, acceleration from the blocks, maintenance of sprinting form over selected distances, and sprinting through the tape.

Critical Features of Technique to Observe During Assessment

Sprint Start

- Positioning of the blocks.
- Body alignment and positioning of the hands, shoulders, and seat following the "on your marks" command.
- Body alignment and positioning of the seat relative to the shoulders.
- Line of vision and angle assumed at the knees following the "get set" command.
- Leg drive, arm action, inclination of the body, and acceleration over the first 5 to 6 meters following the "go" command (sound of the gun).

Sprinting Technique

- Extension of the driving leg and knee lift to horizontal.
- Running on the balls of the feet.
- Relaxation of the hands and facial muscles.
- Position of shoulders (held steady).
- Line of vision (directly ahead).
- Position and movement of arms (held at 90 degrees at the elbows and swung directly forward and backward).
- Moderate inward lean for sprinting on the curve of the track.

Form at the Finish

- Position of chest (thrust forward at the tape).
- Continuation of sprint well beyond the finish.

3. Hold graded competitions to help develop motivation and technique.

   a. Runners use a sprint start and compete over varying distances (40 to 100 meters) on the straightaway.
   b. Runners repeat the start and race distances on the curve.
   c. Runners compete in handicap races held over distances ranging from 60 to 100 meters. You set handicaps according to knowledge of the students' abilities. For example, distance between runners at the finish can be a distance handicap at the start of the next race. An athlete who wins by 5 meters in one race is set 5 meters back at the start of the next. Or, handicap students so that superiority of 1/10 seconds in sprinting 100 meters is translated into a handicap of 1 meter at the start.
   d. Partners measure how far the athletes can run in a certain number of seconds. You control the watch and the whistle.

SUGGESTED PERFORMANCE STANDARDS (SECONDS)

MALE

Distance (m)	80	100	80	100	80	100
Age	Satisfactory		Good		Excellent	
11-12	14.0	16.5	13.0	15.5	12.0	14.5
13-14	13.0	15.5	12.0	14.5	11.0	13.5
15-16	12.0	14.5	11.0	13.5	10.0	12.5
17-19	11.5	14.0	10.5	13.0	9.5	12.0
Distance (m)	200	400	200	400	200	400
11-12	40.0	78.0	36.5	74.0	33.0	70.0
13-14	37.0	74.0	34.0	70.0	31.0	66.0
15-16	32.0	70.0	30.0	66.0	28.0	62.0
17-19	31.0	65.0	27.0	62.0	24.5	57.0

FEMALE

Distance (m)	80	100	80	100	80	100
Age	Satisfactory		Good		Excellent	
11-12	14.5	17.0	13.5	16.0	12.5	15.0
13-14	13.5	16.5	12.5	15.5	11.5	14.5
15-16	13.0	16.0	12.0	15.0	11.0	14.0
17-19	12.5	15.5	11.5	14.5	10.5	13.5
Distance (m)	200	400	200	400	200	400
11-12	43.0	90.0	40.0	82.0	37.0	75.0
13-14	39.0	83.0	36.0	77.0	34.0	72.0
15-16	37.0	78.0	34.0	72.0	31.0	68.0
17-19	35.0	73.0	31.0	68.0	28.0	63.0

CHAPTER

3

SPRINT RELAYS

There are two types of sprint relay in the Olympic Games: the 4 × 100–meter relay and the 4 × 400–meter relay.

The objective in the 4 × 100–meter relay is for runners to pass the baton while both sprint at top speed. A nonvisual (or blind) pass is used, which means that the outgoing runner has no need to look back or turn and reach back for the baton. The 4 × 100–meter relay has three change-over zones, each 20 meters in length, and prior to each change-over zone is a 10-meter acceleration zone. The outgoing runner is allowed to accelerate within the 10-meter acceleration zone provided that the baton is exchanged in the 20-meter change-over zone.

In the 4 × 400–meter relay, only the first lap and the bend of the second lap are run in lanes. There are no change-over zones as in the 4 × 100–meter relay, and a visual exchange is used rather than a blind pass, due to the fatigue and slower speed of the incoming runner. The outgoing runner turns to face the incoming runner and takes the baton out of the incoming runner's hand rather than being given the baton.

In the 4 × 100-meter relay, elite athletes usually place a check mark 20 to 30 foot lengths from the start of the acceleration zone, and the outgoing runner begins accelerating when the incoming runner hits this check mark. A call from the incoming runner indicates when the outgoing runner must reach back for the baton. Usually the exchange occurs approximately 5 meters prior to the end of the change-over zone.

With practice, the outgoing runner learns exactly where the exchange will occur and so is prepared for

the call of the incoming runner. An excellent 4 × 100–meter relay team sprints well and moves the baton at top speed. Good arm stretch must be used during the exchange so that each athlete runs the shortest possible distance during his or her leg of the relay.

There are various methods for passing the baton, each with advantages and disadvantages. Four methods are explained in this chapter: Two are elementary and are recommended for beginners. In both of the elementary exchanges, the receiving runner shifts the baton from one hand to the other. For more advanced performers, this chapter provides two alternate exchanges: the alternate upsweep exchange and the alternate downsweep exchange. With these methods the baton stays in the receiving hand, alternating from right hand to left from one runner to the next. Of the two, the alternate downsweep is recommended.

SAFETY SUGGESTIONS

Relays involve large numbers of athletes, and it is important that change-over zones are well controlled by officials. After passing the baton, competitors must stay in their lanes rather than immediately move to the infield of the track, because slower teams may be coming up on the inside lanes. An athlete who hinders another team will have his team disqualified. Officials should control the movements of athletes to and from baton exchange areas; this will minimize the risk of fatigued athletes wandering into throwing sectors or disturbing those in other events. The safety precautions concerning sprints and sprint starts apply to relays.

TECHNIQUE

There are two fundamental exchange techniques used for passing the baton: the upsweep technique and the downsweep technique.

The Upsweep Technique

The incoming runner passes the baton with an upward, pushing motion and pushes the baton as far as possible into the hand of the outgoing runner. The outgoing runner grips the baton between the *V* formed by the fingers and the thumb of the receiving hand (Figure 3.1a). Figure 3.1b shows a close-up of the baton being passed up into the *V* formed by the hand of the outgoing runner.

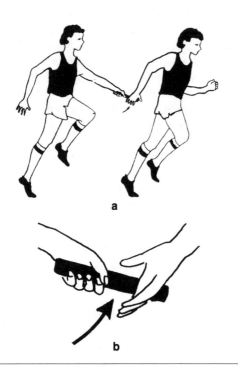

Figure 3.1 Two views of the upsweep baton exchange

The upsweep technique can be applied to three methods of baton exchange: the outside exchange, the inside exchange, and the alternate upsweep exchange. The outside and inside exchanges are considered elementary methods and are recommended for novices. The technique used in the alternate upsweep exchange is advanced and is recommended for more mature and experienced athletes.

The Downsweep Technique

The incoming runner passes the baton with a downward, forward, pushing motion onto a "platform" provided by the hand of the outgoing runner, who reaches back to grip the upper 1/3 of the baton (Figure 3.2a). Figure 3.2b shows a close-up of the baton being passed to the platform formed by the hand of the outgoing runner.

Figure 3.2 Two views of the downsweep baton exchange

The downsweep technique is most commonly used in the alternate (downsweep) exchange. Like the alternate upsweep exchange, the alternate downsweep exchange is an advanced method and is recommended for more mature and experienced athletes. Elite relay teams may use either technique because each exchange has advantages and disadvantages. However, the majority of elite teams use the downsweep exchange.

Outside and Inside Baton Exchanges

The outside and inside exchanges are so named because the runner carrying the baton runs either to the outside or inside 1/2 of the lane for the exchange. In both exchanges, the incoming runner passes the baton with an upsweep motion into the *V* formed by the fingers and thumb of the outgoing runner. The outgoing runner then shifts the baton as quickly as possible from the receiving hand to the other hand in preparation for the next change-over. This aspect of the outside and inside exchanges classifies them as elementary and less efficient than the alternate exchanges, in which the outgoing runner does not shift the baton.

Figure 3.3a shows the outgoing runner receiving the baton, and Figure 3.3b shows the outgoing runner shifting the baton from one hand to the other.

Figure 3.3 Receiving (a) and shifting (b) the baton for inside and outside exchanges

Characteristics of the Outside Exchange

With this exchange, the incoming runner carries the baton in the left hand, passing it with an upsweep motion. The outgoing runner receives the baton in the *V* formed by the thumb and fingers of the right hand (Figure 3.4). During the exchange, the incoming runner runs to the outside of the lane, while the outgoing runner waits on the inside of the lane looking back over the right shoulder, keeping the left foot forward, and using a standing start or modified crouch start. The outgoing runner receives the baton in the right hand and immediately shifts it to the left, running from the inside of the lane toward the outside for the next exchange. Subsequent runners repeat the exchange sequence in the same fashion.

Advantages of the Outside Exchange

The upsweep action of this exchange complements the running arm action. Plus, the outgoing runner receives the baton in the right hand, which is most commonly the favored hand. Because the method of baton exchange is the same for the whole team, substituting or shifting runners from one position to another is made easier. Finally, the outside exchange is easy for youngsters to learn.

Disadvantages of the Outside Exchange

This exchange can hinder the sprinting actions of the second and third runners, who must shift the baton from one hand to the other. (Runner 4 has no need to shift the baton). Also, the first and third runners (the curve-runners) run farther using the outside exchange than using the inside exchange.

Characteristics of the Inside Exchange

The incoming runner carries the baton in the right hand, passing the baton with an upsweep motion. The outgoing runner receives the baton in the *V* formed by the thumb and fingers of the left hand (Figure 3.5).

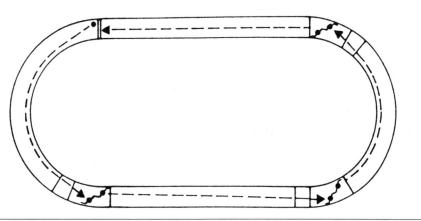

Figure 3.4 Outside exchange

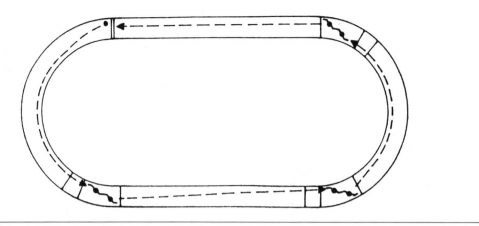

Figure 3.5 Inside exchange

During the exchange, the incoming runner runs to the inside of the lane, while the outgoing runner waits on the outside of the lane, looking back over the left shoulder, keeping the right foot forward, and using a standing start or modified crouch start. The outgoing runner receives the baton in the left hand and immediately shifts it to the right, running from the outside of the lane toward the inside for the next exchange. Subsequent runners repeat the exchange sequence in the same fashion.

Advantages of the Inside Exchange

The upsweep exchange complements the running arm action, and because the method of exchange is the same for the whole team, substituting or shifting runners from one position to another is made easier. The first and third runners (the curve runners) run shorter distances using the inside exchange as compared with the outside exchange. Looking back for the incoming runner is more comfortable when the outgoing runner is standing on the outside of the lane. Finally, the inside exchange is easy for youngsters to learn.

Disadvantages of the Inside Exchange

The second and third runners must shift the baton from one hand to the other, which hinders the sprinting action. (Runner 4 has no need to shift the baton from one hand to the other.) Runners receive the baton in the left hand, which is commonly a less favored hand.

Advanced Exchanges—The Alternate Upsweep Exchange and the Alternate Downsweep Exchange

Advanced relay runners use two advanced baton exchanges: the alternate upsweep exchange and the alternate downsweep exchange.

Alternate Upsweep Exchange

In the alternate upsweep exchange, the incoming runner lifts or swings the baton upward into the V formed by the palm and thumb of the outgoing runner's hand (Figure 3.6). This action is exactly the same as used for the outside and inside exchanges, but the outgoing runner does not shift the baton from one hand to the other. The incoming runner gives as much of the baton to the outgoing runner as possible, and to do this both runners try to make the giving and receiving hands contact during the exchange.

Figure 3.6 Position for the alternate upsweep exchange

Advantages of the Alternate Upsweep Exchange

Runners 2 and 3 do not have to shift the baton from one hand to the other; thus, sprinting action is not hindered. Runners 2 and 3 run the shortest possible distances, and the upward sweep of the baton complements the running arm action.

Disadvantages of the Alternate Upsweep Exchange

Because each runner in the team has a specific task to perform, rearranging or substituting runners within a team is made more difficult. Also, each runner receiving the baton has less of the baton to grasp and is frequently forced to readjust the grip on the baton, often by hitting the base of the baton on the thigh, which greatly increases the risk of dropping the baton (particularly during the last exchange).

Alternate Downsweep Exchange

Using this exchange, the incoming runner grips the base of the baton and passes it with a pushing downsweep action into the palm of the outgoing runner, who grips the upper extremity of the baton (Figure 3.7). Once the outgoing runner's receiving arm is rotated down and forward, the upper extremity of the baton becomes the base, and the baton is ready for the next exchange.

Figure 3.7 Position for the alternate downsweep exchange

Advantages of the Alternate Downsweep Exchange

This exchange allows for the greatest possible distance between the two runners during the exchange. The incoming runner grips the lower 1/3 of the baton, and the outgoing runner grips the upper 1/3; the distance between the two runners is two outstretched arms plus 1/3 of the baton. As with the alternate upsweep exchange, Runners 2 and 3 have shorter distances to

run, and runners do not shift the baton from 1 hand to the other.

Disadvantages of the Alternate Downsweep Exchange

The pushing downsweep action of this exchange is contrary to the running arm action, and efforts to achieve arm stretch and baton distance between the two runners may cause a loss of rhythm and running speed. Because each runner in the team has a specific task to perform, rearranging or substituting runners within a team is made more difficult.

Common Characteristics of the Alternate Upsweep and Alternate Downsweep Exchanges

The alternate upsweep and alternate downsweep exchanges have several common characteristics. These involve positioning and duties of team members.

Positioning of Team Members

The positioning of team members in the lane is the same for both techniques; both exchanges require the first team member to sprint on the inside edge of the lane, the second to sprint and pass the baton on the outside edge of the lane, and the third to sprint and pass on the inside edge of the lane (Figure 3.8).

First Exchange

Runner 1 runs along the inside of the lane, carrying the baton in the right hand. Runner 2 waits on the outside of the lane, looking back over the left shoulder. As Runner 1 approaches, Runner 2 accelerates along the outside of the lane and receives the baton in the left hand, where the baton remains. Runner 2 continues to run along the outside of the lane.

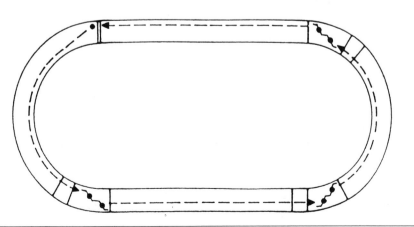

Figure 3.8 Positioning of relay team members in alternate exchanges

Second Exchange

Runner 3 waits on the inside of the lane, looking back over the right shoulder. As Runner 2 approaches (with the baton in the left hand), Runner 3 accelerates along the inside of the lane and receives the baton in the right hand. With the baton remaining in the right hand, Runner 3 continues to run along the inside of the lane.

Third Exchange

Runner 4 waits on the outside of the lane, looking back over the left shoulder. As Runner 3 approaches (with baton in right hand), Runner 4 accelerates along the outside of the lane and receives the baton in the left hand. With the baton remaining in the left hand, Runner 4 runs in a straight line to the finish.

Duties of 4 × 100–Meter Relay Team Members

Each member of a 4 × 100–meter relay team performs specific duties, which apply regardless of whether the team uses an elementary or an advanced exchange.

Runner 1

This runner must be a reliable starter (no false starts), must run well on the curve, and must be skilled at handing off the baton. This runner runs approximately 105 meters from the start to the point where the baton is exchanged.

Runner 2

Runner 2 must be skilled at receiving and handing off the baton and must be able to sprint well over long distances. Runner 2 can be a tall athlete, because this runner has no curves to run. Runner 2 runs approximately 125 meters from the acceleration zone to the point where the baton is exchanged.

Runner 3

This runner must be good at receiving and handing off the baton, must be an excellent curve runner, and must be able to sprint over long distances. Runner 3 runs approximately 125 meters from the acceleration zone to the point where the baton is exchanged.

Runner 4

Runner 4 must be skilled at receiving the baton and able to maintain good form while under pressure; this runner must have plenty of fighting spirit. Runner 4 runs approximately 120 meters from the acceleration zone to the finishing line.

TEACHING STEPS

STEP 1. Lead-Ups
STEP 2. Drills for Elementary and Advanced Baton Exchanges

Step 1: Lead-Ups

The following lead-up activities progress toward the outside and inside exchanges. These lead-up activities emphasize games of chase and tag, sprint starts (see chapter 2), and modified baton exchanges.

Chase

Mark out an area 20 meters by 20 meters. Members of Team 2 run freely within the area; members of Team 1 stand on the perimeter. On the signal, one member from Team 1 attempts to tag any player from Team 2. If tagged, that player must leave the area. The first member of Team 1 sprints back and tags the next member of his or her team, who tries to "capture" another player from Team 2. How much time did Team 1 take to tag all the members of Team 2? Teams change roles when all members of Team 2 have been captured.

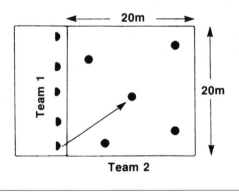

Figure 3.9 Chase

Variations

Set a time limit: How many of the opposing team are captured within the time limit? Or, allow pairs of the chasing team to enter the area to tag their opponents. If you have a larger area, have one complete team chase the other: Who is last to be tagged? How much time did it take?

Red Versus White

Pairs sit facing each other 1 to 2 meters (3 to 6 feet) apart; one member from each pair is "red," the other is "white." When you call "red," red students must react as fast as possible by leaping up, turning, and sprinting to the safety of a line 10 meters to their rear without being tagged by the whites. If the call is "white," the reverse occurs.

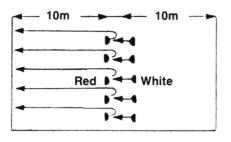

Figure 3.10 Red versus white

Coaching Tips

- Use this lead-up as a chance to practice your sprint start. When you turn to sprint away, roll sideways into the set position and work your arms and legs as powerfully as possible, as though from a sprint start!

Variation

Participants lie, kneel, or sit in their starting positions. This may require some adjustment in the 1- to 2-meter spacing so that the chase remains competitive.

Touch and Go

Team A members assume standing start positions. Members of Team B run to touch with their feet a line 4 to 5 meters from Team A. Team B members turn and attempt to sprint to safety behind a line 15 to 20 meters to the rear. Team A cannot start pursuing until Team B members have touched the 4- to 5-meter line. Team A members attempt to tag Team B members before they reach the safety of the starting line.

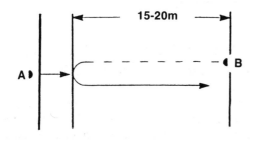

Figure 3.11 Touch and go

Coaching Tips

Team B

- Run slowly to the line; be prepared to accelerate in the opposing direction.
- After you have pivoted around, drive with your legs and work your arms vigorously as you accelerate.

Variation

Team A begins in a set position. On the signal, members of Team B run to pick up tennis balls or relay batons placed on the 4- to 5-meter line. They then turn and sprint to the safety of the 15- to 20-meter line.

Tag

Teams of 3 to 4 athletes line up to the rear of a starting line (A). The first member of each team races to a line 20 to 25 meters away (B) and then back to the starting line to tag the next runner in the team, who repeats the sequence. Each runner goes to the rear of his or her team. Which team finishes first?

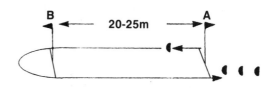

Figure 3.12 Tag

Variations

Students can use different starting positions (e.g., lying, kneeling, sitting, or the sprint-start set position). Or, place cones 20 to 25 meters away from each team; team members run around the cones instead of to a line. For another variation, a baton can be handed (visually from the front) from one team member to the next.

Shuttle Relay With Baton Exchange

Split teams into two groups (A and B), which face each other 20 to 25 meters apart. The first runner from

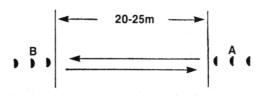

Figure 3.13 Shuttle relay with baton exchange

Group A sprints to pass a baton to the first member of Group B, who sprints back to pass the baton to the second member of Group A. The sequence of exchanges is complete and the race is over when all runners on a team have changed sides.

Pendular Relay

Set up posts 20 to 25 meters apart. Runners from each team sprint around Post B and tag the next runner to the rear of Post A.

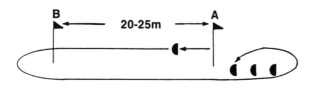

Figure 3.14 Pendular relay

Visual Baton Relay

Holding a baton, the first runner sprints around a post and hands the baton to the next member of the team. Both runners visually control the exchange of the baton. The first runner can use a sprint start.

Figure 3.15 Visual baton relay

Coaching Tips

Outgoing runner

- Begin running when the incoming runner is 3 to 4 strides away. In this exchange, look back and extend your arm backward to receive the baton. This type of exchange is similar to that used in the 4 × 400–meter relay.

Circular Relay

Runners stand in a line inside the circle. The first runner, standing at the circle's edge, sprints around the outside of the circle, and the next team member moves

to the circumference and assumes a sprint-start set position. A tag on the shoulder from the incoming runner sets the next runner going. Be sure to make the circumference of the circle large enough to give sufficient traction; too tight a curve will cause runners to slip.

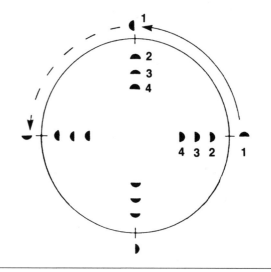

Figure 3.16 Circular relay

Variation

Place a check mark on the circumference of the circle 3 to 4 large strides back from the starting point for each team. When the whistle blows and the first runner has started sprinting around the circle, the second runner moves to the starting point and watches for the first runner to pass the check mark. When the first runner hits the check mark the second runner will turn and start accelerating. Both athletes attempt to pass the baton while sprinting. Don't emphasize a particular exchange at this stage in the teaching sequence. Any type of exchange is acceptable as long as both athletes pass the baton while sprinting.

Coaching Tips

- Look back for the incoming runner, and watch for the point when he or she hits the check mark. Start running at that instant.

Step 2: Drills for Elementary and Advanced Exchanges

Use the following drills for teaching all exchanges, whether elementary or advanced. The main elements of each drill will be the same, although the specifics of the baton pass will depend on the type of exchange you are teaching. The following drills use an elementary (outside) exchange as an example.

Static Baton Exchange Practice

Groups of 3 or 4 students stand 1-1/2 meters apart, one behind the other. This distance is sufficient to require good arm stretch during the baton exchange. The last athlete in each line holds a baton. Students pass the baton with the left hand to the right hand of the runner in front. The baton carrier calls "stick" or a similar verbal command, and on this call the receiving athlete places the right hand back to receive the baton, holding the right arm angled at approximately 45 degrees. The baton is swung up into the *V* formed by the thumb and fingers. The receiving athlete immediately shifts the baton from the right hand to the left. When the front group member receives the baton, all group members rotate 180° and the practice is repeated. Use differing calls for each team and separate the teams sufficiently so that there is no confusion among receiving runners answering the call from the baton carriers.

Coaching Tips

Baton carrier

- Hold the base of the baton and rotate your hand downward so the baton forms a straight line from the forearm.
- Hit the baton into the *V* of the receiving hand, making sure you don't hit the receiver's finger tips!
- Give the receiving runner the top 1/3 of the baton.

Baton receiver

- Hold your receiving hand steady at 45 degrees; don't wave the hand around. Thumb and fingers must be well spread.
- Grip the top 1/3 of the baton with the receiving hand. Immediately bring the hand across the front

of your body and grip the base of the baton with the opposite hand, ready for the next pass.

Static Baton Exchange Using Sprint Arm Action

Groups of 2, 3, or 4 students stand 1-1/2 meters apart, one behind the other. Each athlete assumes a slight forward body lean and mimics the arm action used when sprinting. At the call, the receiver's hand is placed back, and the last person in each line passes the baton to the receiver. The receiver immediately shifts the baton from the right to the left hand, repeats the arm action (but not the leg action) of running 2 or 3 times, and then calls for the next exchange.

Coaching Tips

- Flex your arms at the elbows and swing them back and forth slowly.
- Lean your upper body forward as though sprinting.
- Listen for the call.
- When you receive the baton, mimic running for at least 2 to 3 arm actions, then make the call for the next exchange.

Baton Exchange Practice— Jogging Slowly

Use the same organization as the previous drill. Team members must maintain a distance of two arms' stretch plus 1/3 of the baton between each pair of runners. On the call, the baton is passed forward from one runner to the next as they jog slowly. If runners are in pairs, the rear runner can pass the baton and then run ahead to receive the next pass.

When groups of 3 and 4 are running slowly, the following practices can be employed. The baton can be dropped to the side after the last exchange. The runners pass by, and the rear runner picks up the baton to repeat the sequence of passes. (This method only

Figure 3.17   Static baton exchange

works well if all athletes are sprinting slowly.) Or, the rear runner can sprint to the front of the team immediately after passing the baton; this sequence is repeated continuously. In another variation, the last runner to receive the baton steps to the side and allows the 3 runners to the rear to pass by. Runners then repeat the sequence of passes from the rear of the team.

Coaching Tips

- Run slowly to begin with, and concentrate on the baton passes.
- Position yourself the correct distance from other athletes so that both arms are fully extended when the baton is passed.
- Don't put your arm back until you hear the call.
- Avoid running too close to the athlete in front of you prior to making the call.

Baton Exchange Practice

Students practice this drill at 1/2 to 3/4 speed, then at full speed. When students are running at speed, they must maintain the required distance between runners in order to make these passing practices effective. The front runner should set the pace, and those to the rear then establish the correct distances for passing the baton.

Coaching Tips

Baton receiver

- Hold your arm steady to receive the baton.
- Spread your fingers and thumb wide to provide a good target.

Alternate Upsweep Baton Exchange Practice

Four runners begin sprinting easily in single file. After the front runner has established the pace, students set the passing distance of 2 arms' stretch. The rear runner carries the baton in the right hand, gripping the baton at the base. After the call, the rear runner makes the pass with an upsweep into the outstretched left hand of the receiving runner. Students continue to pass the baton (alternating left- and right-hand passes) to the front of the team.

Coaching Tips

Baton carrier

- Be sure to make your hand contact the receiver's hand during the exchange; give as much of the baton as possible.

- Remember that each receiving runner gets less and less of the baton to hold; runners need to be able to grip as close to the base of the baton as possible.

Baton receiver

- Once you receive the baton, don't shift it from one hand to the other. Grip as close to the base of the baton as possible so you have as much baton as possible above your hand.
- Avoid having to hit the base of the baton on your thigh to reposition your grip.

Alternate Downsweep Baton Exchange Practice

Four runners in file begin sprinting easily. After the front runner has established the pace, runners set the passing distance of 2 arms' stretch plus 1/3 of the baton. The rear runner holds the baton by the base in the right hand. On the call, this runner pushes the baton downward onto the platform formed by the left hand of the receiving runner. Gripping the upper 1/3 of the baton, the receiving runner rotates the arm down and forward and prepares to pass the baton with a downsweep push onto the right hand of the next runner in line. Runners alternate passing the baton in this fashion to the front of the team.

Coaching Tips

Baton carrier

- Push the baton down onto the hand of the receiving runner and give only the upper 1/3 of the baton. The upper 1/3 becomes the base of the baton when the receiving runner brings the arm forward for the next pass.

Baton receiver

- Be sure to hold the receiving arm parallel to the ground. This gives a flat platform as a target for the runner passing the baton.

Introduction to the Acceleration Zone, Change-Over Zone, and Use of Check Marks

Pair runners of approximately equal sprinting ability. One runner stands ready on a midline with a check mark initially placed approximately 4 to 6 meters (5 to 6 long strides) to the rear. The other, as the incoming runner, sprints from a line 25 meters back. When the incoming runner hits the check mark, the outgoing runner turns and sprints as fast as possible

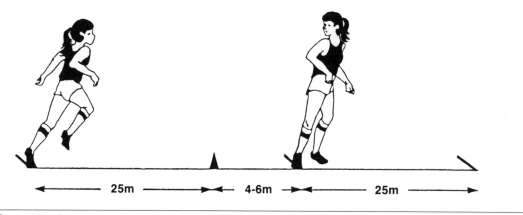

Figure 3.18 Acceleration and change-over zones, and check marks

toward a line 25 meters ahead. The incoming runner attempts to catch up with the outgoing runner by the time they reach the 25-meter line. Adjust check marks so that the tag occurs when both runners are sprinting flat-out (this will usually be close to the 25-meter line). Runners then use a baton in order to practice a selected exchange method. The check mark is shifted back one large stride to allow for the arm stretch and baton distance between the two runners. The outgoing runner waits for the incoming runner to hit the check mark and then turns and accelerates. The baton exchange should occur near the 25-meter line.

Crouched Starting Position of the Outgoing Runner

Use the previous drill to teach the outgoing runner several skills, such as using a crouched position and looking back over the shoulder for the incoming runner. Figures 3.19a and b show two variations for the crouched position, one of which uses a hand for support and more closely simulates the sprint-start set position. Other skills to teach at this time include the correct stance on the outside of the lane, looking back over the left shoulder, and reaching back with the receiving hand only on the call of the incoming runner.

Figure 3.19 Two variations of the crouched starting position

Coaching Tips

Outgoing runner

- Accelerate as vigorously as possible as soon as you see the incoming runner hit the check mark; stay in your 1/2 of the lane until you receive the baton.
- The incoming runner must catch you and give you the baton, so don't slow down.
- Listen for the call; only then do you put your arm back for the baton. Don't put your arm back until you hear the call.
- The complete baton exchange should take no more than 2 to 3 strides.

Incoming runner

- If you are supposed to run to the inside half of the lane, be sure you do so. Don't run directly behind the outgoing runner, otherwise you'll find yourself treading on his or her heels.
- Call and extend your arm only when you are within distance to give the baton, not before.
- Don't run with the baton arm continuously outstretched.
- Reach forward with the baton only when in passing distance.

Baton Exchange on the Track Using Acceleration and Change-Over Zones

Again using the previous two drills, participants work in pairs and practice the required exchange. It is useful to have a third member observe and help to establish the positioning of check marks. For another variation, the incoming and outgoing runners practice the exchange running from straightaway into curve and from curve into straightaway.

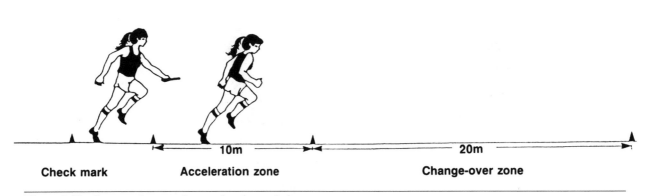

Figure 3.20 Baton exchange using acceleration and change-over zones

Repetitive Acceleration and Change-Over Zone Practice

When Runner 1, the incoming runner, passes the check mark, Runner 2, who is ready at the start of the 10-meter acceleration zone, sprints to receive the baton in the 20 meters of the change-over zone. Runner 2 sprints to pass the baton to Runner 3. The check mark is initially placed 4 to 6 meters back from the acceleration zone and is later readjusted. After passing the baton, Runner 1 takes the starting position of Runner 2, and Runner 2 takes the position of Runner 3.

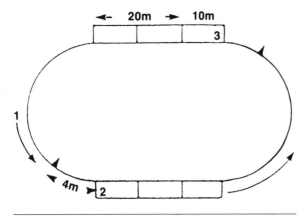

Figure 3.21 Repetitive acceleration and change-over zone practice

You decide the distance run to the next change-over; the recommended distance is 25 meters. Additional runners can also be included in the practice so that each runner has a longer rest period between sprints.

Young athletes need not use the full 10 meters of the acceleration zone. The line indicating the start of the acceleration zone can be used as the check mark for the incoming runner. The outgoing runner then stands well within the 20 meters of the change-over zone. This gives a young sprinter a line to use as a check mark and also ensures that the baton exchange occurs in the change-over zone and not in the acceleration zone (which is illegal!). Adjust the starting position of the outgoing runner and his or her check mark so that the baton exchange occurs approximately 5 meters from the far end of the change-over zone.

Continuous Relay Practice Using 8 Runners

Use check marks, but don't use specific change-over zones. The 8 athletes run 50 meters each. After the exchange, runners jog back to their individual starting positions to receive the baton the second time around.

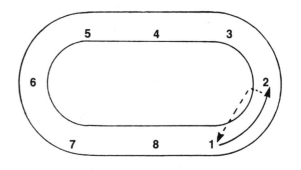

Figure 3.22 Eight-runner continuous relay practice

Continuous Relay Practice Using 9 Runners

Each runner sprints 50 meters; no specific acceleration or change-over zones are used. Runners 1 and 9 are stationed at the start. Runner 1 carries the baton to Runner 2 and stays at that position to receive the baton the second time around. Runner 9 steps onto the track to fill the position vacated by Runner 1.

If runners use an alternate exchange, the first runner carries the baton in the right hand. On the next

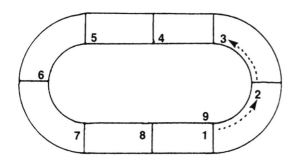

Figure 3.23 Nine-runner continuous relay practice

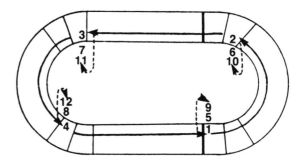

Figure 3.24 Twelve-runner continuous relay practice

circuit, this athlete must receive and pass the baton with the left hand. This variation also requires a shift from the outside to the inside of the lane for the reception.

Continuous Relay Practice Using 12 Runners

Each runner sprints the full 100 meters plus additional distances for acceleration and change-over. Runner

1 sprints around the curve, passes the baton to Runner 2, and then goes to the end of the team stationed at the first change-over. Runner 2 sprints the straightaway, passes the baton to Runner 3, and goes to the end of the team stationed at the second change-over, and so on. Immediately after the first runner from each change-over group has sprinted away with the baton, the next member steps onto the track. An alternate exchange will demand an ability to receive and pass the baton with either hand.

COMMON ERRORS AND CORRECTIONS

ELEMENTARY AND ADVANCED ALTERNATE EXCHANGES

ERROR	REASONS	CORRECTIONS
The outgoing runner is not ready for the exchange and starts too late or too early.	The outgoing runner is unsure of duties and poorly estimates the speed of the incoming runner.	The outgoing runner needs more practice on the exchange; reassess check marks and specific duties of each runner.
The outgoing runner looks back during the exchange.	The runner is afraid of not receiving the baton or of dropping it during the exchange. The runner poorly estimates the speed of the incoming runner and is unsure of the accuracy of the check marks.	Corrections are the same as for the previous error. Provide students with more practice in pairs, and work on developing the confidence of the outgoing runner.
The outgoing runner runs with the hand back (arm extended) for several strides prior to receiving the baton.	The outgoing runner is unsure when he or she is going to receive the baton and is afraid of not receiving the baton.	Corrections are the same as for the previous two errors. The runners need more practice on the exchange. The incoming runner must know when to call, and the outgoing runner should know at what point in the change-over zone the incoming runner will call.

ERROR	REASONS	CORRECTIONS
Runners drop the baton during the exchange.	The incoming runner may not be holding the lower 1/3 of the baton. The outgoing runner may not be spreading the thumb and fingers of the receiving hand to form a *V* or may be allowing the arm to wave around so that it presents an unsteady target. The receiving arm may be held too high or too low.	Provide runners with more practice on the exchange, concentrating on correct arm and hand actions by both runners. The receiving runner's arm should be held at approximately 45 degrees, with fingers and thumb spread to form a good *V*.
The outgoing runner forgets to shift the baton from the receiving hand to the other hand or performs this action immediately prior to passing the baton to the next runner.	The outgoing runner is unsure of duties or is nervous and distracted.	Corrections are the same as for previous drills. Have runners practice reception and immediate shift of baton from one hand to the other. The last runner in the team does not need to shift the baton after receiving it.
The incoming runner stretches out the baton arm too early and disrupts the sprinting rhythm.	The incoming runner is anxious and is unsure of where the exchange is going to occur.	Have runners practice the baton exchange. Establish where the exchange will occur, and have runners practice maintaining good sprinting action until within baton-passing distance.
The incoming runner slows down prior to the exchange.	The incoming runner is anxious about (or afraid of) the exchange and is unsure of where the baton exchange should occur. The runner may have poor sprint endurance.	Establish where the exchange will occur, and have runners practice the baton exchange at full speed. Have runners practice sprint endurance training (see chapter 2).
The incoming runner runs onto the heels of the outgoing runner.	Runners are forgetting which part of the lane they should run in during the exchange. The outgoing runner starts sprinting too late.	Have students practice the baton exchange at full speed. If students use the outside exchange, the incoming runner must run to the outside 1/2 of the lane. For the inside exchange, the incoming runner runs to the inside 1/2 of the lane.
The incoming runner leaves the lane immediately after passing the baton to the outgoing runner.	The runner lacks knowledge of rules controlling relay races.	Make sure all runners know the rules governing the event.
The last member of the team, on receiving the baton, shifts it from one hand to the other.	The runner doesn't understand the duties required of the last runner on the team. Or, the runner is excited or anxious.	More practice will help runners develop control and reduce anxiety. The last runner must learn to receive the baton and run—nothing more.

ADVANCED BATON EXCHANGES
ALTERNATE UPSWEEP EXCHANGE

ERROR	REASONS	CORRECTIONS
The outgoing runner is forced to hit the baton on the thigh in order to shift the grip to the base of the baton.	The incoming runner is not gripping the base of the baton but is holding the middle, so this runner gives the outgoing runner the top of the baton. Runners are too far apart when they complete the exchange, and the outgoing runner receives insufficient baton.	The incoming runner must grip the baton at the base and give as much of the baton as possible to the outgoing runner. Both runners' hands must touch during the exchange.
The incoming runner has great difficulty in passing the baton to the outgoing runner.	The outgoing runner may not be holding the receiving arm at the correct angle (approximately 45 degrees) or may be allowing the arm to wave around, so that it presents an unsteady target.	Have students practice the exchange again. The outgoing runner should accelerate vigorously with good upper lean; the runner should take into account this upper body lean when holding the arm back. The receiving arm should be held steady.

ALTERNATE DOWNSWEEP EXCHANGE

ERROR	REASONS	CORRECTIONS
The incoming runner has great difficulty in passing the baton to the outgoing runner.	The outgoing runner is not holding the receiving arm high enough so that the baton can be placed in the palm of the hand. The outgoing runner may be accelerating without enough forward lean. The outgoing runner may also be allowing the receiving arm to wave around and present an unsteady target.	Have students practice the exchange again. The outgoing runner should accelerate vigorously with good upper body lean. When the arm is placed back, the runner should hold the arm at about 60 degrees—even higher during acceleration when upper body lean is extreme. Arm should be held steady.
The outgoing runner is forced to hit the baton on the thigh in order to shift the grasp to the base of the baton.	The incoming runner has not given the outgoing runner the upper 1/3 of the baton. Both runners are too close together during the exchange.	The incoming runner should hold the baton by its bottom 1/3 and give the upper 1/3 to the outgoing runner. Runners should be 2 arms' length (plus 1/3 of the baton's length) apart during the exchange.

ASSESSMENT

1. Assess the following theoretical elements as taught during instructional sessions.

   a. Fundamental rules governing the 4 × 100–meter relay.

   b. Good safety habits for use in 4 × 100–meter relay.

   c. Basic elements of the technique of the 4 × 100–meter relay.

   d. Basic elements of training for the 4 × 100–meter relay.

2. Assess the performance of technique during the following stages of skill development.

   a. Pairs of runners demonstrate a selected elementary exchange. Use check marks but no acceleration or change-over zones.
   b. Pairs of runners demonstrate a selected advanced alternate exchange. Use check marks but no acceleration or change-over zones.
   c. Pairs of runners demonstrate a selected exchange. Use check marks and acceleration and change-over zones.

Critical Features of Technique to Observe During Assessment

Example: Alternate Downsweep Exchange

- Positioning of the check mark by the outgoing runner.
- Baton carry by the incoming runner and sprinting in the inner or outer 1/2 of the lane as required.
- The call by the incoming runner and the pushing downsweep action with the baton.
- Body position and alignment of the outgoing runner on the inner or outer 1/2 of the lane (as required) while waiting for the incoming runner.
- Line of vision and acceleration of the outgoing runner once the incoming runner passes the check mark.
- Position of the receiving arm and hand by the outgoing runner following the call of the incoming runner.

3. Hold graded competitions to help develop motivation and technique.

   a. Teams of 2 runners race 100 meters using a selected exchange. Use check marks but no specific acceleration or change-over zones.
   b. Teams of 6 runners race 6 × 50 meters—300 meters in total. Use check marks but no specific acceleration or change-over zones.
   c. Teams of 8 runners race 8 × 50 meters: 400 meters in all. Use check marks but no specific acceleration or change-over zones.
   d. Teams of 4 runners race 4 × 100 meters under full competitive conditions.

SUGGESTED PERFORMANCE STANDARDS (SECONDS)

MALE

Age	Distance (m)	Satisfactory	Good	Excellent
11-12	5 × 80	70.0	64.0	61.0
13-14	5 × 80	65.0	62.0	58.0
15-16	4 × 100	57.0	54.0	52.0
17-19	4 × 100	55.0	52.0	50.0

FEMALE

Age	Distance (m)	Satisfactory	Good	Excellent
11-12	5 × 80	70.0	65.0	62.0
13-14	5 × 80	64.0	61.0	58.0
15-16	4 × 100	63.0	59.0	57.0
17-19	4 × 100	62.0	57.0	55.0

CHAPTER
4

HURDLES

Modern hurdling requires a tall athlete who has excellent hurdling technique combined with tremendous sprinting ability. This is particularly the case in the men's 110-meter hurdles, where the hurdles are 3 feet 6 inches (1.067 meters) tall. In other hurdling events (women's 100-meter hurdles and men's and women's 400-meter hurdles), the lower hurdles allow for a less exaggerated technique and greater variation in body size. In all cases, sprinting ability is absolutely essential.

The technique of hurdling has changed little over the past 30 years. In the 100/110-meter hurdles, elite athletes aim for three strides between each hurdle. They also attempt to spend as much time as possible on the ground sprinting and, conversely, as little time as possible in the air over each hurdle. This requires excellent hurdling technique, which can only be developed through a concentrated program of sprinting, hurdling, and related flexibility exercises.

Hurdle height and race distance are adjusted for age and gender. Young athletes run shorter distances using fewer hurdles, which are set at lower heights than those used by adults. Hurdle heights, distances between hurdles, and race distances are also less for females than for males. With age, both males and females work progressively toward adult specifications.

Hurdling teaches rhythm, pacing, and tempo; the athlete learns an appreciation of stride count and stride length. These benefits of hurdle training then carry over into the jumping events, in which pacing, tempo, and stride length are particularly important in run-ups.

SAFETY SUGGESTIONS

Select hurdles that suit the age and ability of the performer. Nothing destroys a student's enthusiasm or ingrains poor technique faster than knowing that contact with a hurdle will cause pain. For this reason, avoid using competitive hurdles until novices have developed sufficient clearance techniques using practice hurdles. Such hurdles can be made from many materials, ranging from light bamboo canes balanced on traffic cones to Styrofoam and rubber hurdles specifically designed and manufactured for the beginner.

During practice, adjust the number and height of hurdles as well as the distance between hurdles to accommodate age, body size, and ability. For beginners, too many hurdles set at competitive heights turn hurdling into a series of mini–high jumps. A large number of hurdles also increases the likelihood of stumbling and tripping as fatigued youngsters struggle to clear all the barriers.

Novices should begin by clearing low obstacles that are 6 inches to 1 foot (15 to 30 centimeters) in height. They can then move to low practice hurdles (at approximately knee height) using short distances between each hurdle and can progress slowly to competitive standards. Once familiar with competitive hurdling over 100/110 meters (where hurdles are all in a straight line), the athlete can then attempt sprint endurance hurdling over longer distances (e.g., 300 and 400 meters). This will demand the ability to hurdle around curves, to hurdle with either leg, and to alter the tempo of running and stride length between hurdles.

Hurdle height and distance must also be varied according to seasonal levels of fitness. In the off-season, reduce heights and distances between hurdles, particularly with the 400-meter hurdles. A simple guide is to check the stride pattern of the athlete and position the hurdles accordingly. Set the hurdle low enough so that an easy clearance is possible and adjust distances and heights as performance improves.

The ability to hurdle cannot be improved solely by clearing hurdles. The closer that the hurdle approaches competitive height, the greater the demand placed on hurdling technique. This technique is improved by related stretching exercises, most of which are aimed at increasing flexibility in the hip area.

Teach novices that hurdles are normally cleared in one direction only, although this does not apply to bamboo canes balanced on traffic cones or to hurdles specifically designed to be hurdled in either direction.

100/110-METER HURDLES

TECHNIQUE

The athlete sprints powerfully toward the hurdle, with the upper body leaning forward at takeoff and the leading leg vigorously extended. The arm on the side of the body opposite the leading leg reaches forward and balances the action of the body. Once the athlete crosses the hurdle, he or she drives the leading leg downward and backward to the ground, forcing the athlete's body forward toward the next hurdle. The trailing leg is brought forward and upward and reaches out toward the next hurdle. Sprinting action between hurdles is powerful and vigorous. The shoulders and hips stay parallel to hurdles throughout, and there is minimal rise and fall of the athlete's body when crossing the hurdle (Figure 4.1).

TEACHING STEPS

STEP 1.	Lead-Ups
STEP 2.	Introduction to Hurdling Technique
STEP 3.	Sprint Start and Approach to the 1st Hurdle

Step 1: Lead-Ups

Select hurdle substitutes that are below hip level for the participants. This will require several lanes of obstacles set at varied heights. Initially, emphasize simply running and clearing the obstacles. Later teach participants to use a 5-pace and thereafter a 3-pace rhythm between the obstacles. Once this is achieved, use low hurdles and emphasize the technique of clearing the obstacles. Progressively increase hurdle height and distance between the hurdles.

Jumping Low Obstacles

Participants run and clear low obstacles. Obstacles can be bamboo canes balanced on traffic cones, elastic

Figure 4.1 Hurdle technique

Figure 4.2 Jumping low obstacles

high-jump crossbars, or mats laid cross-wise. All obstacles are low and easy for the participants to clear.

Clearing Low Obstacles in Shuttle Relays

Include low obstacles (mats) in shuttle relays. The runners clear each mat and tag their teammate for the return run. Don't emphasize clearance technique or the number of paces taken between the obstacles.

Developing a Stride Pattern

Mark pairs of lines on the ground. Distances between pairs of lines (e.g., 1.5 to 2 meters) and from one pair to the next (5 to 8 meters) vary from one lane to the next, which allows for differences in stride length. Students run along a lane and jump the gaps between the pairs of lines, trying to run 3 paces between each pair of lines.

Coaching Tips

For the selection of the leading leg when clearing the obstacle

- Standing with your feet together, lean forward until you overbalance and take a pace forward. The leg that you place forward is your leading leg; clear the gap leading with this leg.
- If you find it too difficult to achieve the 3-pace

rhythm in one lane, move to the next where the lines are closer together.
- Use a rhythm of "over–1–2–3–over–1–2–3–over" to help you as you clear the gap between the lines and run the 3 paces in between.

Developing a Stride Pattern and Clearing Low Obstacles

Set up low obstacles between each pair of lines, placing the obstacles 2/3 of the distance from the first of each pair of lines. Obstacles may be low hurdles, bamboo canes balanced on traffic cones, or ropes held lightly by members of the group. Initially set the height of the obstacles at 6 to 12 inches (15 to 30 centimeters). Each participant takes off from the line to clear the obstacle and runs 3 paces to the next obstacle. Emphasize that each athlete must try to run moderately fast, keeping each clearance low and maintaining the 3-pace rhythm, but do not emphasize clearance technique. This practice teaches an estimation of the takeoff and rhythm between obstacles.

Coaching Tips

- The obstacles are very low, so avoid making your hurdle clearances look like 3 high jumps.
- If you find it difficult to maintain the 3-pace rhythm and clear the hurdles, move to another lane where obstacles are closer together.

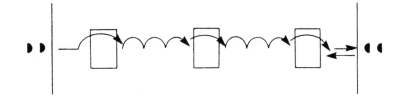

Figure 4.3 Shuttle relay over low obstacles

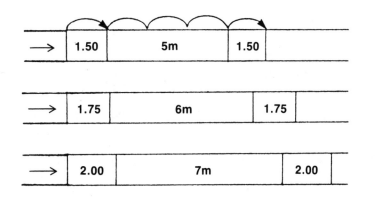

Figure 4.4 Developing a stride pattern

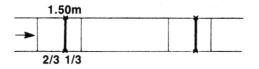

Figure 4.5 Developing a stride pattern and clearing low obstacles

- As you gain confidence and run faster you may want to move back to a lane where the obstacles are farther apart.

Step 2: Introduction to Hurdling Technique

Many of the drills used to introduce good hurdling technique are similar to those used to develop correct sprinting technique. The close relationship between hurdling and sprinting occurs because a successful hurdler must be an excellent sprinter and because the emphasis on high-knee lift, lower leg extension, and vigorous arm action is essential for both sprinting and hurdling.

Some of the following drills will be tiring for beginners. A recommended distance for each drill is 8 to 10 meters.

High-Knee Marching

Each athlete marches forward slowly, driving the thigh of the leading leg forcefully up to horizontal. The arms are bent at 90 degrees at the elbows, and the supporting leg extends fully up onto the toes as the opposing knee is lifted. The athlete works the arms as vigorously as possible, pulling the elbows back and up. Begin the drill by emphasizing one leg only; thereafter, the athlete elevates each thigh in sequence.

Figure 4.6 High-knee marching

Coaching Tips

- Be sure to lift each thigh to horizontal.
- Push up onto your toes with each step.
- Work your arms vigorously forward and backward, not across your body.

High-Knee Marching With Extension of the Lower Leg

Each participant practices high-knee marching with extension of the leading leg in the following sequence. The right leg steps forward normally, and the left thigh is raised and the lower leg extended. Next, the left leg steps forward normally, and the right thigh is raised and the lower leg extended. With each successive step, the right thigh and then the left thigh is raised to horizontal, with the lower leg extended each time. The athlete takes each step precisely and slowly, kicking out the lower leg after lifting the thigh to horizontal.

Figure 4.7 High-knee marching with lower leg extension

Coaching Tips

- Keep your vision directly ahead, and relax your shoulders.
- Keep your arms at 90 degrees at the elbows, and swing them back and forth vigorously.
- Lift your thigh as close to horizontal as possible. When the thigh is in the air, kick the lower leg forward and step down to repeat.

High-Knee Running

Each member of the group practices high-knee lift while moving forward at a slow jog. The thighs are raised to horizontal or above, and the knees remain flexed throughout. Students work their arms vigorously throughout. This drill will be quite strenuous for novices.

Figure 4.8 High-knee running

Coaching Tips

- Look forward and try not to lean backward.
- Concentrate on raising your thighs at least to horizontal.
- Keep your arms moving strongly back and forth to balance the leg action.

High-Knee Running With Lower Leg Extension

This drill, which is quite exhausting for novices, simulates the prancing motion of a horse. The performer can begin with simple high-knee running and then include the lower leg extension once the rhythm of the high knee lift is established.

Coaching Tips

- Set up the rhythm while running in place and then try to move forward at a slow jog. Slowly increase the speed of your legs.
- Use a rhythm pattern of "up–step out, up–step out."

Simulated Hurdling Action

The basic hurdling action is best demonstrated in a mechanical fashion, phase by phase, and as slowly as possible over low hurdles. The participants follow behind and copy your actions. To start, emphasize leg actions.

The sequence of movements is as follows: The left (leading) leg is elevated, the lower leg kicked out forward, and the foot then placed on the ground. As the left leg is elevated the right arm reaches forward to counter-balance it. The right (trailing) leg is turned outward, flexed at the knee, rotated upward and forward at the hip, swung around and forward, and placed down on the ground. To counterbalance the right leg, the right arm will swing backward. At high

Figure 4.9 High-knee running with lower leg extension

Figure 4.10 Simulated hurdling action

speed, arm action will be more vigorous to counterbalance the more powerful leg action.

Coaching Tips

- Lift the knee of the leading leg to above horizontal, kick out the lower leg, and step down.
- Turn the trailing leg out to the side, bend (flex) it at the knee, and bring it forward up and under your arm. Rotate the leg to the front, lower the foot, and step forward.

Leading-Leg Action— No Extension of Lower Leg

Participants walk along the side of low hurdles. If the leading leg is the right, the participant walks on the left side of the hurdles, and vice versa. The participant lifts the thigh of the leading leg so that the foot clears the hurdle; no lower leg extension occurs. The performer places the foot of the leading leg on the ground and moves on to the next hurdle; no trailing-leg clearance of the hurdle occurs. Participants walk to the next hurdle and repeat the sequence over 3 low hurdles.

Figure 4.11 Leading-leg action with no lower leg extension

Coaching Tips

- Be sure to flex your leading leg at the knee as you lift your leg upward.
- Lift the leading leg directly forward and upward; don't swing it sideways and up.
- Concentrate on the action of the leading leg only. Don't worry at this point about the action of your arms or the trailing leg.

Leading Leg—High-Knee Lift With Lower Leg Extension

Participants jog very slowly with high-knee lifts along the side of the low hurdles. Each participant lifts the thigh of the leading leg to horizontal, extends the lower leg over the hurdle, and brings the trailing leg around the side of the hurdle. The athletes maintain high-knee lift throughout the jog.

Coaching Tips

- Lift the thigh of your leading leg above horizontal and kick the heel forward to extend the lower leg.
- Position yourself so that the leading leg can be extended without hitting the hurdle.

Partner Practice for Trailing-Leg Action

Participants work in pairs. The performer stands on his or her leading leg at the side of a low hurdle, and a partner holds the performer's outstretched arms. The performer brings the trailing leg slowly over the hurdle and down to the ground, then repeats the action.

Coaching Tips

- Concentrate on bringing the trailing leg around, forward, and up under your arm.

a   b

Figure 4.12 Two views of the high-knee lift with lower leg extension

Figure 4.13 Partner practice for trailing-leg action

- Perform the action slowly and mechanically at first, and then slowly increase speed.

Trailing-Leg Action Only

The athlete walks, then jogs, along the side of low hurdles so that only the trailing leg clears the hurdle. The athlete raises the leading leg to clear an imaginary hurdle; the thigh of the leading leg is raised to horizontal, but no lower leg extension occurs. When the performer places the leading leg on the ground, the trailing leg is brought over the hurdle.

Coaching Tips

- Imagine you are clearing a low hurdle with the leading leg. Reach forward with the opposite arm.

a

b

Figure 4.14 Trailing leg practice

- Lift the thigh of the trailing leg upward and outward to clear the hurdle.
- Raise the heel of the trailing leg so that your heel does not hit the hurdle.
- Bring the knee of the trailing leg up and forward, simultaneously swinging the arm on the same side to the rear.

Walking Hurdle Clearance With No Leading-Leg Extension

The performer approaches the hurdle directly from the front at walking speed. The hurdle is set low enough so that full leading-leg extension is not required. The leading leg crosses the hurdle and is placed down on the ground. The performer then brings the trailing leg quickly over the hurdle and walks to the next hurdle to repeat the action. Each performer should get close enough to the hurdle so that the leading leg can easily clear the hurdle and be placed on the ground. You can increase the intensity of this activity by having the performer move from one hurdle clearance to the next with a prancing, high-knee lift. This is a strenuous activity for beginners; 2 to 3 hurdles in sequence are recommended.

Figure 4.15 Walking hurdle clearance with no leading-leg extension

Coaching Tips

- Lean your upper body forward as you raise the leading leg. Maintain this lean, because it will make the clearance of the trailing leg easier.
- Place the foot of the trailing leg on the ground directly ahead of where the leading leg lands.
- Work your arms vigorously during the hurdle clearance to counter-balance leg action.

Walking Hurdle Clearance With Leading-Leg Extension

The performer walks between the hurdles, raising and extending the leading leg for the hurdle clearance and

Figure 4.16 Walking hurdle clearance with leading-leg extension

bringing the trailing leg quickly over the hurdle. You can increase the intensity of this drill by requiring a high-knee lift at jogging speed between the hurdles.

Coaching Tips

- After raising the thigh of the leading leg, kick out the heel of the lower leg.
- Aim for fast, snappy actions during the hurdle clearance.
- Move slowly between the hurdles, concentrating on the actions needed to clear the hurdle.

Hurdle Clearance From a Running Approach

Students use the normal hurdling action, approaching the hurdle at a jog. Over low hurdles, participants will not need to incline their upper bodies excessively. As participants gain confidence, progressively increase the speed of approach. Use only 1 hurdle for this drill.

Coaching Tips

- Begin with fast leg actions and moderate knee lift during the approach to the hurdle.
- Initially, move slightly faster than walking speed. With each approach, increase your speed.
- The faster you approach, the farther back your takeoff must be. Work your arms and legs vigorously during clearance.
- Make the clearance as fast as possible and sprint for another 8 to 10 meters. Don't slow down immediately after clearing the hurdle.

Clearance of 2 Hurdles

Set up 3 or 4 lanes (containing 2 hurdles each) that alternate with lanes containing no hurdles. Each lane with hurdles has them set progressively farther apart, at distances ranging from 6 to 10 meters. In the empty lanes, athletes test their approaches and their pacing alongside the hurdles, and partners mark the takeoff positions for the first and second hurdles. Judging from the takeoff marks, participants choose the lane in which they are able to perform 3 paces between each hurdle. Challenge the athletes to see if they can progress to the lane where the hurdles are farthest apart.

Coaching Tips

- If you find yourself on top of the second hurdle with no room to take off, move to a lane where hurdles are farther apart.
- In an empty lane sprint fast, putting in 2 simulated hurdle clearances with 3 paces in between. Your partner checks your takeoff spot for the 1st and 2nd hurdle.
- Drive low and hard at the first hurdle and sprint to the next.
- Avoid high-jumping the second hurdle.
- Don't jump the hurdle: Get over it and back to sprinting. Work your arms and legs vigorously.

Step 3: Sprint Start and Approach to the First Hurdle

A sprint start for hurdling may require the performer to place the trailing leg forward in the blocks and set the leading leg to the rear. Therefore, if the hurdler uses 8 strides to reach the first hurdle, he or she should position the trailing leg forward and the leading leg back in the blocks. Some long-legged athletes use 7 strides, in which case the leading leg is put forward in the blocks. Using 9 strides is also acceptable for beginners (Figure 4.17).

The performer accelerates throughout the drive to the first hurdle and over the next 2 to 3 hurdles. The body becomes upright after the 5th and 6th stride in the approach to the first hurdle.

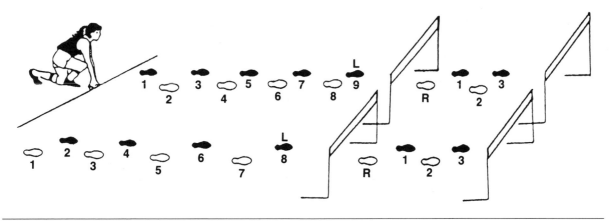

Figure 4.17 Sprint start and approach to first hurdle

Drills

Clearance of 1 Low Hurdle From a Standing Start

Set up low hurdles in lanes that alternate with lanes containing no hurdles. Vary the distance between hurdles 11 to 13 meters from the starting line. The participant begins by running in a vacant lane along the side of the hurdles. The participant uses a standing start with the left foot forward if the right leg is the leading leg. You or a partner counts the number of strides and marks the 8th stride, which will be the takeoff spot for the hurdle clearance. The distance of the takeoff spot from the hurdle should be approximately 2/3 the total distance taken to clear the hurdle. If you find during these preliminary practices that the hurdle is too far away, use the following options.

Move the hurdle closer until the participant's confidence improves and speed increases. Then shift the hurdle progressively farther back. Or, instruct the performer to switch legs at the start and use 9 strides to the first hurdle. The performer can revert back to 8 strides as confidence improves and speed increases.

Coaching Tips

- Aim for good acceleration from the standing start.
- Drive aggressively toward the hurdle.
- Don't slow down as you approach the hurdle.

Clearance of 2 Hurdles From a Sprint Start

During practice with 2 hurdles, you can vary the distance of the second hurdle from the first, and also set the second hurdle lower in height than the first hurdle. As speed and confidence increase, the athlete works toward taking 8 strides to the first hurdle and 3 strides to the second.

Competition Over Two Hurdles

Competition helps to develop an aggressive approach to the hurdles. For this practice, vary hurdles in distance from the start in each lane: Set some hurdles at 11 meters from the start, some at 12, and others at 13. The second hurdle in each lane may also vary in distance from the first. The total distance to the finish (25 meters) is the same for each lane.

Coaching Tips

- Get the leading leg down to the ground as fast as possible after clearing each hurdle.
- Be aggressive with arm action, and bring your trailing leg past the hurdle as fast as possible.
- Drive hard between the hurdles and through the finish.
- Aim for continuous acceleration.

Increasing the Number of Hurdles

As the performers' abilities improve, progressively increase the number of hurdles from 2 to 5. Initially reduce the height of the hurdles and the distance between each hurdle, although urge students to work toward competitive distances and heights. Further improvement in hurdling technique will occur through repeated hurdle clearance, sprinting, practice, and improved flexibility.

COMMON ERRORS AND CORRECTIONS

ERROR	REASONS	CORRECTIONS
The athlete's approach to the first hurdle is irregular, and the stride pattern from the start varies. The athlete shows hesitation.	The athlete is anxious, unsure of approach and pacing to the hurdle, and afraid of the hurdle clearance. The athlete straightens up too soon from the blocks, and his or her vision is not on the 1st hurdle. The athlete has insufficient body lean and drive at the hurdle and poor leg power.	Use a low, lightweight (e.g., foam rubber) practice hurdle. Instruct the athlete to run alongside the hurdle, practicing starts and pacing to the 1st hurdle. Have the athlete maintain forward lean until the 5th and 6th stride, and then attack the hurdle with aggressive acceleration and body lean. Power exercises will improve the athlete's drive from the blocks.
The athlete jumps over the hurdle, using "breaststroke" arm action when crossing the hurdle.	The athlete straightens up prior to clearing the hurdle. The approach is too slow to the hurdle, and the athlete overstrides prior to the takeoff. The athlete has weak use of leading leg and opposing arm.	The athlete must maintain upper body lean immediately prior to and during hurdle clearance. The athlete should drive the opposing arm and the upper body low and forward during hurdle clearance. The athlete must also sprint aggressively at the hurdle so that takeoff position is correct.
The leading leg is excessively flexed throughout the hurdle clearance.	The takeoff is too close to the hurdle, and the athlete has no forward extension of the lower leg after the thigh is elevated. The athlete may have poor flexibility.	Adjust the athlete's approach stride pattern to the hurdle. Have the athlete practice hurdle technique with and without hurdles, emphasizing extension (kick-out) of lower leg after lifting the thigh close to the horizontal. Stretching and flexibility exercises may be necessary.
The leading leg is not lifted directly at the hurdle.	The takeoff is too close to the hurdle, and the athlete uses poor hurdling technique. The athlete may have poor flexibility.	Readjust the athlete's stride pattern approaching the hurdle. Have the athlete practice hurdle technique with low hurdles set on a line. During clearance, the athlete should concentrate on driving the leading leg forward along the line. Work on flexibility exercises for the hip and thigh area.

ERROR	REASONS	CORRECTIONS
The trailing leg and foot are not raised sufficiently. The knee or foot hits hurdle.	The athlete uses poor hurdling technique. The athlete does not bring the trailing leg forward parallel to the hurdle and allows the foot of trailing leg to hang down. The athlete may have poor hip flexibility.	Work on flexibility and stretching exercises for the hip and thigh area. Use partner exercises, emphasizing trailing-leg action.
The trailing leg is brought through far too early. Both feet hit the ground at the same time after hurdle clearance.	The downward drive of the leading leg after clearing the hurdle is too slow. The athlete does not bring the trailing leg through high enough after crossing the hurdle or drive the trailing leg "down the track" after clearing the hurdle. The athlete jumps the hurdle.	Emphasize downward-backward thrust of the leading leg. Instruct the athlete to drive "low" at the hurdle with the leading leg and opposing arm. Check takeoff position and stride pattern prior to hurdle, and readjust them if the athlete is jumping the hurdle. The athlete should try trailing-leg practice with a partner over a low hurdle.
The athlete straightens up immediately after clearing the hurdle.	The athlete jumps the hurdle and slows down after clearing the hurdle. The upper body is elevated after hurdle clearance.	The athlete must correct stride length prior to hurdle takeoff, using strong forward drive of upper body, leading leg, and opposing arm. The athlete must keep the upper body forward so that the center of gravity does not shift backward.
The athlete lands too far away from the hurdle.	The takeoff is too close to hurdle; the athlete is jumping the hurdle. The downward and backward action of the leading leg is slow after hurdle clearance.	Readjust the athlete's stride length so that the takeoff position is farther from the hurdle. The athlete must speed up the downward and backward "stabbing" action of the leading leg.
The athlete loses speed between hurdles.	The athlete's hurdling technique is poor. There is no drive toward the next hurdle, and the body is too upright. The athlete is jumping the hurdle and using poor arm and leg action between hurdles.	Have the athlete practice driving at the hurdle and getting into sprint action as fast as possible after clearance. The athlete can improve arm action and leg drive with repetitive bounding and hopping.

ASSESSMENT

1. Assess the following theoretical elements as taught during instructional sessions.

   a. Fundamental rules governing the 100/110-meter hurdles.

   b. Good safety habits for use in the 100/110-meter hurdles.

   c. Basic elements of 100/110-meter hurdles technique.

   d. Basic elements of training for the 100/110-meter hurdles.

2. Assess the performance of technique during the following stages of skill development.

   a. Clearance of 1 hurdle from a flying start.
   b. Clearance of 1 hurdle from a sprint start using starting blocks.
   c. Clearance of 2 hurdles using 3 strides between the hurdles. The student approaches the 1st hurdle from a sprint start using blocks, and the second hurdle is adjusted in distance to accommodate the individual.
   d. Clearance of 2 hurdles using 3 strides between the hurdles, with hurdles set at competitive distances.
   e. Clearance of 3, 4, and 5 hurdles using 3 strides between the hurdles. The student approaches the 1st hurdle from a sprint start using blocks.

Critical Features of Technique to Observe During Assessment.

- Aggressive sprinting from the blocks to the first hurdle and between hurdles.
- Upper body lean toward the hurdle.
- Extension of the leading leg and opposing arm toward the hurdle.
- Forceful downward drive of the leading leg after crossing the hurdle.
- Movement of the trailing leg (forward, upward, and reaching out toward the next hurdle).
- Minimal rise and fall of the hips and minimal break in sprinting form when the student crosses the hurdles.
- Shoulders and hips remaining parallel to the hurdles throughout.

3. Hold graded competitions to help develop motivation and technique.

   a. Competitors sprint 25 meters, crossing 1 hurdle. Adjust hurdle height and distance to the hurdle for each individual.
   b. Competitors sprint 50 meters, crossing 3 hurdles. Adjust hurdle height and distances between hurdles for each individual.
   c. Competitors compete over 5, 7, and 10 hurdles, with hurdle height and distances set according to age level.

SUGGESTED PERFORMANCE STANDARDS (SECONDS)

Age	Race distance (m) / Hurdle height (cm) / Number of hurdles — Male	Female	MALE			FEMALE		
			Satisfactory	Good	Excellent	Satisfactory	Good	Excellent
11-12	60m	60m	14.0	13.0	12.0	14.5	13.5	12.5
	76.2 cm							
	6 hurdles							
13-14	80	60	16.5	15.0	14.0	14.0	13.0	11.8
	76.2							
	6							
15-16	80	80	15.5	14.0	13.5	17.0	16.0	15.0
	84	76.2						
	6							
17-19	100	80						
	84	76.2	17.0	16.0	15.0	16.5	15.5	14.5
	10	6						
17-19	110	100						
	91.5	84	19.0	18.0	17.0	18.5	17.5	16.5
	10							

400-METER HURDLES

The 400-meter hurdles event is an extension of the sprint hurdle races and is usually considered an event for more mature athletes. Occasionally, 200-meter and 300-meter hurdle races are held, but these distances are now more commonly used as training for the 400-meter distance.

The 400-meter hurdles event demands excellent hurdling ability combined with a high level of sprint-endurance. As such, it is an event built upon a foundation of long sprints (i.e., 400-meter sprints) and sprint hurdling (i.e., 100- and 110-meter hurdles). Coaches normally introduce young athletes to the 400-meter hurdles after building a background in endurance training, sprinting, and sprint hurdling. Because of this, the 400-meter hurdles tends to be a specialist event for the more senior of school-age competitors.

Besides being an excellent 400-meter runner, the 400-meter-hurdles specialist must also be able to lead with either leg over the hurdles; run the 400-meter hurdles in any lane; hurdle efficiently irrespective of the tightness of the bend; and change stride pattern between hurdles as fatigue increases.

The hurdling technique in the 400-meter hurdles is similar to that of the 110-meter and 100-meter hurdles but is less exaggerated because the hurdles are lower in height—3 feet (91.4 centimeters) for males and 2 feet 6 inches (84 centimeters) for females. The positioning of the hurdles is the same for males and females (i.e., 45 meters to the first hurdle and 35 meters between each of 10 hurdles).

TECHNIQUE

Because the hurdles are lower in 400-meter hurdles, the clearance action is less exaggerated than that used in the 100/110-meter hurdles. The upper body is more upright, and there is less forward lean during the actual hurdle clearance. The leg action for 400-meter hurdles is similar to that of the 100/110-meter hurdles; the performer lifts the thigh of the leading leg to horizontal and extends it forward for the clearance and brings the opposing arm forward to balance this action. The trailing leg is flexed at the knee and rotated forward horizontally to clear the hurdle, and the knee of the trailing leg is rotated upward and inward as the leg is brought forward and into line for the next stride (Figure 4.18).

The athlete aims for a smooth, fast clearance, changing tempo and stride pattern between hurdles and leading with left or right leg as the need arises.

TEACHING STEPS

STEP 1. Lead-Ups
STEP 2. Development of Sprint Endurance
STEP 3. Hurdling With a Right- and Left-Leg Lead
STEP 4. Establishing a Stride Pattern for the Approach to the First Hurdle (and to Subsequent Hurdles)

Step 1: Lead-Ups

Review lead-ups and drills for the 100/110-meter hurdles; review lead-ups and drills for sprinting and sprint starts, chapter 2.

Step 2: Development of Sprint Endurance

Review drills for the improvement of sprint endurance, chapters 2 and 5.

Step 3: Hurdling With a Right- and Left-Leg Lead
Drills
Review drills for 100/110-meter hurdling.

Figure 4.18 400-meter hurdles technique

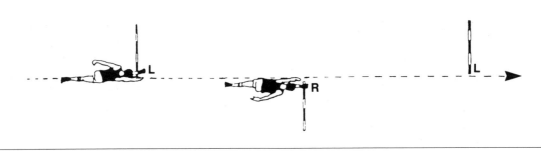

Figure 4.19 Hurdle clearance at walking speed

Hurdle Clearance at Walking Speed

Set 3 to 4 hurdles 6 to 9 inches (15 to 23 centimeters) below competitive height, arranging them so that only the athlete's leading leg crosses the hurdle. Participants walk and step over each hurdle, leading with the right leg over the first and the left leg over the second, or vice versa. On each occasion, the participant brings the trailing leg around the side of the hurdle.

Coaching Tips

- Be slow and precise in your actions to begin with.
- Try to get comfortable leading with your non-favored leg.
- Mimic the action of the trailing leg, but concentrate more on the actions of the leading leg.

Hurdle Clearance at Jogging Speed

Set up hurdles as for hurdle walking. The performer slowly jogs toward each hurdle, emphasizing high-knee lift. The leading leg crosses the hurdle, and the trailing leg is brought around the side.

Coaching Tips

- Use the high-knee lift only as you get close to the hurdle.
- Lift the thigh and extend the lower leg to cross the hurdle.
- Your favored leg will feel comfortable crossing the hurdle.
- Work on lifting your nonfavored leg directly toward the hurdle. Kick the heel forward to extend the lower leg.

Hurdle Clearance With Even Strides Between Hurdles

Set up hurdles so that students take 4 to 6 easy running strides between each hurdle. Only the leading leg crosses the hurdle; the trailing leg is brought around the side of the hurdle. The even number of strides between the hurdles will require an alternate leg lead.

Coaching Tips

- Be sure to lead with an alternate leg each time. Do not alter the stride pattern so that you lead with the favored leg throughout.

Hurdle Clearance With Two Strides Between Hurdles

Reduce the distance between low hurdles so that students take 2 easy strides between each hurdle. This will demand good coordination and an alternate leg lead over each hurdle. Only the leading leg crosses the hurdle; the trailing leg is brought around the side.

Coaching Tips

- Concentrate on the nonfavored leg. Clearances with the other leg will cause no difficulty.
- Use a rhythm of "drive–1–2–drive–1–2–drive–1–2" as you cross the hurdles.
- Reach forward with the opposing arm to balance the leading-leg action.

Lead Leg Clearance Only— 2 Strides Between Hurdles

Adjust the distance between 2 hurdles so that students can run 2 strides in between at greater speed. Only the leading leg crosses the hurdle.

Trailing Leg Clearance Only— 2 Strides Between Hurdles

Have students repeat the previous 4 drills with only the trailing leg crossing the hurdle.

Coaching Tips

- Walk up to the hurdles and lift the trailing leg slowly and mechanically over each hurdle. Concentrate on developing the correct action, particularly when using the nonfavored trailing leg.

- When running faster, use strong arm actions and good body lean over the hurdle. This will help the trailing leg clear the hurdle.
- Simulate the action of the leading leg even though it is not crossing a hurdle.

Hurdle Clearance—
Alternate Leg Lead

Place the hurdles in a line; the athlete crosses them directly from the front (i.e., both leading and trailing legs cross the hurdle). Arrange the hurdles to give the athlete 4 or 6 strides in between with an alternate leg lead. Initially reduce the hurdle height, and later increase it. The athlete can also practice over hurdles that are set up to allow 2 strides in between each hurdle.

Alternate Leg Lead Over Hurdles
Set on the Curve of the Track

In the 400-meter hurdles, 5 of the 10 hurdles are set on the curves of the track. To prepare for this situation, arrange hurdles as in the previous drill, but place them on the curve of the track. Students practice taking 6 or 8 strides between each hurdle.

Coaching Tips

- This drill will show you that it is more efficient (and comfortable) to have a left-leg lead over hurdles set on the curve, particularly when running on the tighter inside lane.
- The inward lean to the left as you run around the track will help to clear the right (trailing) leg.
- A right-leg lead is awkward but frequently has to be used, particularly on the last curve, when you are tired. Be sure to run directly at the hurdle so the leading leg crosses the hurdle well toward the outer edge of the hurdle. If you do this, the

Figure 4.20 Illegal 400-meter hurdle clearance

trailing leg (and foot) will completely cross the hurdle. If they don't cross the hurdle, you will be disqualified! (See Figure 4.20 for an illustration of an illegal clearance.)

- As a beginner, you will find it easier to run directly at hurdles set on the curve of the track for at least 2 strides prior to the hurdle and run straight at least 2 strides after the hurdle. This will help you avoid disqualification.
- When you are more experienced, you will be able to cross the hurdles at more of an angle.

Alternate Leg Lead With 10 to 14
Strides Between Each Hurdle

Progressively increase distances between hurdles so that students take 10, 12, and 14 strides between each hurdle. The even number of strides demands an alternate leg lead over each successive hurdle. The athlete can begin with hurdles set in adjacent lanes and arranged for leading-leg clearance only. As the athlete's confidence increases, place the hurdles in the same lane so that both the leading leg and trailing leg cross the hurdle.

Hurdle Clearance Using
Uneven Strides Between Hurdles

Set distances between hurdles so that the athlete takes an uneven number of strides (9, 11, or 13) between each hurdle. This will require the same leg lead over each hurdle.

Step 4: Establishing a
Stride Pattern for
the First Hurdle (And Between
Subsequent Hurdles)

The number of strides taken to the first hurdle (competitive distance is 45 meters) varies considerably for each athlete. The number of strides the athlete takes will depend on which leg is forward in the blocks and the stride length taken to the first hurdle. The athlete's natural stride length and level of fitness will determine the number of strides taken between hurdles throughout the race. The stride pattern and tempo of approach to the first hurdle will determine the number of strides taken between the next 5 to 6 hurdles. Fatigue during the remaining 4 to 5 hurdles will require changes in stride pattern, normally an increase in the number of strides taken between hurdles. For example, at the 5th hurdle a 15-stride pattern may be changed to a 17-stride pattern; in this case the stride length must be shortened to include the additional 2 strides. It is not uncommon for athletes to change their stride patterns 3 times within a race.

The stride patterns that elite athletes take to the first hurdle vary from 21 to 24 strides. These athletes then use stride patterns ranging from 13 to 17 strides to the next 5 to 6 hurdles and thereafter up to 19 strides for the remaining hurdles. The stride pattern depends upon the athlete's level of sprint endurance and other factors such as tempo and stride length.

Approach to the First Hurdle

The method for teaching the approach to the first hurdle is the same as for the 100/110-meter hurdle race. The number of strides the athlete uses will depend on the individual. An even number of strides in the approach to the first hurdle will require the starting blocks to be set with the trailing leg forward.

The athlete runs by the side of the first hurdle, noting pacing and takeoff position for the first hurdle and deciding the number of strides to use (e.g., if a 22-stride rhythm is too difficult, the athlete switches to 23 or 24 strides). Starting blocks are readjusted accordingly.

Approach and Clearance of 2 Hurdles—Competitive Distance (35 Meters) Between the Hurdles

Initially place the second hurdle in the adjacent lane. The athlete clears the lst hurdle (e.g., 22 paces) and runs past the second hurdle, noting the pacing and deciding on the number of strides to use (e.g., 15) prior to takeoff for the second hurdle. The second hurdle is then placed in the lane, and the athlete repeats the start and attempts both hurdle clearances. A partner can assist in assessing the stride pattern and determining the number of strides to take between hurdles.

Stride and Tempo Variation Using 2 Hurdles

The athlete uses varying stride patterns (e.g., 17, 18, and 19) while running between the hurdles. This familiarizes the athlete with the "change-up" to a shorter stride length, faster tempo, and increased number of strides between the hurdles.

Approach and Clearance of 3, 4, and 5 Hurdles Set at Competitive Distance

Set 5 hurdles at competitive distances and add 15 meters after the last hurdle. The distance of 45 meters

to the first hurdle, 35 meters in between the hurdles, and 15 meters at the finish totals 200 meters. Repetition of this distance, with specific controls set on the speed of the run, the number of repetitions, and the rest period becomes an excellent form of interval training.

Variation

Elite athletes will frequently set 3 to 4 hurdles on the straightaway facing one direction, and in the adjacent lane 3 to 4 hurdles facing the opposing direction. In repetitions using a flying start athletes run up one lane and immediately down the other. Placing the hurdles in adjacent lanes reduces the amount of labor required to place hurdles around the track.

Combinations of Hurdles and Distances

Variations in distance and the number of hurdles help the athlete develop stamina and a feel for pacing and rhythm between the hurdles. The athlete practices changes in the rhythm of running, as well as change-up in tempo to differing stride patterns, over distances in which hurdles are included in the latter part of the run. Assign the number of repetitions of each run and the rest periods taken in between according to the level of fitness. The type of interval training used by the 400-meter hurdler is similar to that of the 400-meter sprinter. Following are some examples.

200 meters (with 5 hurdles) followed by 100 meters flat

200 meters (with 5 hurdles) followed by 150 meters flat

50 meters followed by 200 meters (with 5 hurdles)

100 meters followed by 200 meters (with 5 hurdles)

150 meters followed by 200 meters (with 5 hurdles)

Variations

200 meters (with 5 hurdles) followed by 200 meters flat

300 meters (with 7 hurdles) followed by 100 meters flat

200 meters flat followed by 200 meters (with 5 hurdles)

100 meters flat followed by 300 meters (with 7 hurdles)

This type of training will help to improve the athlete's level of sprint endurance. The athlete must try to clear the last 2 hurdles successfully and maintain the required stride pattern in between the hurdles. The competitor with the greatest endurance and best hurdling technique will be least affected by fatigue and will be forced to make fewer adjustments in tempo, stride length, and hurdling technique.

Checking the Athlete's Pace Judgment Over 400-Meter Hurdles

Compare times taken at various parts of the race by timing the contact of the leading leg with the ground after the leading leg passes over specific hurdles. This check is of great assistance to the athlete and to you, because it indicates the quality of sprint endurance and hurdling technique. In general, the second half of the 400-meter hurdle race should be run no more than 2 seconds slower than the first half.

COMMON ERRORS AND CORRECTIONS

(Errors in basic hurdling technique are found in 100/110-meter hurdles.)

ERROR	REASONS	CORRECTIONS
The athlete is disqualified because the trailing leg does not cross the hurdle.	The athlete leads with the right leg over hurdle and runs too close to the inside edge of the lane.	The athlete should aim to cross the hurdle in the center. Two strides prior to takeoff, the beginners should line up with the center of the hurdle (rather than approaching at an angle). The athlete should work to improve sprint endurance and alter stride pattern so that the left leg leads over hurdles on the curve.
The athlete hits the hurdles, struggles to reach the hurdles, and slows down prior to hurdles. The athlete has difficulties with stride rhythm and pacing between the hurdles.	The athlete does not reach the first hurdle with the correct pacing and cadence, thus destroying subsequent stride rhythm and cadence. In the latter part of the race, the athlete uses poor change-up to an increased number of strides between hurdles. The athlete has inadequate sprint endurance and may be anxious.	Improve sprint endurance. Work on approach to the first hurdle and pacing between hurdles. Have the athlete practice change-up in tempo and reduction in stride length to accommodate fatigue in the latter part of the race.

ASSESSMENT

1. Assess the following theoretical elements as taught during instructional sessions.

    a. Fundamental rules governing the 400-meter hurdles.

    b. Good safety habits for use in the 400-meter hurdles.

    c. Basic elements of 400-meter hurdling technique.

    d. Basic elements of training for 400-meter hurdles.

2. Assess the performance of technique during the following stages of skill development.

    a. Approach and clearance of 2 hurdles. Require an even number of strides between the hurdles so that both right- and left-leg leads are required.

    b. Approach and clearance of 2 hurdles set at competitive heights and distances. Set the hurdles on the straightaway and then on the curve of the track.

c. Approach and clearance of 5 hurdles over 200 meters set at competitive heights and distances.

d. Approach and clearance of 5 hurdles set over the final 200 meters of a 400-meter track. The first 200 meters do not contain hurdles.

e. Running of 400-meter hurdles under full competitive conditions.

Critical Features of Technique to Observe During Assessment

- Stride control and approach to the first hurdle and between subsequent hurdles.
- Less exaggerated clearance of the hurdle (see 100/110-meter hurdles for other features of hurdle clearance).
- Hurdle clearance on the curve using left- and right-leg lead.
- Tempo and stride adjustment over hurdles set on last 200 meters.

3. Hold graded competitions to help develop motivation and technique.

a. Participants compete using 3 hurdles set over 150 meters. Two hurdles are set on the straightaway, and hurdle height is adjusted to the age and gender of the individual.

b. Participants compete using 3 hurdles set over 150 meters. All hurdles are on the curve, and hurdle height is adjusted to the age and gender of the individual.

c. Participants compete using 5 hurdles set over 200 meters. Hurdle height is adjusted to the age and gender of the individual.

d. Participants compete over 300 meters, with 5 hurdles set over the first 200 meters.

e. Participants compete over 400 meters, with 5 hurdles set over the first 200 meters.

f. Participants compete over 400 meters, with 5 hurdles set over the final 200 meters.

g. Participants compete over 400 meters under full competitive conditions.

SUGGESTED PERFORMANCE STANDARDS (SECONDS)

MALE (age 17-19)

	300-meter hurdles	
Satisfactory	*Good*	*Excellent*
58.0	54.0	50.0
	400-meter hurdles	
80.0	75.0	70.0

FEMALE (age 17-19)

	300-meter hurdles	
Satisfactory	*Good*	*Excellent*
64.0	60.0	56.0
	400-meter hurdles	
88.0	84.0	78.0

CHAPTER

5

DISTANCE RUNNING

Events from the 800-meter race to the marathon are usually considered distance races. Although the elite athlete might consider the 800 meters a long sprint, for beginners this race falls into the category of a distance race.

Training for all races from sprints to the longest distance requires improvement of the athlete's anaerobic and aerobic endurance. Aerobic endurance is controlled by the capacity of the heart, lungs, and circulatory system to supply oxygen to the muscles for a long, sustained effort. Training for aerobic endurance is characterized by long runs at moderate speed. Anaerobic endurance is local muscular endurance, or the capacity of the muscular system to operate using stored fuel. Training for anaerobic endurance is characterized by all-out effort over distances that are frequently shorter than the race distance.

Sprinting places extreme demands on an athlete's anaerobic capacity. As the competitive distance increases, there is progressively less demand for anaerobic endurance and greater demand for aerobic endurance. Figure 5.1 shows the relative demands placed on the athlete's anaerobic and aerobic energy systems in relation to race distance. This diagram also indicates that no distance runner can be satisfied with only aerobic training; the distance runner must be able to maintain as fast a pace as possible and be able to sprint whenever it is required. For this reason, the training of the distance runner is designed to improve both aerobic and anaerobic endurance.

Novices training for long-distance races must begin in the off-season and work progressively toward the competitive season. Stressing volume (long, slow

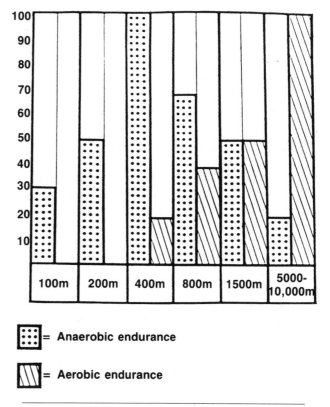

= Anaerobic endurance

= Aerobic endurance

Figure 5.1 Energy demands of distance running

runs) before intensity (repetitive, high-speed runs), a novice approaches the season in the following manner:

1. Begin training with work on aerobic endurance.
2. After developing a base of aerobic endurance,

	Precompetition Period		Competition Period
	(off-season)		(in-season)
Training emphasis	Mostly ---------------- aerobic	A mix of of aerobic and anaerobic	---------------- Mostly anaerobic
Distance	Long -- Short		
Intensity	Light ----------------	Moderate	---------------- Heavy
Repetitions	Few ----------------	Many	---------------- Few

Figure 5.2 Season's training program for distance running

shift to a mix of aerobic and anaerobic endurance exercises.

3. Complete the program with training that emphasizes anaerobic endurance and is specific to the event. The longer the competitive distance, the less emphasis is needed on anaerobic endurance.

Figure 5.2 shows a simplified form of the season's program.

To plan a season's training for novices, work through Steps 1, 2, 3, 4, and 5 listed later in this chapter. For example, fall, winter, and spring are the precompetition or off-season and summer is the competitive period. Adjust accordingly when the competitive period occurs in the spring instead of the summer.

SAFETY SUGGESTIONS

The popularity of distance running—from jogging to serious marathon running—has increased dramatically in recent years. Unlike many other track and field events, distance running can be practiced virtually anywhere and requires minimum equipment. However, in spite of the simplicity of distance running, both you and the performer must consider many safety factors.

Carefully consider safety when planning cross-country, fartlek, and jogging trails. If possible, plot the course so it does not cross other traffic lanes, particularly those used by vehicles. Inform the police if you plan to hold a race that is likely to disturb local traffic patterns. Check the course for potholes, tree roots, and sharp rocks and for trail bottlenecks that might cause the runners to collide.

When running on roads, athletes should run facing the traffic and wear bright, easy-to-see colors. Runners should be particularly careful at intersections and run with partners during training. Running alone is potentially dangerous—especially on lonely trails.

For both training and competition, you must consider the ages of those taking part as well as the length of the run, the number of participants involved,

and the type of weather expected during the run. Excessive heat will demand fluid replacement, and extreme cold will require warm clothing such as a hat, gloves, and tights or a track suit. Runners should wear comfortable clothing that will not scratch or chafe the skin. Good quality running shoes are also essential. Tennis shoes are major culprits in causing injury.

The start and finish of a cross-country race must be well marshaled. In particular, the start must be wide enough and long enough so that the runners can separate themselves with the minimum of jostling. The finish must be wide enough to allow exhausted runners to sprint directly to the finish without bumping or spiking each other. Course marshals must be able to position each runner according to finish with the minimum of fuss.

The warm-up is an essential part of distance training and should include loosening activities followed by easy running in which athletes emphasize stretching out and striding. Some accelerative running (''pick-ups'') may be used to get the legs moving fast.

The actual sequence and duration of activities in a warm-up will vary according to the preferences of the instructor and the athlete. The intent is to have the body warm and the cardiovascular system working well; for many, the warm-up is as much psychological as physiological.

A distance-running program for young children must be developed slowly and carefully and should emphasize variety and maintenance of interest. Distance running should not dominate a physical education program but should be mixed in with other sports so that children are exposed to a wide selection of activities. Many of these sports can emphasize aerobic development.

Avoid placing excessive demands on young athletes; making them run too often and too far can destroy interest and drive away promising runners. Children who complain frequently of soreness or who try to avoid running may indicate that your approach is wrong. Fun, variety, and progressive development are the keys.

Be aware of what is "enough": what produces a training effect and what is excessive and can lead to injuries. With beginners, use game situations that allow rests or run-walks during which you visually assess participants; red faces and other obvious signs of discomfort are signals to cut back on the demand. This chapter provides some recommended distances and times for beginners.

Aerobic workouts should predominate in distance-running programs for young children. Anaerobic training is particularly demanding for a young developing body and should occupy a minimal part of the program until the child is in the late teens. Rest and recovery days should occur after demanding training sessions; this is of benefit both physiologically and psychologically.

Athletes concentrating on both cross-country races in the fall and winter and distance competitions in the summer find themselves faced with two competitive seasons. A break should be taken between the two seasons.

TECHNIQUE

The distance runner's technique is characterized by an upright body position, although some slight forward lean may occur during phases of acceleration.

The stride length in shorter distances is moderate to long and in longer distances is somewhat shorter (Figure 5.3). When the athlete increases speed or sprints, the stride length may be reduced as the tempo of running increases.

Knee lift and leg drive depend upon the distance and the phase of the race. During sprinting phases, the knee lift will be high; during nonsprinting phases, knee lift is minimal. The arm action must balance that of the legs; arm action should be vigorous and powerful during the sprinting phases and moderate to minimal during the nonsprinting phases.

TEACHING STEPS

STEP 1. Lead-Ups
STEP 2. Aerobic Endurance Training
STEP 3. Power and Resistance Training
STEP 4. Mixing Aerobic and Anaerobic Training
STEP 5. Anaerobic Endurance Training

Step 1: Lead-Ups

Relays, Chase, and Tag

Although these activities do not normally require continuous running (which best produces a base of aerobic endurance), they do help condition the muscles and

Figure 5.3 Distance running technique

the cardiovascular system, and the fun of these activities diverts the participant's attention from the amount of running involved. See chapters 2 and 3 for examples of various types of relays and games of chase and tag.

Games

Sports such as basketball and soccer, which emphasize repetitive running, help prepare novices for more specific aerobic training that will follow later. Repetitive running and passing a ball over selected distances (e.g., the width or length of a soccer field) are also good aerobic lead-ups.

Step 2: Aerobic Endurance Training (Off-Season Precompetitive Period)

Long-Distance Running

Long-distance running is considered the best method for developing an aerobic base and building aerobic endurance. The following examples suggest ways for introducing this form of training to beginners. You need not introduce these activities in sequence, because all develop aerobic endurance. By varying the activity, you will maintain interest.

Long Runs

Long runs are usually performed in a "steady state," in which the athlete works at a rate at which oxygen demands and oxygen use are balanced. Athletes can run on trails, fields, roads, and tracks at slow to moderate speed. Emphasize variety, and instruct athletes to progressively increase intensity by running the same distance at a faster speed or running a longer distance at the original speed.

The recommended distance for beginners is 2 to 3 kilometers (1.2 to 1.8 miles).

Timed Runs

The athlete runs continuously for a specific time period rather than for a particular distance. The athlete increases intensity by attempting to run for a longer time period. A recommended time period for beginners is 8 to 15 minutes.

Long Runs in Performance Groups

Divide students into groups according to levels of performance; choose a leader for each group. The leaders carry stopwatches and take their groups on 14-minute runs (7 minutes out and 7 minutes back). Faster groups will run farther during the 14-minute time period. Increase time periods according to fitness.

Quality Distance Runs

Quality runs are distances run with greater intensity. Use these runs after students have developed aerobic conditioning from long, steady runs and from fartlek. Have students run, with greater intensity, distances that were previously run at an easy pace, and emphasize the maintenance of speed. Quality runs are usually considered the first step toward paced or tempo training, in which the athlete learns to maintain a particular pace over a selected distance. In a quality distance run, an athlete runs a measured route (usually run easily in 15 to 20 minutes) 1 to 2 minutes faster in order to improve the quality of the work.

Handicap Distance Races

Athletes can also perform a quality run in the form of a handicap distance race. Runners start singly or in pairs with time handicaps so that the fastest runners start last. Attempt to set the handicaps so that all runners arrive at the finish close together. This type of run is ideal for cross-country course and provides motivation for both slow and fast runners.

Fartlek

The objective of fartlek (Swedish for "speed-play") is to provide variation in terrain and running intensity (Figure 5.4). Fartlek also provides considerable choice in the activities performed, which can range from calisthenics to sprinting. The course is usually varied and interesting and provides opportunities for running fast, for running moderate inclines, and for long periods of slow, easy jogging and walking. For adults, the choice of when to run fast or slow is frequently left to the individual. For beginners, you control the pace and the activity; fartlek should not become a meaningless social excursion. A course lasting 12 to 15 minutes and including walks and calisthenics is recommended for beginners.

Step 3: Power and Resistance Training (Off-Season Precompetitive Period)

Power and resistance training actually occurs at the same time of the year as aerobic endurance training—during the off-season precompetitive period. The objective of power and resistance training is to develop muscular power that will assist distance running; this

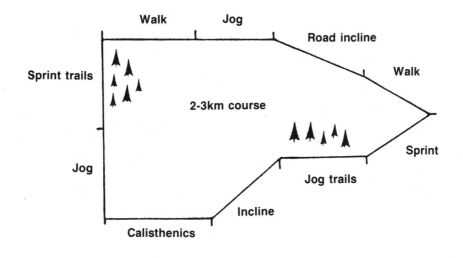

Figure 5.4 Fartlek training

training is not intended to develop needless muscular bulk. This type of training can include light weight training as well as running in sand, in snow, up hills, and in water.

Deep-water running is a popular form of resistance training for distance runners. Using flotation devices where necessary and keeping their bodies upright, distance runners literally "run" circuits in the deep end of the pool, working against the resistance of the water. Normally no contact with the bottom of the pool is allowed. You can also adapt land workouts for use in the pool so that the drills simulate the long runs of aerobic training or the run–recovery–run characteristics of interval training. Pool training is excellent for maintaining the fitness levels of injured athletes while they recover. Exercising in water allows the injured athlete to continue to train and to use joint areas such as the foot, ankle, knee, and hip, which could become more seriously injured (through compression and concussion) if training were to continue on land. Deep-water running also provides diversion, a means of increasing mileage, and an alternative method of training.

Distance runners can also practice various forms of weight training circuits using light weights (30 to 50 percent of maximum), high repetitions (15 to 30), and short recovery periods (30 to 60 seconds).

Step 4: Mixing Aerobic and Anaerobic Training (Midseason Precompetitive Period)

Once you have helped the athlete develop an aerobic base through long runs, fartlek, and quality runs,

intensify training by increasing the pace or tempo of each run, carefully regulating the length and type of recovery taken between runs, and specifying the length of each individual run and the distance accumulated in each workout.

Achieving the desired training effect is contingent upon the way you design the workouts. You may gradually change the workouts so that more anaerobic training and less aerobic training are included; introduce this change in training by having the group work on intensified fartlek. Thereafter, introduce the group to paced or tempo running, which in itself is a preparation for interval training, which follows.

Intensified Fartlek

In intensified fartlek the terrain is still varied and interesting, and the distance is the same as before, but greater effort is required. Replace walking recovery periods with jogging, make sprinting sections longer and more vigorous, and intensify and quicken the pace throughout. This activity differs considerably from the more leisurely approach taken to fartlek when it is initially introduced.

Pace or Tempo Training

Pace or tempo training refers to the rate that an athlete must run in order to cover a particular distance in a set time. Students are initially introduced to pace or tempo training through the quality distance runs and intensified fartlek. A feeling for running at the correct speed becomes very important when the athlete begins work on interval training.

Introducing Pace or Tempo Training to Novices

Start a stopwatch and ask the group (or individuals in the group) to estimate when 30 seconds have elapsed. Compare their estimates with the correct time. Then repeat this practice with other times (e.g., 20 seconds, 45 seconds).

Coaching Tips

- Close your eyes and imagine the second hand moving on a clock. Say "now" and raise your hand when you think the stopwatch has reached 30 seconds.

Estimating the Duration of a Run

Team members run in single file. Instruct leaders to take their teams over a random course and bring their teams back to the starting place in exactly 45 seconds. Change leaders and times with each run.

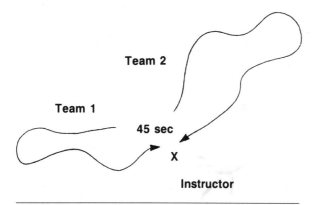

Figure 5.5 Estimating the duration of a run

Coaching Tips

- Stay together in your teams.
- Run any direction you wish; arrive back as a group.

Estimating Pace and Tempo on the Straightaway

Instruct groups to run 50 meters in 15 seconds on the straightaway. Call times as the runners pass the 50-meter mark (55 yards approximately). Do not allow athletes to suddenly increase speed to arrive at the finish on time. They must try to set the correct pace from the start. Participants walk or jog back to the start. Use the same distance and time requirement two or three times so runners can establish a feel for

the required pace. Then use differing times for subsequent occasions so that students can practice faster and slower paces of running.

Coaching Tips

- Try to get a feel for how quickly you must run to cover the distance in the required time.
- Don't bound when you run. Keep your stride length the same throughout.

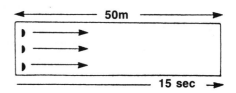

Figure 5.6 Estimating pace and tempo on a straightaway

Estimating Pace and Tempo on a Triangular Course

Three groups begin at the corners of a 3 × 50–meter triangular course laid out on the grass. Tell the groups how long they must spend running to the next corner and that they must arrive as the whistle blows. You blow the whistle at selected times (e.g., 15 seconds for beginners). Those who arrive early must run in place. Those who are slow must catch up and then adjust their paces to be more accurate over the next 50 meters. A short rest period (10 seconds light jogging on the spot) may be necessary at each corner to allow slower runners to recover.

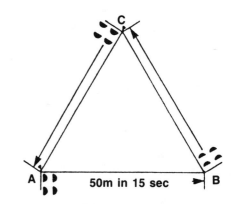

Figure 5.7 Estimating pace and tempo on a triangular course

Coaching Tips

- This is basically the same as repetitively running 50 meters in 15 seconds on the straightaway.

- Try to arrive at the corner flag exactly on the whistle blast.

Variation

Participants run a full circuit of the course in 45 seconds. A double blast indicates that athletes must run a circuit in 40 seconds. After one slow and fast circuit, athletes can take a walking recovery period. Later add larger courses (e.g., a square course rather than triangular), jogging rests rather than walking, and faster circuits to increase intensity.

Estimating Pace and Tempo on a 400-Meter Track

Set up flags or traffic cones at 50-meter intervals around a 400-meter track. Runners must maintain a set pace (e.g., 15 seconds for 50 meters), arriving at the flags on a whistle blast.

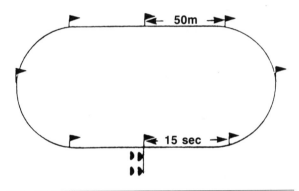

Figure 5.8 Estimating pace and tempo on a track

Pace and Tempo Training in Groups

Two groups of runners start together but run in opposing directions around the track. Each group must maintain the correct tempo (e.g., 200 meters in 40

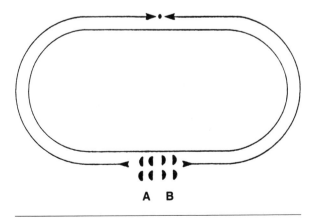

Figure 5.9 Group pace and tempo training

seconds) in order to arrive exactly together on the opposing side of the track. They pass each other and continue to run, meeting on the side of the track on which they started. Flags placed every 50 meters around the track, coupled with 10 second whistle blasts, can help athletes pace themselves. Require a faster pace for more experienced athletes.

Pace Training, Varying Distances

Athletes run different distances in the same time period (e.g., 50, 60, and 70 meters, each in 20 seconds), forcing a change in pace for each distance.

Coaching Tips

- Reduce stride length and tempo for the short distances.
- Increase stride length and tempo for the longer distances.
- Try to relax as you run, loosening the muscles of your arms, hands, and face.
- Swing your arms forward and backward, not across your body.
- Keep your vision forward and your head up. Don't roll your head or let it drop back.

Interval Training

There are many variations of this form of training, each type depending upon the balance of aerobic and anaerobic endurance you want to achieve. Interval training systematically varies the following:

- distance run
- number of times distance is run
- speed of each run
- length of recovery period between each run
- type of recovery (walk, jog) taken during recovery period

Thus, by using recovery periods after each run, the athlete is able to run repetitively at race pace or even faster. No other form of distance training provides this benefit.

Most forms of interval training use an incomplete or partial recovery during recovery periods. This means that the heart is not allowed to fully return to a resting level. By starting the next run when the cardiovascular system has only partially recovered, the athlete progressively adapts to the training, and the cardiovascular system becomes more efficient.

Interval training is usually performed on the track and as such is highly formal, repetitious, and disciplined, a fact you must take into consideration when working with school-age athletes.

The variables used in interval training (e.g., distance or number of runs) are interrelated. How much or how many of each ultimately depends upon the athlete's level of fitness and the specific intent of the training, such as the race distance the athlete is training for. These variables are as follows:

- Distance. Training distances vary considerably (50 to 1,500 meters) and depend upon the length of race the athlete is training for. The distance the athlete runs is related to the speed of each run, the number of repetitions performed, and the duration and type of the recovery periods.
- Number of Repetitions. The number of repetitions depends on the distance of the run, the speed of the run, and the duration and type of each recovery period.
- Speed. The speed of the run is usually modified so that the heart rate returns to 120 at the end of each recovery period. The speed depends on the distance of the run, the number of repetitions, and the duration and type of the recovery period.
- Type of Recovery. The type of recovery used by the athlete may be a walk, a slow or fast jog, or a slow run. The type of recovery (and its duration) will depend upon the speed of the run, the distance, and the number of repetitions performed.
- Duration of Recovery. The recovery period may last from less than 1 minute to 5 minutes or more. As with the type of recovery, the duration of the recovery depends upon the speed of the run, the distance, and the number of repetitions performed. The type and duration of recovery period depend upon the speed with which the athlete's heart returns to 120 beats.

Interval Training Designed to Develop Aerobic Endurance

This form of training develops stamina and basic endurance and forms a foundation for the other types of interval training that follow. It is characterized by short distances (50 to 200 meters), short recovery periods (1 minute or less), and a large number of repetitions (10 to 15). Because of the short recovery periods, the athlete is forced to run the next repetition with an incomplete recovery. In this way, the cardiovascular system continuously works under stress and develops the capacity to recover quickly.

Athletes who compete in the long sprints (400 meters) need less aerobic endurance than anaerobic endurance. However, they do train to improve their aerobic endurance, and for this reason the 400 meters is included in Table 5.1.

Introduce beginners to interval training at the same time they work on paced or tempo training. The repetitive runs around the triangular course (Figure 5.7), although used to develop a feel for paced or tempo running, are also a simplified form of interval training. This triangular course can be expanded to a square course, as shown in Figure 5.10.

Introduction to Interval Training on a Square Course

Groups start at the corner flags and run to reach the next corner flag on the whistle (e.g., 15 seconds). Require a specific recovery period (jogging in place)

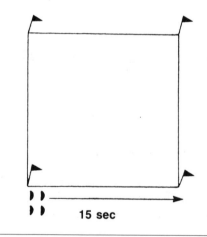

Figure 5.10 Interval training on a square course

Table 5.1 Example of Aerobic Interval Training

Competitive distance (m)	Training distance (m)	Speed of run	Repetitions	Recovery (s)	Type of recovery
400	50-200	Fast–moderate	10-15	10-60	Walk, jog, or run
800	100-200	Moderate	10-15	10-60	Walk, jog, or run
1,500	100-200	Moderate	10-15	10-60	Walk, jog, or run
3,000	100-300	Moderate	10-15	10-60	Walk, jog, or run

at each flag. Set the speed of the run, the number of repetitions, and the length of the recovery period according to the levels of fitness of the participants. Recommended time and rest period for novices are as follows: Athletes run each 50-meter side of the square in 15 seconds followed by a 15-second recovery (easy jogging in place). After 4 circuits, assign the groups a circuit of walk recovery.

Introduction to Interval Training on the Track

Groups of novices walk around the track. Group A runs at medium tempo to catch up with Group B; at that point Group A walks again. Group B then runs to catch up with Group C, and groups repeat the process around the track. The recovery period is the walk, and the distance is determined by how far the groups are apart. Determine the tempo of running and the number of repetitions according to the fitness levels of the participants.

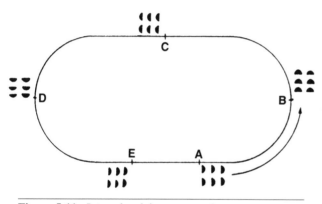

Figure 5.11 Interval training on a track

Interval Training Designed to Develop a Mix of Aerobic and Anaerobic Endurance

Interval training that includes fast to moderately fast runs builds stamina at a pace close to competitive con-

ditions. Basic endurance improves, and at the same time the muscles become used to working anaerobically. Because the runs are generally fast, the recovery periods are longer. Distances vary considerably. The number of runs depends upon the intent of the training (i.e., aerobic or anaerobic) and the athlete's level of fitness. Table 5.2 shows an example of this type of training. It is best to start with a light work load and then progressively increase the intensity.

There are many ways you can design interval training to develop a mix of aerobic and anaerobic endurance.

Interval Sprints

Students run short distances (50 to 100 meters) at high speed, then have a walking recovery of 50 to 100 meters. The number of repetitions will depend upon fitness. Increase the intensity of the training by changing the walk to a jog.

Equal Distances and Recovery Periods

The athlete sprints for 25 seconds and recovers for 25 seconds by jogging slowly. This sequence is performed for 3 or 4 repetitions.

Interval Relay

Form a team of 3 runners. Runner A sprints at top speed to pass the baton to Runner B, then jogs to recover. Runner B runs to pass the baton to Runner C and recovers after the pass. Each runner sprints 5 × 200 meters to cover a distance of 1,000 meters (3,000 meters in total for the team).

Pyramid (Ladder) Sprints

Progressively increase the sprint distance or duration of the sprint; after the athletes reach the top of the "pyramid" or have climbed the "ladder," then

Table 5.2 Example of Aerobic/Anaerobic Interval Training

Competitive distance (m)	Training distance (m)	Speed of run	Repetitions	Recovery (min)	Type of recovery
400	100-300	Fast	3-10	1-5	Walk, jog, or run
800	200-600	Fast–moderate	3-10	1-5	Walk, jog, or run
1,500	200-1,000	Fast–moderate	3-10	1-5	Walk, jog, or run
3,000	200-1,500	Moderate	3-10	1-5	Walk, jog, or run

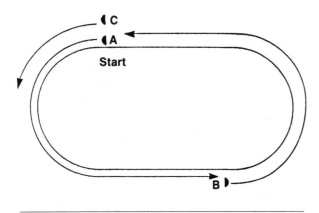

Figure 5.12 Interval relay

progressively decrease distance or duration. For example, athletes run 50, 100, 150, 200, 150, 100, and 50 meters. Or, they sprint for 10, 15, 20, 15, and 10 seconds. The type and duration of recovery period will depend on the athletes' levels of fitness.

Step 5: Anaerobic Endurance Training (In-Season Competitive Period)

Frequently called quality or speed training, this training requires the athlete to run at maximum or close

to maximum speed. Although it uses a run–recovery–run sequence, like other types of interval training, quality or speed training is not considered true interval training because it does not work on the principle of partial recovery after each run. Instead, the high speed of each run requires a complete recovery. The types of drills used are similar to those designed to develop a mix of aerobic and anaerobic endurance. However, the difference is that quality or speed training always requires maximum or close to maximum speed, to enable the athlete to develop sheer speed and the stamina to maintain relaxed and controlled form while running flat-out. Because of the high speed, fewer repetitions are used. This type of training adds a final polish to the athlete's preparation and establishes a "feel" for the pace that will be used during the race. This training is performed immediately prior to and also during the competitive season. Table 5.3 provides an example.

Table 5.3 Example of Quality Training

Competitive distance (m)	Training distance (m)	Speed of run	Repetitions	Recovery	Type of recovery
400	100-200	Fast	2-4	Sufficient to allow full recovery	Walk, jog, or run
800	200-600	Fast	2-4	Sufficient to allow full recovery	Walk, jog, or run
1,000	200-800	Fast	2-4	Sufficient to allow full recovery	Walk, jog, or run
2,000	300-1,000	Fast	2-4	Sufficient to allow full recovery	Walk, jog, or run
3,000	300-1,000	Fast	2-4	Sufficient to allow full recovery	Walk, jog, or run

COMMON ERRORS AND CORRECTIONS

DISTANCE-RUNNING TECHNIQUE

ERROR	REASONS	CORRECTIONS
The athlete uses an uneconomical style of running.	The athlete's leg drive is too much upward and not sufficiently forward.	The athlete practices bounding and hopping, stressing correct leg drive. Emphasize running without rise and fall of the hips.
The athlete leans backward while running. The head is back or is allowed to "roll around."	The athlete has incorrect chest (torso) and head position, and the vision is not directly ahead. The athlete may have weak abdominal and trunk muscles.	The athlete practices running technique activities, running with the head forward and vision ahead. Also assign strengthening exercises for the abdomen.
The athlete swings the shoulders (and head) from side to side while running.	The arms swing across the chest. The athlete has poor concentration on running technique, and vision is not directly ahead.	Stress running technique activities, as with the previous error. Have the athlete practice arm swinging—parallel and in the direction of the run—standing and then while running.
The athlete uses poor drive or extension of the leg while running. The athlete has an appearance of "sitting" while running, or "bent-legged" running.	The athlete uses no extension or leg thrust during the run and has poor leg power and hip flexibility.	Assign exercises for increasing leg power and hip flexibility: hopping, bounding, and jumping, and hurdler's flexibility exercises.
The athlete appears tense while running.	Tension results from poor running technique, exhaustion, poor preparation, and inadequate flexibility.	The athlete must work to relax the face, loosen the lower jaw, and relax the hands (no fists). Arms should be held at an angle of 90 degrees at the elbow. Work to improve the aerobic/anaerobic base, and improve flexibility through related stretching exercises.

ASSESSMENT

1. Assess the following theoretical elements as taught during instructional sessions.

   a. Fundamental rules governing distance running.
   b. Good safety habits for distance running.
   c. Basic elements of distance-running technique.
   d. Basic elements of training for distance running.

2. Assess the performance of technique during the following stages of skill development.

   a. Long runs of varying types.
   b. Pace and tempo runs.
   c. Interval training.
   d. Quality/speed training.

   Critical Features of Technique to Observe During Assessment

   - Overall appearance of relaxed, easy running style.
   - Upright body position with minimal body lean during periods of acceleration.
   - Moderate knee lift and arm swing.
   - Arms and legs work directly forward and backward.
   - A rolling support from the heel to the ball of the foot.
   - Minimal lift and fall of the hips with each stride.
   - Variation in tempo and stride control according to demand.

3. Hold graded competitions to help develop motivation and technique.

   a. Participants compete in a 12-minute run. How much distance is covered?
   b. Participants compete over distances selected according to age and ability.
   c. Participants compete singly in a handicap distance race. Start each individual on the basis of prior performances, giving the weakest runner the greatest time advantage.
   d. Participants compete in pairs in a handicap race; members of each pair pace each other. Start each pair on the basis of prior performance, giving the weakest pair the greatest time advantage.
   e. Students predict the times they can achieve in running a specified distance, and scores are awarded for proximity to the predicted time. You set a maximum time for the course on the basis of previous performances.
   f. Groups compete against each other, simulating a cycle pursuit race. Here, two groups of runners start on opposing sides of the track; the group that gains distance on its opposition at the end of a specified time is the winner.
   g. Individuals compete against each other on an orienteering run. Using markers positioned around the course, maps and a compass, athletes compete over a specified distance. Base the distance and difficulty level on the ability levels of the competitors.

SUGGESTED PERFORMANCE
STANDARDS (MINUTES)

MALE

Age	Distance (m)	800	1,500	3,000
11-12	Satisfactory	3.20	7.00	16.00
	Good	3.10	6.30	15.00
	Excellent	3.00	6.00	13.30
13-14	Satisfactory	3.10	6.30	15.00
	Good	2.50	6.00	13.30
	Excellent	2.40	5.30	11.50
15-16	Satisfactory	2.50	6.00	13.30
	Good	2.40	5.30	11.50
	Excellent	2.30	5.00	10.50
17-19	Satisfactory	2.45	5.30	11.50
	Good	2.35	5.00	10.50
	Excellent	2.20	4.50	10.30

FEMALE

Age	Distance (m)	800	1,500	3,000
11-12	Satisfactory	3.30	8.00	18.00
	Good	3.20	7.30	17.00
	Excellent	3.10	7.00	16.00
13-14	Satisfactory	3.20	7.30	17.00
	Good	3.10	7.00	16.00
	Excellent	3.00	6.30	15.00
15-16	Satisfactory	3.10	7.00	16.00
	Good	3.00	6.30	15.00
	Excellent	2.50	6.00	13.30
17-19	Satisfactory	3.00	6.30	15.00
	Good	2.50	6.00	13.30
	Excellent	2.40	5.30	12.00

CHAPTER

6

STEEPLECHASE

Steeplechase, which is derived from cross-country running and obstacle course races, is a combination of distance running, hurdling, and water jumps and as such combines the training necessary for the distance runner and the hurdler. At present steeplechase is a track event for males only.

The laws of the event allow the athlete to jump on and off the water-jump barrier and to use the same technique in clearing the steeplechase hurdles. The athlete is also permitted to vault over the barriers, although this method is seldom used because it is extremely inefficient. The hurdles and the water jump barrier used in the steeplechase are solid, heavy barriers designed to support the weight of several athletes at the same time. The barriers are not designed to fall or to be knocked over in the manner that occurs in the 100/110-meter and 400-meter hurdles.

Clearance of the water jump requires a technique similar to that used in jumping on and off steeplechase hurdles. The two types of obstacles differ in that the water jump not only has a barrier but also a 3.66-meter (12-foot) water pit, which the athlete must jump across or run through. The common practice is to jump up onto the 91.4-centimeter (3-foot) barrier with one leg and use the same leg to drive across the water. Occasionally an athlete will jump from the barrier and totally clear the water, but most athletes land with 1 foot in the water and step out with the other.

For athletes over 19 years of age, the competitive steeplechase distance is 3,000 meters with the water jump most frequently on the inside of the track. Each lap is slightly less than 400 meters (approximately 390 meters). At the senior level, a 3,000-meter race contains 28 hurdles and 7 water jumps. A 2,000-meter steeplechase race has 18 hurdles and 5 water jumps, and the 1,500-meter race 12 hurdles and 3 water jumps. The latter two races are usually run by athletes below senior age level.

An athlete who concentrates on steeplechase needs to be an excellent distance and cross-country runner and a good hurdler and must be strong enough to perform efficiently over the water jump. One of the biggest difficulties that the steeplechaser will face is estimating takeoff positions for the hurdles and the water jump throughout the race relative to an increasing level of fatigue. All steeplechasers jump on and off the water-jump barrier. Some use the same technique on the hurdles, whereas others use a hurdle clearance similar to a 400-meter hurdler. Whatever the method, the athlete must cross the barriers as efficiently as possible and with minimum wastage of energy.

SAFETY SUGGESTIONS

Steeplechase is a demanding distance race. In terms of fatigue, a 1,500-meter steeplechase race is generally considered equal to a 3,000-meter race on the flat. Young athletes are usually introduced to steeplechase by way of cross-country running. Their initial experiences with steeplechase should be short competitions that have the minimal number of hurdle and water-jump clearances.

It is particularly important that the young athlete learn to jump on and jump off the barriers before learning to hurdle. In addition, the athlete should develop a good aerobic base through long runs and interval training. The stamina that the athlete develops with this kind of training will mean that fatigue will take longer to affect the quality of the clearance technique used. Part of the young athlete's training will be to recognize and gauge the onset of fatigue and to decide when to switch from actually hurdling steeplechase hurdles to the easier technique of jumping on and off.

To maintain a high level of safety, check all steeplechase hurdles and the water-jump barrier to make sure that they are stable and capable of withstanding the force applied by several athletes jumping on and off at the same time. Replace the tops of barriers when they become splintered, and be sure the floor of the water-jump pit is smooth and covered either with the same rubberized surface used on the track or with a mat. This cushions the athlete's landing when he jumps down into the water. Empty the water from the water-jump pit when it is not in use.

Competitors should wear well-fitting spikes that drain well and are comfortable to run in when wet. A good safety practice is to have athletes walk into the water-jump pit with their spikes on, totally immerse their feet (and shoes), and then retighten the soaked laces. Nylon shoes stretch when they become wet, and this precaution prevents shoes from becoming loose and uncomfortable during a race.

In physical education classes in which students do not wear spikes, it's best to use a simulated water jump: Students jump onto a steeplechase hurdle and then into the sand of the long-jump pit (Figure 6.5). Even though the surface of the hurdle is likely to remain dry, be aware that wet grass or sand on top of the hurdle can cause an athlete not wearing spikes to slip. When students wear rubber-soled shoes, all surfaces should be dry and the hurdle surface brushed clean of sand and dirt.

The preparation for clearing the hurdles and the water jump is an important part of steeplechase technique. Elite athletes become accustomed to occasional bumping and jostling and to maneuvering and adjusting their approach for each of the barriers. Even though bumping occurs, athletes are expected to respect the rules and avoid cutting in and disrupting the approaches of others. The first barrier (hurdle) in a steeplechase race is purposely made longer so that at the start of the race, athletes who are bunched close together can clear the hurdle without incident.

Teach the athletes to approach all barriers straight on so that the contact of the foot with the barrier is at a right angle. This becomes even more important when the barriers become wet on top. When the water jump is on a curve of the track, the athlete should run wide so that the approach to the water jump is in a straight line.

The athlete must not run closely behind an opponent when approaching the barriers. It is better to shift away from the opponent and get a clear view of the barrier, so that if the opponent trips and falls, the athlete behind is not involved in the same incident. Also, teach athletes to avoid pausing after landing in the water at the water jump. Other athletes will be following and preparing to jump down from the barrier.

For indoor training, vaulting boxes safely substitute for steeplechase barriers providing that spotters stabilize the boxes. Outdoors, a steeplechase barrier set in front of the long-jump pit provides a good substitute for the water jump, particularly as landing in the sand simulates the drag of the water.

When you work with young athletes, the most important feature of training is careful and progressive development. Increase the competitive distance and the number and height of the barriers as fitness and maturity develop. For beginners, 1 or 2 vaulting-box sections 30 to 60 centimeters (1 to 2 feet) tall set in front of the long-jump pit substitute adequately for a water jump.

TECHNIQUE

At about 10 to 15 meters prior to the water jump, the athlete accelerates in order to jump up onto the barrier and then clear the water. The takeoff usually occurs 1.5 to 2 meters (5 feet to 6 feet 6 inches) prior to the barrier. The upper body leans forward, and the free leg is flexed so that the instep can be placed on the barrier.

Once on the barrier, the supporting leg flexes to approximately 90 degrees and the upper body is kept low so that the athlete passes low over the barrier, rather than jumping upward.

When the athlete's body has passed over the supporting leg, the spikes grip the forward edge of the barrier in preparation for the drive over the water. The athlete drives forward and downward with the leading leg, aiming at landing 30 to 40 centimeters (12 to 16 inches) before the end of the water jump. The athlete extends the arms sideways on the landing to maintain balance (Figure 6.1).

TEACHING STEPS

STEP 1.	Lead-Ups
STEP 2.	Development of Aerobic and Anaerobic Endurance
STEP 3.	Steeplechase Hurdle and Water-Jump Clearance

Figure 6.1 Steeplechase technique

Step 1: Lead-Ups

All lead-up drills used for distance running and for hurdling are excellent preparation for the steeplechase, because a steeplechaser is in essence a cross-country runner competing on the track. Lead-ups that develop stamina (see chapter 5), hurdling ability (see chapter 4), and explosive leg power (see chapter 9) are excellent preparation for the steeplechaser. Flexibility exercises will improve hurdling technique, and weight-training leg exercises and rebound jumping (plyometrics) are excellent for improving leg strength and assisting in the clearance of the water jump.

The developmental sequence for teaching steeplechase consists of combining endurance training with drills that teach the young athlete to jump on and off the steeplechase hurdles.

Because the steeplechase hurdle has the same dimensions as the barrier in front of the water jump, a common practice is to use a hurdle as a substitute for the water-jump barrier and the long-jump pit as a substitute water jump. Once accustomed to landing in the sand, the athlete then progresses to clearing the actual water pit. Throughout these practices, the athlete can work to develop a reasonable hurdling technique over low sprint hurdles. When the athlete can easily clear 91.4-centimeter (3-foot) sprint hurdles, he can apply the same technique to steeplechase hurdles.

Step 2: Development of Aerobic and Anaerobic Endurance

See chapter 5 for drills to develop aerobic and anaerobic endurance.

Step 3: Steeplechase Hurdle and Water-Jump Clearance

Jumping On and Off a Vaulting Box

The vaulting box is progressively built up in sections to the competitive steeplechase height of approximately 3 feet (91.4 centimeters). Students can initially practice in the gym, starting with lower heights and using a mat to cushion the landing. The athlete jumps onto the box and, using the same leg, drives forward onto the mat (the takeoff leg from the floor is not the same leg used to drive from the box). Each athlete should learn to lead with either leg and to judge the takeoff position relative to the approach speed. The athlete must drive forward and upward with the arms and free leg to help jump onto the box. Once on the box, the athlete rotates forward over a flexed supporting leg, keeping the body low and the torso inclined forward during the clearance. The athlete uses a strong drive forward with the leading leg to jump from the box and uses the arms to maintain balance during the landing. Bounding and hopping activities used in triple jump (chapter 9) are useful preparatory exercises for steeplechase hurdle and water-jump clearance.

Use spotters to assure that the vaulting box is stable and will not tilt when the performer jumps onto it. The athlete must approach and jump onto the box at a 90° angle; any other angle may cause the athlete to fall when jumping onto a wet steeplechase barrier. The athlete must approach the box at right angles.

Coaching Tips

- To begin with, use your favored leg to jump up onto the hurdle from the ground. (Chapter 8 contains activities to select the favored leg.)

Figure 6.2 Jumping on and off a vaulting box

- Run wide from the curve and line up directly at the center of the vaulting box.
- Swing the thigh of the leading leg upward and drive strongly from the jumping leg.
- Swing both arms forward and upward to assist you in jumping up onto the box.
- Stay low over the box; don't straighten up.
- Jump long and low down to the ground.
- Put your arms out sideways to help maintain balance in the landing.
- Keep moving forward; don't pause at the landing. In a race other competitors will follow.

Inclusion of a Vaulting Box and Two Low Sprint Hurdles in a Circuit

This practice is for the athlete who can hurdle over low hurdles and adjust the approach for takeoff to the hurdles.

Variations in the size of the circuit and the positioning of the box and hurdles develop the athlete's abilities to assess the distance of the jump takeoff and to clear the hurdles. At least 15 meters should be available for acceleration toward the box. Use check marks set at 6 to 8 strides prior to the box to help beginners

Figure 6.3 Steeplechase training circuit

judge the approach distance for takeoff. You can also set the box low and then progressively move it higher. Initially set the hurdles well below 91.4 centimeters (3 feet).

Figure 6.3 shows a circuit that you can set up indoors. You can also use the vaulting box on the track or place the box in front of the long-jump pit to simulate the water jump.

Coaching Tips

- Try to lengthen your stride rather than shorten it when assessing the distance for the takeoff to the box.
- Accelerate toward the box; don't slow down.

Jumping On and Off a Steeplechase Hurdle

The steeplechase hurdle substitutes for the barrier in front of the water jump, because both are the same height and width. Draw a line on the ground to indicate the 3.66 meters (12 feet) of the water jump. Teach the athlete to adjust the approach so that the takeoff is accurate for jumping onto the hurdle, to correctly place the foot on the top of the hurdle, and to clear a distance approximating that of the water jump.

Coaching Tips

- Be sure to accelerate toward the hurdle.
- Contact the hurdle with your instep; allow your foot to roll on the top of the hurdle so that the instep of the foot grips the far side of the hurdle.
- Lean forward and flex the supporting leg on the hurdle so that your body rotates low over the hurdle. (Do not try standing up on the hurdle.)
- Drive low and forward for the landing.

- Use the swing of the leading leg to assist in driving your body outward for the landing.
- Use your arms for balance in the landing.

Combining a Steeplechase Hurdle and the Long-Jump Pit to Simulate a Steeplechase Water-Jump Clearance

Place a steeplechase hurdle at the edge of the long-jump pit, and include other steeplechase hurdles or sprint hurdles in a circuit. Athletes jump up onto the hurdle and jump down into the sand of the long-jump pit. The "drag" of the sand simulates the effect of the water in the water jump. Intensify the drill by including more hurdles and increasing the distance run.

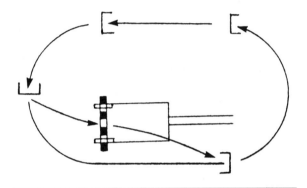

Figure 6.5 Simulated steeplechase water-jump clearance

Coaching Tips

- Concentrate on driving low and forward into the landing.
- Do not relax in the landing; try to keep moving forward.

Figure 6.4 Jumping on and off a steeplechase hurdle

Jumping Onto the Water-Jump Barrier and Clearing the Water Jump

The performer jumps up onto the barrier and aims to clear all but the final few centimeters of water. One foot lands in the water and the other steps forward out of the water to continue running. Teach the performer that the single-legged landing in the water is an active landing from which the athlete quickly moves forward. The next stride should be well clear of the water.

Coaching Tips

* The single-legged landing in the water is an active landing: Don't relax when you land, but keep driving forward. The next stride should be clear of the water.

Improvement of Steeplechase Hurdle Clearance

Remember steeplechase hurdles cannot be set at a height lower than 91.4 centimeters (3 feet). They are built to support several athletes jumping on them at the same time. Consequently, the novice should continue to jump on and off steeplechase hurdles until an adequate hurdle clearance technique is developed over sprint hurdles. It is an advantage to be able to hurdle with either leg leading, although this is not absolutely necessary. For greater confidence in clearing the 91-centimeter (3-foot) steeplechase hurdles, the athlete must be comfortable in hurdling sprint hurdles set at 98 centimeters (3 feet 3 inches). (See chapter 4 for drills and coaching tips to develop hurdling technique and the ability to hurdle with an alternate leg lead.)

Clearing a Steeplechase Water Jump and Steeplechase Hurdles in Distance Training

Place the steeplechase water jump and steeplechase hurdles in various sections of middle-distance training runs. By varying the positions of the barriers, you force the athlete to adjust approach and stride pattern relative to various levels of fatigue. If several athletes train together, this drill forces each athlete to assess stride patterns for takeoff under competitive conditions. The level of fatigue will vary according to the run.

For example, set the course so the athlete clears the steeplechase water jump and hurdles several times in the 1st part of a middle-distance training run and completes the remaining part of the run without barriers to clear. Or, the athlete clears the steeplechase water jump and hurdles in the midphase of a middle-distance training run and completes the 1st and latter parts of the run without barriers to clear. Another variation is to set the course so the athlete clears the steeplechase water jump and hurdles in the last part of a middle-distance training run.

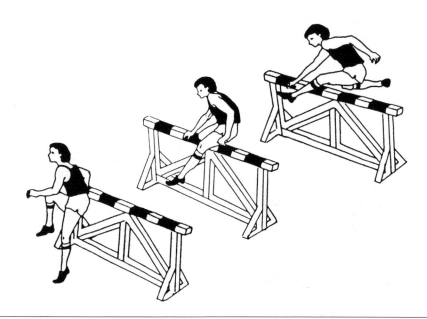

Figure 6.6   Steeplechase hurdle clearance

COMMON ERRORS AND CORRECTIONS

STEEPLECHASE WATER-JUMP CLEARANCE

ERROR	REASONS	CORRECTIONS
The athlete's pacing and rhythm of approach to the water jump are poorly judged. The athlete takes stutter steps prior to takeoff.	The athlete has had insufficient practice on the approach. The athlete is anxious and has poor endurance.	The athlete needs repetitive practice of approach and clearance of the water jump. Use check marks to help the athlete develop a feel for distance in final strides prior to takeoff. Work on endurance training.
The athlete loses momentum after jumping onto the barrier and hesitates prior to clearing the water jump.	The athlete takes off from too far away or jumps too high and lands on the barrier with an erect upper body and/or straight legs.	Instruct the athlete to keep the upper body low and forward when landing on the barrier. The athlete must flex at the hips and knees to keep the center of gravity low and to provide drive over water jump.
The athlete lands in the middle of the water. The jump is either too high or too short.	The approach to the water jump is too slow. The athlete has poor drive from the barrier with the supporting leg and poor transfer of forward momentum from the arms and leading leg. The jump from the barrier may be upward rather than forward.	Help the athlete improve aerobic endurance, and work to speed up the approach to the water jump. Use repetitive bounding and jumping to improve jumping technique and to strengthen legs. Instruct the athlete to flex the supporting leg on the barrier, keep low, and drive forward.
The athlete loses speed after landing in the water.	The athlete jumps upward from the barrier and relaxes and hesitates after landing in the water.	The athlete must lean forward and drive forward and outward, concentrating on keeping the body moving forward after landing in the water.

ASSESSMENT

1. Assess the following theoretical elements as taught during instructional sessions.

   a. Fundamental rules governing steeplechase competition.
   b. Good safety habits for use in steeplechase training.
   c. Basic elements of steeplechase technique.
   d. Basic elements of steeplechase training.

2. Assess the performance of technique during the following stages of skill development.

   a. A simulated water-jump clearance using a steeplechase hurdle and the long-jump pit, or a simulated water-jump clearance using a vaulting box and gymnastics mats.
   b. A water-jump clearance using the competitive equipment.
   c. A jump-on/jump-off steeplechase hurdle clearance.

d. A steeplechase hurdle clearance using hurdling technique.

e. A series of steeplechase hurdle and water-jump clearances occurring during the start, middle, or end of a distance run. (Tempo and stride adjustment in the run-up for the hurdle and water-jump clearances are challenged by the differing levels of fatigue that occur.)

Critical Features of Technique to Observe During Assessment

Water-Jump Clearance and Jump Clearance of a Steeplechase Hurdle

- Stride adjustment and acceleration toward the steeplechase water-jump hurdle.
- Vigorous drive with the supporting leg, forward body lean, and flexion in the leading leg at takeoff toward the hurdle.
- Low carriage of the upper body over a flexed (90 degrees) supporting leg on the hurdle.
- Strong forward and downward drive from the hurdle with the arms spread for balance on the landing.
- An active landing with the leading leg, from which the athlete immediately continues running.
  (For the steeplechase hurdle clearance using hurdling technique, see 100/110-meter hurdles and 400-meter hurdles in chapter 4.)

3. Hold graded competitions to develop motivation and technique.

   a. Individuals compete in cross-country runs that include water jumps, hurdles, and similar obstacles.
   b. Runners compete in steeplechase competitions that are graded according to age and experience. Runners compete over 1,500, 2,000, and 3,000 meters.

SUGGESTED PERFORMANCE STANDARDS (MINUTES)

MALE

Distance
1,500-m steeplechase

Age		Satisfactory	Good	Excellent
15-16		8.00	7.20	6.40
17-19		7.20	6.40	6.00

7

HIGH JUMP

In recent years the Fosbury Flop technique of high jumping has superseded the straddle, and the world records for both males and females are held by flop jumpers. The preference for the flop technique also exists in the multidiscipline competitions of the decathlon and the heptathlon. Although a few athletes still use the straddle, most prefer the flop. Most athletes find the flop technically less demanding than the straddle and considerably easier to learn. Youngsters tend to grasp the fundamentals quickly and find the flop's dramatic method of bar clearance more attractive than that of the straddle.

SAFETY SUGGESTIONS

The drop from height and the backward rotation in the Fosbury Flop frequently cause jumpers to land on their shoulders and then roll backward. Landing pads that have insufficient depth and are too low to the ground allow too much backward rotation in flight, which, combined with drop from a height, cause compression injuries in the neck and shoulders. You should use landing pads that are specified by the manufacturer to accommodate the flop. Such pads are noted for their absorbency and large landing area (5 meters by 4 meters). The landing surface is at least 1-1/2 meters above the ground, which is essential in stopping athletes from overrotating backward while in flight.

Flop jumpers also tend to have flight paths that cause them to cross the landing pads diagonally and land in the corners, so the corners should have as much support as the centers. Don't use any landing pad that might allow the athlete to "bottom out." Nor should you try to create a landing area out of a stack of gymnastic crash pads. Even when the mats are tied together, an athlete could fall into the separation between them.

Surgical tubing or elastic rope is an excellent teaching aid and is preferable to competitive crossbars for training. Take care to ensure that the high-jump standards are well anchored at the base and that the rubber "crossbars" can stretch adequately so the standards do not pull in toward the athlete during a poor jump.

Run-ups should be firm and give good traction and support for each successive jumper. Grass and artificial surfaces may become slippery and dangerous when wet unless spikes are used. The design of high jump spikes is critical for good traction on the takeoff. The shoe on the jumping foot normally has 6 spikes on the sole and more on the heel to prevent slipping during the last stride prior to takeoff. Many athletes use short spikes or none at all on the leading (swing-up) leg.

One of the most important factors in successful flop high jumping at the elite level is an extreme back arch during bar clearance. This high degree of flexibility is developed slowly and systematically over a long period. It is unnecessary for novices and recreational jumpers; they can achieve good performance with minimal hyperextension of the back during bar clearance. It is important that instructors who work with young athletes realize that the back arch is not a natural position for the body and that extreme spinal flexibility is not a prerequisite to enjoying high jumping at the elementary level.

TECHNIQUE

The athlete leans into the final curve of a fast, long run-up. At takeoff the athlete drives directly upward off the jumping foot, simultaneously forcing the leg nearest the bar both upward and back toward the run-up. This action helps to rotate the athlete into a back layout position.

The arms, which assist in takeoff, may be brought into the sides of the body, or one arm can reach out along the line of the bar. When the jumper's shoulders cross the bar, the back is hyperextended and the hips pressed upward. Once the athlete's seat has passed over the bar, there is a powerful flexion at the hips as the legs are brought toward the chest. The head and shoulders lift upward and assist in clearing the legs over the bar. The athlete relaxes to land on the back and shoulders (see Figure 7.1).

TEACHING STEPS

STEP 1.	Lead-Ups
STEP 2.	Flop High Jump Using a Short (3-Stride) Run-Up
STEP 3.	Flop High Jump Using an Extended (Curved) Run-Up

Step 1: Lead-Ups

All jumping, bounding, and sprinting activities are excellent preparation for the high jump. Lead-ups used for the long jump (chapter 8), the triple jump (chapter 9), and sprinting (chapter 2) can also be used for the high jump.

Figure 7.1 Two views of the flop high jump technique

High-Knee Marching

With each step the athlete drives the thigh of the leading leg up to horizontal or above. The athlete drives up onto the toes of the supporting foot, works the arms vigorously, and drives the knee upward as powerfully as possible.

Figure 7.2 High-knee marching

High-Knee Running

Each participant runs slowly, concentrating on raising the thigh of the leading leg to horizontal or above. The athlete drives up onto the toes of the supporting foot throughout.

Figure 7.3 High-knee running

Long Bounding Strides

With each stride the athlete drives both forward and upward to cover as much ground as possible. The athlete drives the thigh of the leading leg up to horizontal and works the arms vigorously throughout. The driving leg extends powerfully and vigorously throughout.

Coaching Tips

- Swing your arms forward and upward with each bounding stride.
- Try to achieve a wide stride position at the midpoint of each bounding stride.
- Try to get a feeling of "floating" at the midpoint of each stride.

Jumping to Head a Suspended Volleyball or Soccerball

Suspend balls 30 to 60 centimeters (1 to 2 feet) above the heads of the participants. From a run-up of 3 to 5 strides, each athlete jumps to head the ball, using a 1-footed takeoff.

Coaching Tips

- Try to lean slightly backward prior to takeoff.
- Jump directly upward.
- Swing your arms and leading leg upward as vigorously as possible.

A Stride Jump Over the Bar

Substitute surgical elastic tubing for a competitive crossbar. Participants approach directly from the front and stride-jump over the substitute crossbar to land on both feet in a standing position. This drill encourages the athletes to jump directly upward and also develops the correct rolling action from the heel and toe on the takeoff (jumping) foot.

Figure 7.4 Bounding strides

Figure 7.5 Heading a suspended ball

Coaching Tips

- Drive up vigorously with the leading leg and your arms at takeoff.
- Stretch up and extend your body at takeoff.
- Keep your head up; don't lean forward in the jump.

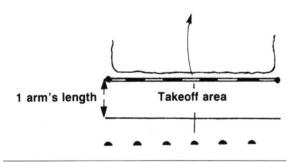

Figure 7.6 Stride jumping over a simulated bar

Marking a Takeoff Line for a Stride Jump Over the Bar

Set the elastic crossbar 2 to 3 inches (7 centimeters) above the top of the landing pads. Mark a takeoff line

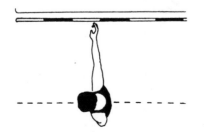

Figure 7.7 Marking a takeoff line for a stride jump

on the ground at approximately one arm's length back from the bar. Participants are not allowed to jump from farther back than the line; this forces them to high jump rather than long jump.

A Stride Jump Using a Three-Stride Approach

Set the takeoff spot 1 arm's length back from the bar. Starting with the feet together, each participant measures 3 running strides from the takeoff spot at an angle of 35 to 40 degrees to the bar. This angle allows the athlete to rotate onto the back for the bar clearance and will be required later for a curved run-up. Use traffic cones to guide the run-up. A jumper approaching from the left begins with the feet together and starts the run-up with the right foot. The jumper will use a right–left–right run-up and take off with the right leg.

Coaching Tips

- Use a powerful bounding jump to ''stride'' up onto the landing pads.

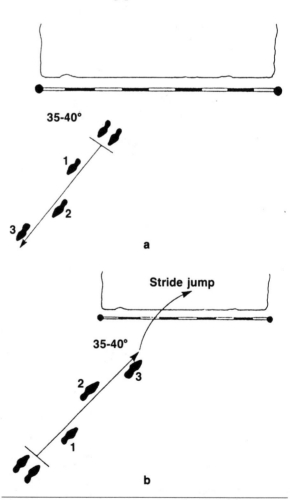

Figure 7.8 Stride jump with a three-stride approach

- Drive the thigh of the leading (left) leg up to horizontal or above.
- Hold your head high and keep your upper body straight.
- Swing your arms to help you jump upward.

Step 2: Flop High Jump Using a Short (3-Stride) Run-Up

Orientation to Backward Jumping

Each participant jumps backward to land flat-backed on the landing pads. The jumper's heels are no more than 2 foot lengths away from the base of the landing pad at takeoff. No elastic crossbar is used in this drill.

Figure 7.9 Backward jumping

Coaching Tips

- Lift the hips upward during the jump so that the body lands flat on the landing pad.
- Spread your arms to cushion the landing.

Backward Jumping With Leg Elevation

The starting position is the same as for the previous drill. Each athlete now lands on the back with legs

Figure 7.10 Backward jumping with leg elevation

elevated. The performer must jump upward, arch the back, then flex at the hips to lift the legs upward. No elastic crossbar is used.

Coaching Tips

- Think of this drill as a jump followed by a sit-up in the air.
- Jump upward, drop your shoulders and head back, and then pull your knees to your chest.

Backward Jumping With Leg Elevation—Elastic Crossbar Set at Hip Height

The athlete performs the same action as in the previous drill but uses the elastic rope as a crossbar. Initially set this substitute crossbar just above the height of the landing pad. For better performers in the group, raise the elastic beyond hip height to shoulder height.

Figure 7.11 Backward jumping over a simulated bar

Use of Minitrampoline by Experienced Jumpers

Experienced athletes often use minitrampolines to gain additional height and time in the air in the backward jumping drill. This drill enables the jumper to concentrate on visually timing the bar clearance. Position

Figure 7.12 Using a minitramp to assist backward jumping

the minitrampoline to slope toward the landing area. This drill is not recommended for novices.

Coaching Tips

- Look across your shoulder at the bar to time the bar clearance of your legs.
- Arch your back above the bar, and when your seat has crossed the bar, pull your knees toward your shoulders to clear your legs.
- Be sure to flex the legs at the knees.

Elementary Flop Using a Straight Three-Stride Run-Up

Initially set the takeoff at 1/4 of the crossbar's length in from the nearest standard, and 1 arm's length away from the bar. Use an angle of 35 to 40 degrees for the run-up. Starting with feet together the jumper runs back 3 fast strides from the takeoff spot. A partner marks the third stride. The jumper begins the run-up from the left side starting with the right foot (i.e., "right foot, left foot, right foot, jump"). Use markers to guide the foot positions.

Figure 7.13b shows a run-up occurring from the right side of the bar. The jumper begins the run-up taking the first stride with the left foot.

Coaching Tips

- Accelerate toward the bar during the run-up.
- Place the takeoff foot down quickly (directly in line with the run-up) and drive the knee of the leading leg vigorously upward.
- Once the knee is as high as possible, turn it back toward the center of the run-up.

Step 3: Flop High Jump Using an Extended (Curved) Run-Up

Technique

The run-up for the flop is straight to start with and curved prior to takeoff with the greater part of the

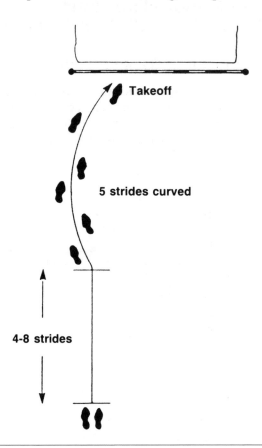

Figure 7.14 Technique for the curved run-up

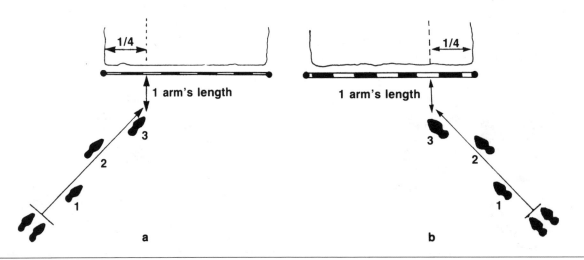

Figure 7.13 Elementary flop with a straight three-stride run-up from the left (a) and from the right (b)

curve usually occurring in the last 5 strides before takeoff. The number of strides taken in the run-up varies greatly, ranging from 9 to 15 or more. Frequently elite athletes use 2 check marks, the first positioned where the first stride falls in the approach to the bar and the second frequently placed 5 strides prior to the takeoff (Figure 7.14). The run-up is characterized by continuous acceleration.

Body Position During the Run-Up

The athlete leans forward at the start of the run-up and accelerates toward the bar. During the curved part of the run-up, the athlete leans in toward the center of the curve but straightens again at the takeoff (Figure 7.15). The penultimate (second to last) stride is usually longer than the last stride before takeoff. The characteristic curve in the run-up used by the flop jumper helps the jumper to assume a good takeoff and an optimal layout position over the bar.

Drills

Curve Sprinting

This activity is a preparation for the curved flop run-up. Participants sprint a figure eight, alternately curving to the left and then to the right. Each runner leans the body weight (center of gravity) well into each curve. The curves are moderate and should not slow the running speed.

Coaching Tips

- Be sure to lean into the curve of the run-up so that the body weight is on the inside of the curve each time.

Orientation to a Curved Run-Up

Mark a circle of 6 to 7 meters (approximately 20 to 23 feet) in diameter on the ground. Jumpers who approach the bar from the left side and take off with the right foot run clockwise. The speed of the run should be sufficient to give the athlete a feel for the outward pull of centrifugal force and the need to lean in toward the center of the circle. The amount of lean will depend on the speed of run.

Coaching Tips

- Run fast and lean well into the curve.

Lean

Figure 7.15 Body position during the run-up

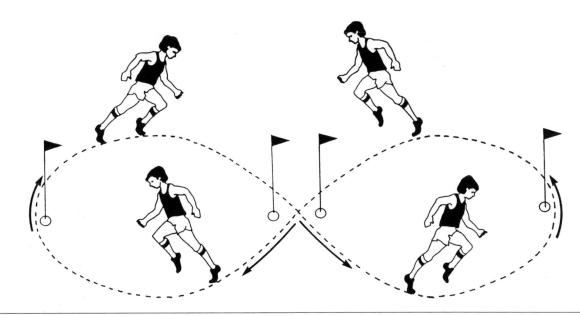

Figure 7.16 Curve sprinting

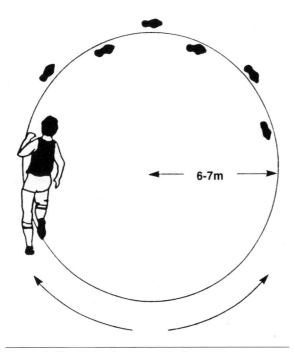

Figure 7.17 Orientation to a curved run-up

- Place each foot parallel with the curve of the run-up.

Elementary Curved Run-Up

This run-up is adequate for young novices (12 to 15 years of age) attempting the flop from a curved run-up. Measure the takeoff for an athlete approaching from the left in the following manner.

Set the takeoff 1 arm's length from the bar and 1/4 of the crossbar's length in from the left high-jump standard. Take 1 large stride to the left from the left high-jump standard, and take 2 strides from this point back into the run-up. Mark this position, which will be the third to last stride in the run-up. Measure out the strides, making allowance for the ages and sizes of the participants.

Measure a 5-stride run-up from the takeoff spot. When the athlete is approaching the bar, the first 2 strides will be straight and the final 3 strides will be curved. The run-up will resemble an inverted *J*. Each run-up will differ slightly according to individual stride length. Increasing confidence and faster approaches will necessitate a longer run-up.

Figure 7.18b shows a similar run-up from the right side of the bar. The 1st pace of the run-up is taken with the left foot.

Increasing the Length of the Run-Up

As participants develop confidence, they will need to enlarge and adjust the run-up to allow for greater approach speed. The takeoff spot will still be 1/4 of the crossbar's length in from the nearest high-jump standard. The following sequence will assist in setting up a 9-stride run-up. Adjustments will have to be made relative to individual stride length and speed of approach.

The take-off spot is 1/4 of a crossbar length in toward the center of the crossbar, measured from the nearest high-jump standard. The takeoff spot is shifted

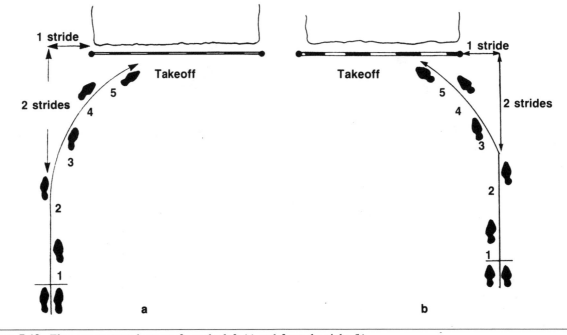

Figure 7.18 Elementary curved run-up from the left (a) and from the right (b)

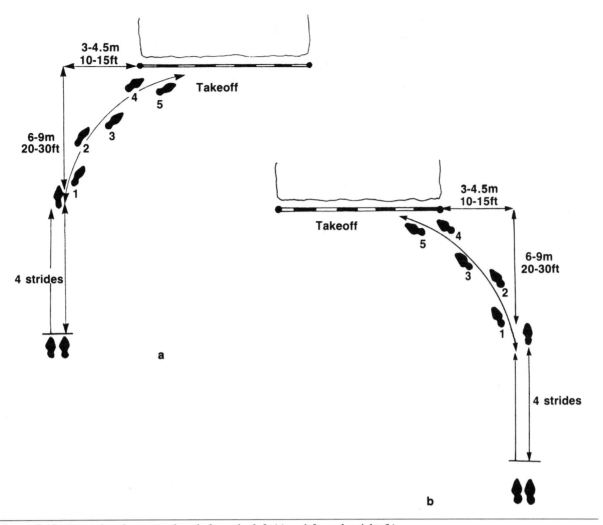

Figure 7.19 Increasing the run-up length from the left (a) and from the right (b)

back from the bar to just beyond 1 arm's length (i.e. 75 to 90 centimeters or 30 to 36 inches). This allows for an increase in the speed of approach.

Measure 3 to 4.5 meters (10 to 15 feet) directly to the left from the left standard and 6 to 9 meters (20 to 30 feet) back into the run-up (5 paces from the bar). This marks the start of the curved part of the run-up. Measure 4 more strides in a straight line back from the 5th stride to give a 9-stride run-up.

An athlete will begin a 9-stride run-up from the left side with the right foot (starting with the feet together); one or two check marks on the run-up assist in making the run-up accurate. If 2 check marks are used, place the 1st where the first stride falls in the approach to the bar. Place the 2nd check mark 5 strides prior to takeoff. With improved technique (and leg strength), the athlete can lengthen the run-up in order to gain additional acceleration.

Figure 7.19b shows the same run-up for a jumper approaching from the right side of the bar. The first stride of the run-up is taken with the left foot.

Developing the Arm Action and Stride Length During the Last Three Approach Strides

This action closely resembles the technique used in the last three strides by the straddle jumper. Figure 7.20 shows the last two strides taken by a flop jumper approaching from the left side of the bar. Notice the forward-backward movement of the arms and the backward lean of the body prior to takeoff.

Lead the group through the required movement pattern of the last three strides, which the students then practice freely on grass. The actions are performed slowly and mechanically to begin with and then progressively increased in speed to a slow run.

Figure 7.20 Arm action and body position during the last two approach strides

The sequence of actions for jumps approaching the bar from the left side (and jumping from the right foot) is as follows:

- The jumper stands with feet together and the arms extended at the side of the body.
- The jumper steps forward 1 medium-size stride with the right foot, keeping the arms at the side of the body.
- Next is a step forward, using one long stride with the left foot and allowing the hips to "slide" ahead of the shoulders.
- Both arms move in a circular fashion (similar to breaststroke arm action) ahead of the body.
- The jumper steps forward 1 short stride with the right foot, emphasizing a backward lean, and at the same time rotates the arms backward.
- Finally, the athlete jumps directly upward from the right foot, driving the thigh of the left leg up to horizontal and simultaneously swinging the arms upward.

Coaching Tips

- Stretch forward into the penultimate stride.
- Place the jumping foot down on the ground for the last stride as quickly as possible.

Skipping Backward With a Rope While Moving Forward

One difficulty for jumpers in learning the last 3 strides of the flop run-up is rotating the arms backward while simultaneously moving the body forward. Skipping backward with a rope while moving forward is an excellent method to teach the backward rotation of the arms.

Coaching Tips

- Start skipping in place with the rope rotating backward, then slowly move forward. Keep the rope rotating backward.

Figure 7.21 Backward rope skipping

Long Bounding Strides With Arm Swinging

If skipping backward while moving forward is too difficult, the athlete can practice bounding forward with long strides, swinging the arms forward on one stride and backward on the next.

Figure 7.22 Bounding with arm swings

Arm Action and Stride Length Adjustment During the Run-Up

This drill does not use a crossbar. Place marks on the run-up or use traffic cones to indicate the size of the last 3 strides. The performer "slides" the hips

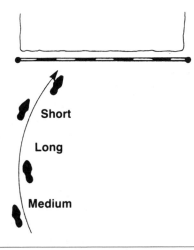

forward in the penultimate stride, maintaining the backward lean into the last stride. The arms are shifted from forward to backward as the athlete steps quickly forward for the last stride.

Coaching Tips

- Step well forward in the penultimate stride and lean back.
- Push your hips ahead of your chest and swing your arms backward.
- Put the jumping foot down quickly for a short stride, and swing your arms and nonjumping leg forward and upward for takeoff.

Figure 7.23 Arm action and stride length adjustment

COMMON ERRORS AND CORRECTIONS

ERROR	REASONS	CORRECTIONS
The athlete leans forward toward the bar at takeoff.	The last two strides of the run-up are too small.	The athlete practices the run-up with the last strides marked on the ground. Emphasize placement of the jumping foot with the heel placed down first and good backward body lean prior to takeoff.
The athlete leans the upper body sideways towards the bar at takeoff.	The takeoff foot is placed parallel to the bar at takeoff.	Mark the run-up with a line and draw the position of the takeoff foot on the ground (diagonally toward the crossbar).
The athlete takes off with the back already rotated toward the bar.	The athlete is anticipating the back-layout position. The takeoff foot is pointing back toward the run-up. The curve of the run-up is too tight.	Mark the correct position of the takeoff foot. Use visual cues ("Look along line of the crossbar") to control body position. The athlete should reduce the "tightness" of the curve.
The jumper has difficulty getting into a back-layout position over the bar.	The athlete has insufficient curve in final part of run-up and does not lean into the curve of the run-up. The jumper has poor rotary action of the leading leg.	Mark the correct position of the takeoff foot. Instruct the athlete to increase the curve of the run-up and lean into curve. Have the athlete emphasize the upward thrust and rotation of the free leg back toward the run-up at takeoff.

ERROR	REASONS	CORRECTIONS
The athlete crosses the bar in a sitting position, knocking the bar off with the seat.	The athlete lifts the thighs or shoulders too early during the bar clearance. The head is lifted to look at the bar during the clearance.	After the takeoff, the athlete must drop the leading leg downward and press the hips upward. The athlete should drop the head back and use sideways vision toward the crossbar to give timing for the elevation of the legs.
The athlete crosses the bar with the side of the body nearest the bar rather than with the back.	The athlete uses insufficient rotation around the long axis of the body and insufficient rotation of the leading leg back toward the run-up.	Instruct the athlete to use a 3-stride run-up emphasizing the upward and inward rotation of the leading leg. The athlete should emphasize strong lean into the curve when using a longer run-up. A tighter curve in the run-up may be necessary.
The takeoff foot placement varies with each jump.	The stride length in the run-up varies with each approach. The run-up is poorly established, and the athlete does not know the correct stride length.	Measure the run-up and use control markers. Work on building uniform acceleration throughout the run-up.
The athlete slows down before takeoff.	The athlete is anxious about the takeoff. Stride length is incorrect in final phase of run-up.	Have the athlete practice run-up and takeoff without using a crossbar. Use markers for positioning the last 3 strides.
Run-up speed is not translated into height.	The run-up is too fast. The athlete uses no backward body lean at takeoff or inward lean into curve. The takeoff foot is incorrectly placed. Leg power may be poor.	The athlete should start the run-up slowly and accelerate throughout, tighten the curve of the run-up, and/or lean more into curve. The athlete should point the takeoff foot diagonally toward the crossbar and lean back at takeoff. The athlete can also improve leg power to assist in takeoff.

ASSESSMENT

1. Assess the following theoretical elements as taught during instructional sessions.

   a. Fundamental rules governing the high jump.
   b. Good safety habits for use in the high jump.
   c. Basic elements of high-jump technique.
   d. Basic elements of training for the high jump.

2. Assess the performance of technique during the following stages of skill development.

   a. Backward jumping and flop bar clearance (elastic crossbar is used)
   b. Flop high jump from a 3-stride noncurved run-up.
   c. Flop high jump from a 5-stride curved run-up.
   d. Flop high jump from 9- and 11-stride curved run-ups.

Critical Features of Technique to Observe
During Assessment

- Measurement of the run-up and positioning of check marks.
- Acceleration through the run-up and inward lean into the curve of the run-up.
- Shift of the hips ahead of the upper body in the final strides of the takeoff. Backward rotation of the arms.
- Positioning and alignment of the takeoff foot immediately prior to takeoff.
- Upright trunk and elevated head at takeoff.
- Upward drive of the arms and knee of the leading leg during takeoff.
- Rotation of the thigh of the leading leg back toward the run-up at takeoff.
- Lowering of the leading leg and the elevation of the hips over the bar.

- Rotation of the body to a layout position.
- Vision along the line of the crossbar.
- Flexion at the knees and hips to clear the bar.
- Relaxed landing on the shoulders with the arms spread.

3. Hold graded competitions to help develop motivation and technique.

   a. Jumpers use a backward jump and flop clearance to clear an elastic crossbar.
   b. Jumpers compete in a flop high-jump competition using a straight 3-stride run-up.
   c. Jumpers compete in a flop high-jump competition using a curved 5-stride run-up.
   d. Jumpers compete in a flop high-jump competition using a run-up with stride length chosen according to individual preference.

SUGGESTED PERFORMANCE STANDARDS (CENTIMETERS)

MALE

Age	Satisfactory	Good	Excellent
11-12	95	115	130
13-14	120	130	150
15-16	130	140	155
17-19	140	150	160

FEMALE

Age	Satisfactory	Good	Excellent
11-12	90	100	120
13-14	100	120	130
15-16	115	130	140
17-19	130	135	145

CHAPTER

8

LONG JUMP

For many years long jumping was an event that sprinters enjoyed as a diversion from sprinting. Today, athletes specialize in long jumping, although it is still common for sprinters to be great jumpers, and vice versa.

Two major techniques are used in long jumping: the hang technique and the hitch-kick technique. The hitch kick is the more popular, but both techniques have been used by elite athletes to reach distances in excess of 8.83 meters (29 feet).

The hang and the hitch kick are patterns of movements used by the athlete while in flight. Each technique is intended to counteract the unfavorable forward rotation imparted to the athlete at the moment of takeoff. If the hang or the hitch kick were not performed, the athlete's feet and legs would contact the sand earlier than necessary and the resultant distance would be shorter.

Both hang and hitch kick require the same fast run-up, similar body positions at takeoff, and similar actions for the landing in the sand. Most young athletes will have difficulty performing the hitch kick, because it requires considerable speed and spring to perform well. However, an elementary long jump and a rudimentary form of the hang technique are well within the reach of young athletes. Remember that the most important requirements of long jumping are speed and spring and that an athlete does not have to perform a hitch kick to achieve excellent distances.

SAFETY SUGGESTIONS

The sand in a long-jump pit should be fine, well raked, level, and slightly wet to avoid dust. It should be deep enough (i.e., no less than 38 centimeters, or 15 inches) to prevent jarring and should be frequently searched for debris. It should be covered when not in use. The edges of the pit should be designed so as not to injure the athlete, although they must be well defined so that sand does not scatter onto the grass. The pit should be surrounded by a wide grass area or open area that is well clear of walls, trees, fences, and other obstacles. The pit should be positioned so that athletes are not in any danger from throwing events.

Brooms, rakes, and spades must always be stacked well clear of the pit, not left lying around. You as well as officials should ensure that no jump is made while the pit is being raked or dug. The takeoff board should be firmly fixed to the ground and should lie flush with the surface of the run-up. The run-up should provide a firm but comfortable approach and should be kept clean and swept clear of dirt, sand, and other debris. Depressions near the takeoff board should be filled in and made level, and takeoff boards narrower in width than 20 centimeters (8 inches) should not be used, because these are likely to cause foot injuries. Another consideration is that grass and certain types of artificial surfaces can become slippery when wet and can be dangerous unless the athletes wear spikes.

Elite athletes in the long jump and the triple jump prepare in the off-season by practicing sprinting, sprint endurance training, and a variety of dynamic jumping activities that develop the explosive elastic quality of the legs. In these activities, variously called rebound activities, depth jumping, and more commonly ''plyometrics,'' the athlete simulates the rebound of a bouncing ball. These activities place considerable stress on the joints and muscles of the legs and are not recommended for the young and physically immature athlete.

99

TECHNIQUE

The following descriptions of the hang and hitch kick give the main elements of each technique. Elite athletes will perform the techniques with some individual variations. Nevertheless, the main elements remain the same.

The Hang Technique

After a fast run-up, the athlete drives up powerfully at takeoff, extending the leading leg and driving it backward to join the trailing leg. Both arms circle downward, backward, and then forward in clockwise rotation, and the athlete momentarily "hangs" in the air. The legs are flexed and driven forward, and as the legs extend for the landing, the arms reach forward and rotate backward again at the shoulders. As soon as contact with the sand is made, the legs flex at the knees and the upper body moves forward and over the feet (Figure 8.1).

The Hitch-Kick Technique

After a fast run-up, the athlete drives up powerfully at takeoff. The leading leg, which is flexed at takeoff, is extended so that the athlete assumes stride position in flight. The leading leg is rotated back in an extended position, and both legs are flexed and brought forward for the landing. The arms rotate clockwise, balancing the action of the legs; this characteristic cycling action of the legs is called the hitch kick. The athlete extends both legs for the landing, as the arms circle forward and then backward. Upon contact with the sand, the knees flex and the upper body moves beyond the feet (Figure 8.2).

Figure 8.1 The hang technique

Figure 8.2 The hitch-kick technique

TEACHING STEPS

STEP 1. Lead-Ups
STEP 2. Elementary Long Jump and Run-Up
STEP 3. The Hang Technique
STEP 4. The Hitch-Kick Technique

Step 1: Lead-Ups

Long jump and triple jump use similar lead-up and preparatory activities, and both events require excellent sprinting ability and explosive leg power. Following are some demanding activities that develop leg power. For beginners, 3 to 4 repetitions with short rests between each are recommended. For activities that develop sprinting ability, see chapter 2.

Hopping for Distance and Finding the Favored Jumping Leg

Measure the distance each participant can achieve in 3 successive hops from a standing start with the right leg only. Measure the distance gained from the same action performed with the left leg only. Which leg hopped the longer distance and is therefore the preferred jumping leg?

Coaching Tips

- On each hop drive the thigh of the leading leg (i.e., nonjumping leg) to horizontal.
- Jump for distance with each hop, not height.
- The leg with which you jump farther is your favored leg.
- Remember whether it is the right or the left leg.

Bounding for Distance

In this lead-up activity, the thigh of the leading leg is lifted to horizontal with each bounding stride. The performer should strive for long strides, reaching for distance.

Coaching Tips

- Swing your arms up and forward with each bounding stride.
- Try to achieve a wide stride position at the midpoint of each bounding stride.
- Try to get a feeling of "floating" at the midpoint of the stride.

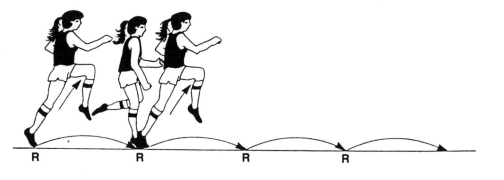

Figure 8.3 Hopping for distance

Figure 8.4 Bounding for distance

Standing Long Jump Using a Two-Legged Takeoff

The athlete uses a strong swing of the arms coupled with a double-legged drive to cover as much distance as possible.

Coaching Tips

- Extend your legs as powerfully as possible and combine that action with a strong swing of the arms.
- Pull the legs forward underneath your body to cover as much distance as possible.

Standing Long Jump Using a Single-Legged Takeoff

This is similar to a bounding stride except that both legs are brought together for the landing. Participants jump using their favored and nonfavored legs for the takeoff and then compare distances.

Coaching Tips

- Extend the jumping leg as powerfully as possible.
- Swing the leading leg up to horizontal.
- Use your arms in the same fashion as with the two-leg jump. Swing both of them up and forward in unison with the leading leg.

Distance Jumping Competition

From a line, participants see how far they can jump in total with 3 successive two-footed jumps (rabbit hops). Who can go the farthest?

Coaching Tips

- Don't put everything into the first of the 3 jumps.
- For optimal distance, all 3 jumps must be fairly equal in length.
- Avoid jumping upward. Jump low and forward.

Variation

The first member of a team completes 3 two-footed jumps (or 3 bounding strides). The next member of the team adds 3 more jumps to increase the distance achieved. Which team can accumulate the greatest distance?

Circle Jumping

Lay a series of hoops (3 or 4) on the grass in front of each team. Each team member hops or bounds as

Figure 8.5 Standing long jump with a two-legged takeoff

Figure 8.6 Standing long jump with a single-legged takeoff

Figure 8.7   Distance jumping competition

Figure 8.8   Circle jumping

required from hoop to hoop. Initially place the hoops close to each other, then set them progressively farther apart to demand long reaching strides and explosive leg action. The hoops should not slip if an athlete lands on them. If there is any likelihood of this occurring, use traffic cones; the participants attempt to land next to the cones.

Coaching Tips

- Use a forward and upward swing of the arms to help with each jump.

- Drive forward as vigorously as possible from the jumping leg.
- Concentrate on lifting the leading thigh to horizontal with each successive jump.
- Keep your vision forward, don't let your head drop backward.
- Don't relax when you land; try to "claw" the ground backward immediately upon landing with the supporting foot.
- Experiment by starting the series of jumps from the right foot and then from the left. Which gives you the greatest distance?

Hopping and Bounding Over a Series of Low Obstacles

Each participant hops, bounds, or jumps (as required) over a series of low obstacles. The arms are driven upward and the thigh of the leading leg is driven up to horizontal with each jump.

Heading Suspended Volleyballs or Soccer Balls

Suspend volleyballs or soccer balls from ropes at various heights. Participants use a 3-stride run-up to head

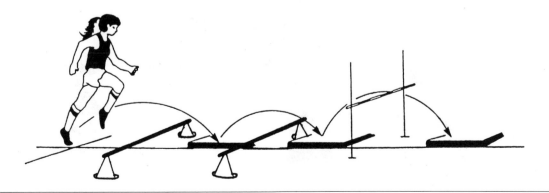

Figure 8.9   Hopping and bounding over low obstacles

Figure 8.10 Heading suspended balls

the ball. If they are successful heading 1 ball, they shift to the next highest.

Coaching Tips

- Work out a 3-stride run-up so that you jump from your favored leg.
- Lean back slightly prior to takeoff.
- Swing your arms and the leading leg upward to help in gaining height.
- Keep your trunk upright at takeoff and extend the jumping leg as powerfully as possible.

Jumping From a Beat Board and a Low Box

Participants pace a 3-stride run-up from the beat board. They step from the beat board onto a low box and take off from the favored leg to land on mats or

in sand. Athletes practice different types of flight patterns (e.g., tuck, straddle, or stride).

Coaching Tips

- Approach the beat board and box at the same speed that you "measured" your run up.
- Start your run-up from the other leg if you find yourself jumping from your nonfavored leg.
- Drive up strongly from the box so that you have time to complete the required maneuver.
- Use your arms and the leading leg as before. Swing them upward as strongly as possible.

Step 2: Elementary Long Jump and Run-Up

Technique

At takeoff, the athlete fully extends the jumping leg and flexes the leading leg with the thigh raised to horizontal. The upper body is perpendicular, the vision is ahead and upward, and the arms complement the action of the legs.

When the athlete is in flight, the leading leg extends and the jumping leg trails behind so that the jumper is momentarily in a stride position. For the landing, the jumping leg is brought forward and both legs are extended. The arms and upper body reach forward, and the legs flex at the knees on contact with the sand (Figure 8.12).

Drills

Elementary Long Jump From 3 Bounding Strides

The athlete takes 3 bounding strides in sequence. On the third, the jumper takes off from the favored leg, holding the thigh of the leading leg at horizontal

Figure 8.11 Jumping from a beat board and a low box

Figure 8.12 Elementary long jump technique

Figure 8.13 Jumping to kneeling from three bounding strides

through to the landing in the sand pit. The jumper lands in a one-legged kneeling position with the leading leg forward and flexed at the knee. Be sure the pit is well dug for this drill.

Coaching Tips

- At takeoff, swing (drive) the thigh of the leading leg to horizontal and hold it in this position through to the landing. Don't be tempted to lower it while you're in the air.

Standing Jumps Over a Mound of Sand

Build up a mound of sand lengthwise down the center of the long-jump pit. Fashion the mound of sand to become progressively higher along the length of the sand pit. The mound forces the jumper to flex and pull the legs up and under the seat and then extend them forward for the landing. Participants jump from the side of the pit. If they are successful in jumping one cross section of the mound they move to attempt

Figure 8.14 Standing jumps over a mound of sand

a higher section. Each participant jumps taking off with both feet together, then taking off from a stride position with the jumping foot placed forward.

Coaching Tips

- Extend your legs strongly at takeoff, then flex them quickly.
- Pull the legs up under your seat and extend forward into the landing.
- Flex at the knees and hips on the landing.
- Reach forward with your arms in order not to sit backward on the landing.

An Elementary Long Jump From an Elevated Takeoff

The performer uses a short run-up (3 strides), steps onto a low box (1 section), and takes off from the box to jump into the sand. Those who prefer jumping off the left foot will start with the right foot forward. The run-up sequence for a left-footed jumper is as follows: left foot, right foot, left foot, jump. The elevated takeoff allows time in the air in order to achieve a good stride position and bring both legs forward successfully for the landing.

Beat-Board Takeoff

Athletes repeat the previous drill but from a lower elevation (e.g., substitute a gymnastic beat board for the top section of the vaulting box).

Ground Takeoff

Remove the gymnastic beat board and have athletes repeat the drill from ground level.

Measuring a Run-Up

A sequence for determining a run-up for beginners is as follows:

1. Each jumper stands in stride position, facing back down the run-up with the toes of the nonjumping (i.e., nonfavored) foot placed against the leading edge of the takeoff board.
2. The jumper runs 9 strides down the long-jump run-up, with the 1st stride taken by the jumping foot.

Figure 8.15 Elementary jump from an elevated takeoff

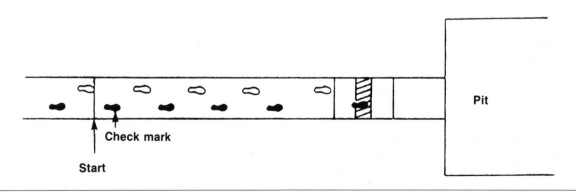

Figure 8.16 Measuring a run-up

3. You or a partner counts each footfall of the jumping leg, in a sequence of 1, 3, 5, 7, and 9 (this is easier and less confusing than counting every stride).

4. Mark the 9th stride, which gives an approximate starting point for the run-up. The athlete then places the nonjumping foot on the mark and takes the 1st stride toward the pit with the jumping foot. The uneven number of strides in the run-up will put the jumping foot on the board for the takeoff.

5. You can use check marks at the 1st and 5th strides of the run-up for additional accuracy.

Variation

You may use the following variation to determine an approximate run-up for beginners.

- Lay out a 100- to 150-foot tape next to the curb of the track straightaway.
- Starting at the zero end of the tape, the athlete sprints down the straightaway.
- Approximate the position where the athlete reaches top speed, and mark the distance.
- Before sprinting the athlete calls out "right" or

"left" to indicate the jumping foot, and then sprints down the straightaway a second time.

- Note the placement of the jumping foot nearest the top speed marker as a partner counts the athlete's strides. The partner tells the athlete the number of strides used to reach the top-speed marker.
- Transfer the distance to the long-jump run-up. The athlete counts the number of strides while accelerating down the run-up and jumps from a takeoff area.

Using a Takeoff Area Instead of a Takeoff Board

It is recommended that beginners jump from a takeoff area rather than from a takeoff board. Using a takeoff area helps make beginners more relaxed during the run-up and less concerned about hitting an exact spot for takeoff. The competitive takeoff board is 20 centimeters (8 inches) in width and is 1 meter from the edge of the pit. A takeoff area can be a chalk-marked area or a large board 80 centimeters to 1 meter in width, set flush in the runway with the position of a regular takeoff board marked on it in a central

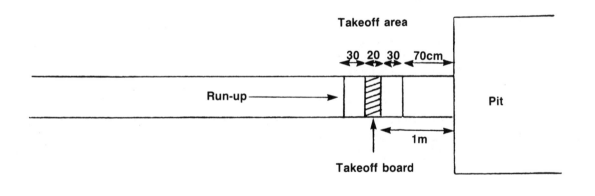

Figure 8.17 Using a takeoff area

Figure 8.18 Shortening the final stride

position. For competitive purposes, all jumps taken from within the takeoff area are valid.

9-Stride Run-Up

As each participant attempts the 9-stride run-up, you stand by the takeoff area and note the relationship between the position of the takeoff foot and the takeoff board. Help the athlete adjust the start of the run-up to bring the takeoff as close to the board as possible.

Shortening the Last Stride in the Run-Up

Long jumpers must learn to lengthen the penultimate stride and shorten the final stride prior to takeoff. This lowers the body, tilts it backward, and places it in an optimal position for takeoff.

Coaching Tips

- Use vocal cues to establish long-jump rhythm.

  Stride: 5 4 3 penultimate last jump
  Vocal cues: da da da   daaaa   da dap

Teaching the Rhythm and Placement of the Last Two Strides

A mark positioned on the run-up used with a beat board and the top of a gymnastic vaulting box can help teach athletes to stretch the penultimate stride and reduce the length of the final stride before takeoff.

Position the marker by the side of the run-up to indicate the start of the penultimate stride. Place the beat board a sufficient distance from the marker so that the athlete must stretch to reach the beat board. Position the box top beyond the beat board half the distance of marker to beat board. The athlete uses a short 5-stride run-up. Direct the athlete with vocal cues from the previous drill. Jumping from the box top will give height in the flight of the long jump.

Coaching Tips

- Stretch your body upward immediately prior to takeoff.
- Look forward, not downward, at takeoff.
- Reach out with your stride onto the beat board, then shorten the last stride onto the box top for the takeoff.

Increasing the Length of the Run-Up

Place a check mark to indicate the first stride and another to indicate the 5th stride prior to the board. Elite athletes will use 19 strides or more for their run-ups. For a 19-stride run-up, use check marks in the same fashion, placing them at the 1st stride and at 5 strides prior to the board. After hitting the 1st check mark, the elite athlete sprints 13 strides to gain maximum acceleration. When the athlete reaches the 2nd check mark, the trunk is upright and the body begins to sink a little. The shorter last stride is used in preparation for the upward drive of the takeoff.

Step 3: The Hang Technique

See Figure 8.1

Learning to Drive the Hips Forward

Each performer runs, takes off as for an elementary long jump, and attempts to drive the hips forward toward a bamboo cane that is held by a partner or

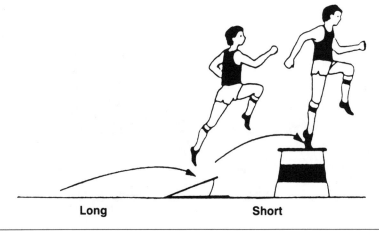

Long   Short

Figure 8.19 Rhythm and placement of the last two strides

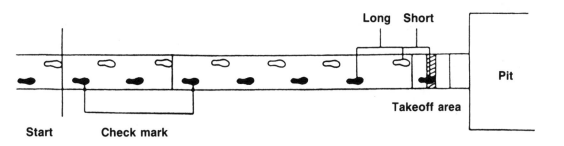

Figure 8.20 A nine-stride run-up with two check marks

Figure 8.21 Driving the hips forward

by you. For a variation, 2 partners stand 1 meter away from the takeoff with their arms outstretched to form a double "gate"; the jumper must open the gate.

Coaching Tips

- At takeoff, lift the thigh of the leading leg up and forward as normal.
- Drive powerfully with the jumping leg.
- Once in the air, lower the leading leg and push the cane forward or open the gate with the stomach or hips.

Figure 8.22 Arm action of the hang technique

Learning the Arm Action of the Hang Technique

The performer jumps upward, and a partner assists by holding the performer's waist and lifting upward from the rear. As the performer jumps he or she practices the clockwise circling of the arms.

Emphasizing the Arm Action in the Hang Technique

The participant stands in stride position with the leading leg on a box top and the favored or jumping foot to the rear, a stance that simulates the position that the jumper assumes after driving upward from takeoff. The athlete places both arms forward and pushes off with the leg that is on the box top. The arms simultaneously circle clockwise (downward and backward and then forward), and the athlete lands with feet and arms forward.

Practicing the Complete Hang Technique From Height

Place two vaulting boxes (using 2 to 3 sections each) lengthwise, one behind the other. Performers step

Figure 8.23 Emphasized arm action in the hang technique

Figure 8.24 Practicing the hang technique from vaulting boxes

along the top of the boxes, taking off from the end. The additional height provides time to attempt the hang technique.

Coaching Tips

- After takeoff, drop the leading leg backward and push your stomach forward.
- Circle your arms backward and then forward.
- As your arms come forward and downward, lift your legs up to meet them for the landing.

Practicing the Hang Technique From Reduced Height

Set a beat board 1 stride (1 meter) away from 1 or 2 sections of a vaulting box set crosswise. Using a slow 3-stride approach, the performer steps onto the beat board with the jumping foot, then up onto the box top with the leading leg to attempt the hang technique. The extra height will give the performer time to "hang" the legs and pull them through for the landing.

Coaching Tips

- Be sure to measure the 3 strides so that your favored leg lands on the beat board. The step onto the vaulting box simulates the position of the leading leg in the air at takeoff.
- Walk through the approach to begin with, then gradually speed up your run-up.
- Circle your arms forward and down from beat

Figure 8.25 Practicing the hang technique from reduced height

Figure 8.26 Jumping on a sand incline

board to box top, then backward from box top to the sand.

• Try to complete the whole action before landing in the sand.

Variation

Using the favored leg, the jumper takes off at the top of an incline. The extra time in the air provides better opportunity to complete the leg and arm action of the hang technique.

Attempting the Hang Technique From Reduced Height

The performer attempts the hang technique from a single section of a vaulting box (or from a beat board).

The performer uses a 3- to 5-stride run-up and takes off from the favored leg.

Hang Technique With Extended Run-Up

The athlete performs the hang technique from the ground into the pit using an extended (7-, 9-, or 11-stride) run up.

Step 4: The Hitch-Kick Technique

See Figure 8.2

Figure 8.27 The hang technique from reduced height

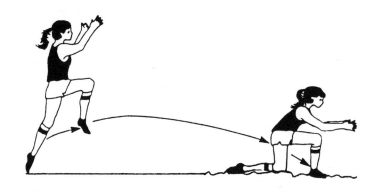

Figure 8.28 Swinging the leading leg up and forward

Swinging the Leading Leg Up and Forward

Using a short run-up, the participant jumps from the edge of the sand pit, holding the leading leg forward throughout. The participant lands in the sand in a flexed stride position (i.e., kneeling, with 1 leg forward and 1 leg back).

Coaching Tips

- Swing (drive) the thigh of the leading leg to horizontal and hold the leg in that position through the landing.

Swinging the Leading Leg Up in a Flexed Position, and Extending at the Knee

From a 3-stride run-up, and using a beat board (or single section of a vaulting box) for takeoff, participants jump, landing in a kneeling position. Each jumper should attempt to drive the thigh of the leading leg upward and swing the lower leg forward prior to the landing. Each jumper should maintain a good stride position in flight. Be sure the pit is well dug for this drill.

Coaching Tips

- Lift the thigh of the leading leg to horizontal and then extend your lower leg forward.
- Land in a kneeling position; don't bring your legs together for the landing.

Practicing the Hitch-Kick Leg Action

Using a 5-stride run-up, the jumper takes off from a beat board or a single section of a box and while in the air pedals backward (i.e., kicks backward) with the foot of the leading leg. The jumper tries to kick a bamboo cane that is placed approximately 1.5 to 2 meters (5 to 6 feet) beyond the takeoff and .5 to .75 centimeters (1 to 2 feet) from the ground.

Coaching Tips

- Lift the leading thigh to horizontal, then straighten the leg and pedal backward. Try to kick the cane backward.

Figure 8.29 Extending the lower leg before landing

Figure 8.30 Practicing the hitch-kick leg action

- The leading leg should end up in a stride position to the rear of the jumping leg when you land.

Variation

A partner holds the cane in position and the jumper practices the same action.

Completing the Hitch-Kick Action

The jumper takes off from a beat board, "cycling" the leading leg to the rear and bringing it forward again in a flexed position for the landing. The arms rotate and balance the actions of the legs. The bamboo cane can still be used if it helps the jumper initiate the backward rotation of the leading leg.

Coaching Tips

- Begin by concentrating on the leg action during this drill. Don't worry about your arms to begin with.
- Lift the thigh of the leading leg, then straighten it and pedal the foot backward.

- Then flex your leading leg and bring it forward for the landing.

Practicing the Hitch Kick Without Additional Takeoff Height

Because the hitch kick must be performed without assistance of any type at takeoff, jumpers now attempt the hitch kick without any additional height and using an extended run-up. If the athlete does not have sufficient speed and spring, the hitch kick can easily dissolve into an aimless wriggling of the legs and can detract distance from the jump. Most jumpers at the elementary level will find that they cannot complete a full hitch-kick action and that they have more success with the hang technique.

A 2-1/2-stride hitch kick is completed in the following manner. The athlete extends the leading leg forward at takeoff (Stride 1). The leading leg is cycled to the rear and the jumping leg brought forward (Stride 2). Finally, the leading leg is brought forward to join the jumping leg for the landing (Stride 2-1/2).

Figure 8.31 Completing the hitch-kick action

COMMON ERRORS AND CORRECTIONS

ELEMENTARY LONG JUMP AND RUN-UP

ERROR	REASONS	CORRECTIONS
During the run-up, the athlete appears tense and does not run in a straight line.	The head position and line of vision are incorrect; the athlete closes the eyes or looks down during the run-up. The athlete uses poor acceleration and sprinting technique.	Emphasize uniform acceleration and correct head and arm action.
The athlete stutter steps and takes off on the wrong foot. There are repeated irregularities in the run-up.	The run-up, starting position, and stride length vary between jumps. The athlete becomes tense when anticipating the takeoff.	Remeasure and check the accuracy of the run-up and check marks. Have the athlete practice sprinting and acceleration on the track, emphasizing controlled acceleration. The athlete should begin the run-up in the same manner each time.
The athlete looks down at the takeoff board or takeoff area at the moment of takeoff.	The athlete is unsure of the run-up and takeoff and is tense prior to takeoff.	Have the athlete perform repetitive run-up practice, using check marks on the run-up. Instruct the athlete to keep the vision horizontal.

ERROR	REASONS	CORRECTIONS
The jumper obtains height but not distance.	The run-up is not accurate; the athlete uses the wrong stride length on the last stride. The athlete has too much backward body lean prior to and during takeoff.	Have the athlete practice the run-up with the penultimate stride occurring on the beat board and the takeoff occurring from a single section of the box. A predetermined distance from beat board to box top forces the jumper to assume correct stride length. Markers on the run-up prior to takeoff will also do same job.
The flight path of the jump is close to the ground; the athlete has no time in the air. The feet hit the sand too early.	There's no drive from the takeoff leg, and the upper body leans forward at takeoff. The thigh of the leading leg is poorly elevated at takeoff, and the athlete uses no extension of the legs at the end of flight. The athlete is weak in the legs and abdomen.	Have the athlete practice repetitive bounding and jumping, keeping the upper body perpendicular and the thigh of leading leg horizontal at takeoff. Emphasize reaching out with the feet for distance immediately prior to landing. Have the athlete remeasure and check run-up and stride lengths for accuracy.
The jumper lands in the sand in a sitting position (sits back after landing in the sand).	The athlete leans backward at takeoff and during landing and has no flexion at the knees when the feet hit the sand. The arms are not used during the landing to help shift the upper body forward.	Have the athlete practice standing long jumps from 1- and 2-footed takeoffs. Emphasize flexion at the knees during landing to allow hips to move forward. Arm swing assists in this action.

HANG TECHNIQUE

ERROR	REASONS	CORRECTIONS
The athlete has poor elevation and upward drive of the leading leg. The leading leg is not lifted to horizontal at takeoff.	The athlete is too concerned with backward thrust of the legs in the hang technique. The take-off is rushed.	Have the athlete repeat the elementary long jump, emphasizing leading-leg action. The athlete should also practice the hang technique from elevation, emphasizing good leading-leg action before driving both legs backward.
The athlete lands upright in the sand pit with the legs virtually perpendicular.	The athlete has too much forward lean at takeoff. There's no height in the jump, thus no time for the legs to act. The athlete has poor flexion at knees and hips, so legs are not brought forward from hang position. The athlete also has weak abdominals.	Instruct the athlete to practice the hang technique from elevation, emphasizing upward drive of the leading leg. The athlete should practice the standing long jump (2-footed) and work on abdominal strength.

ERROR	REASONS	CORRECTIONS
The flight is performed in "bunched" or "squatting" position.	The jumping leg is not fully extended at takeoff and does not remain to the rear for the hang action. The legs are not driven to rear for hang action.	Have the athlete repeat lead-up activities for the long jump (repetitive hopping, bounding, and 2-legged jumps), emphasizing drive with the jumping leg. Work through lead-ups for the hang technique.

HITCH-KICK TECHNIQUE

ERROR	REASONS	CORRECTIONS
Leg actions in the hitch kick lack amplitude, appear hurried and reduced in range, and frequently are incomplete by the time the jumper hits the sand.	The jumper has insufficient time in the air to complete the action. The physical requirements of the hitch kick are too difficult for the performer.	The athlete should return to the elementary long jump and progress to the hang technique. Assess the value of the hitch kick; the hang technique may produce better distances. Leg power activities will assist in improving spring and speed.
The leading leg is bent throughout the hitch kick.	The athlete does not kick out or extend the leading leg or drive it backward after takeoff.	Repeat drills for landing in a stride position in the sand and "pedaling" back on a bamboo cane with the leading leg.

ASSESSMENT

1. Assess the following theoretical elements as taught during instructional sessions.

    a. Fundamental rules governing long-jump competition.
    b. Good safety habits for use in long jump.
    c. Basic elements of long-jump technique.
    d. Basic elements of training for the long jump.

2. Assess the performance of technique during the following stages of skill development.

    a. Jumping from an elevated takeoff and using a short (3- to 5-stride) run-up.
    b. Jumping from a takeoff area and using a short (3- to 5-stride) run-up.
    c. Jumping from a takeoff area and using an extended (9- to 11-stride) run-up.
    d. Jumping from a takeoff board and using an extended (9- to 11-stride) run-up.

Critical Features of Technique to Observe During Assessment

Hang Technique

- Use of an extended run-up with 2 check marks.
- Stride adjustment prior to takeoff.
- Backward inclination of the body at contact with the board.
- Forward body angle at takeoff.
- Strong upward drive at takeoff.
- Elevation of thigh of leading leg to horizontal.
- Lowering of thigh of leading leg and backward thrust of both legs in an extended position.
- Forward, downward, and backward circling of arms.
- Forward motion of legs to a flexed position; extension of legs to join the arms for the landing.
- Flexion at the knees and hips, which allows the body to move beyond the point of contact with the sand.

Hitch-Kick Technique

- Use of an extended run-up with 2 check marks.
- Stride adjustment prior to takeoff.
- Backward inclination of the body at contact with the board.
- Forward body angle at takeoff.
- Powerful upward drive at takeoff.
- Elevation of the thigh of the leading leg to horizontal or above at takeoff.
- Extension and backward rotation of the leading leg.
- Wide stride position in the air.
- Rotation of the arms to balance cycling action of the legs.
- Flexion and extension of both legs for the landing.
- Forward rotation of the arms for the landing.
- Flexion at the hips and knees to allow the body to move beyond the point of contact with the sand.

3. Hold graded competitions to help develop motivation and technique.

   a. Jumpers compete for distance using a standing long jump. Each uses a 2-footed takeoff, then a single-footed takeoff with the takeoff foot placed forward.
   b. Jumpers compete for the total distance of 3 two-footed jumps in sequence, 3 bounding strides in sequence, and 3 hops in sequence.
   c. Jumpers compete from an elevated takeoff and from a run-up of 5 strides. Require a selected technique (e.g., hang technique).
   d. Jumpers compete for distance from a takeoff area, using a 5-stride run-up. Require a selected technique (e.g., hang technique).
   e. Jumpers compete for distance from a takeoff area, using an extended run-up (9 strides or more). Require a selected technique (e.g., hang or hitch kick).
   f. Jumpers compete for distance from a takeoff board, using an extended run-up (9 strides or more). Require a selected technique (e.g., hang or hitch kick).

SUGGESTED PERFORMANCE STANDARDS (METERS)

MALE

Age	Satisfactory	Good	Excellent
11-12	3.1	3.6	4.1
13-14	3.6	4.2	4.6
15-16	4.2	4.7	5.2
17-19	4.6	5.0	5.7

FEMALE

Age	Satisfactory	Good	Excellent
11-12	3.0	3.4	3.9
13-14	3.1	3.8	4.0
15-16	3.6	4.0	4.2
17-19	3.8	4.2	4.4

CHAPTER
9
TRIPLE JUMP

The triple jump was included in the Olympic Games of 1896 and until recently was a men's field event. Today, triple jump competitions are held for men and for women.

Like the long jump, the triple jump demands great speed and spring; however, the 2 events differ in that the triple jump involves three jumps in sequence, all of which are interdependent. To achieve the greatest possible distance, the athlete must balance the distribution of effort between the three jumps. Another unique feature of the triple jump is its tremendous demands on rebound ability (i.e., the ability to jump, land, and jump again). This means that the triple jumper must not only be an excellent sprinter but must have the muscular power and resilience to rebound for three successive jumps.

SAFETY SUGGESTIONS

Although the triple jump is an attractive and fun event, you must be aware of the intense physical demands that training for this event places upon the athlete. The triple jump places considerable stress on the heel, knees, hips, and joints of the feet. Consequently, the intensity of training should be increased slowly and progressively. No instructional period should be devoted solely to triple jump until the participants develop sufficient muscular power and endurance. During the introduction, keep repetitive jumping and rebounding to a minimum, and limit sequences of jumps to 3 or 4. To ease the shock of repetitive jumping and bounding, have athletes perform on surfaces that provide adequate cushioning, such as grass or mats. During indoor training, gymnastic floor-exercise

mats are excellent for this purpose. Heel pads provide additional protection.

This chapter offers some examples of rebound exercises which are an integral part of power training for the triple jumper, indeed for all athletes requiring explosive power in the legs. Called "plyometrics," "depth jumping," or simply "rebound jumping," these are activities in which the athlete simulates the bounce of a ball by repetitively jumping down from a height and immediately rebounding up again. This vigorously stretches and then explosively contracts or shortens the muscles involved. Such exercises are extremely demanding and are recommended only for the mature and experienced athlete; they should not be attempted until the legs have been strengthened through less stressful activities.

Be aware of the problems that can arise from asking young athletes to double up (i.e., compete) in both the long jump and the triple jump. The demands of both events greatly increase the stress placed on the athlete's legs and feet. In addition, there is the technical conflict between the differing takeoffs in the 2 events: The long jump requires great upward thrust at takeoff, the triple jump a low, flat trajectory.

A large "instructional pit" is as useful for teaching the triple jump as it is for teaching the long jump. The larger the pit and the more run-ups that are available, the greater the opportunity for a high level of activity. Takeoff distances for run-ups both from the side of the pit and on the regular run-up will vary according to students' ages and the activity being practiced. The adult distance of the takeoff board for triple jump is 13 meters from the pit. For school-age participants, this distance can vary from 5 to 8 meters.

A takeoff area such as this book suggested for the long jump enhances the young athlete's chance for success when attempting a triple jump. A takeoff area is much easier to hit than a competitive takeoff board and all jumps that occur within the takeoff area are measured. The dimensions of the takeoff area are the same as for long jump (see chapter 8).

TECHNIQUE

The technique of triple jumping has changed very little over the past 20 years. Some variations have occurred in the use of arms in gaining lift during each jump.

But the main elements of the technique have remained basically the same.

The Hop

After a fast run-up, the athlete takes off with a strong forward drive from the jumping leg. The body is upright during takeoff, and a flat horizontal trajectory conserves takeoff speed for use in each of the jumps. The athlete drives the leading (nonjumping) leg up to horizontal and then swings it back to the rear. The

Figure 9.1 Triple jump technique: the hop (a), the step (b), and the jump (c)

thigh of the jumping leg is lifted upward so that a wide stride position exists at the midpoint of the hop.

At the end of the hop, the athlete brings the jumping leg forward and reaches out for distance. As the jumping leg lands, it flexes in preparation to drive the athlete forward in the step. The arms work vigorously to balance the body and assist in driving the body forward. The hop is approximately equal in length to the jump.

The Step

The step is usually shorter than the hop or the jump. The body is upright in the takeoff for the step, and the leading leg is flexed and vigorously swung forward to become the active leg at the end of the step. At the midpoint of the step, the athlete has a wide stride position.

The Jump

The athlete vigorously swings the leading leg forward from the step into the jump, aiming for distance and a good landing position (feet together well in front of the body).

TEACHING STEPS

STEP 1.	Lead-Ups
STEP 2.	The Triple Jump

Step 1: Lead-Ups

Training for the triple jump is excellent preparation for the high jump and long jump. Likewise, all the lead-up activities and run-up practices for long jump are excellent preparation for the triple jump. The demands of triple jump training improve leg power, muscular endurance, and coordination, which benefit not only the jumper but the thrower as well. Repetitive bounding, jumping, and hopping activities are excellent preparation for the triple jump.

Repetitive Bounding

Participants bound with long, reaching strides (3 to 4 strides in total) from a standing start and from a short relaxed run-up (3 to 5 strides). Methods for measuring a run-up and choosing the jumping or favored leg are taught during instruction in long jumping (see chapter 8).

Coaching Tips

- Drive forward vigorously with the jumping leg.
- Swing the leading leg up to horizontal with each bounding stride.
- Try to hold a wide stride position at the midpoint of each bounding stride.
- Swing your arms forward as powerfully as possible at the takeoff for each bounding stride.

Hopping for Distance

The athlete performs 3 to 4 hops for distance on the right leg, then on the left leg.

Coaching Tips

- Swing the leading leg and the arms forward and upward to assist with each hop.
- Drive as powerfully as possible with the hopping leg.

Rabbit Hops

Each member of the group performs 3 to 4 repetitive 2-legged jumps (rabbit hops).

Figure 9.2 Repetitive bounding

Figure 9.3 Hopping for distance

Figure 9.4 Rabbit hops

Coaching Tips

- Extend both legs as powerfully as possible for each jump.
- Lean forward and swing your arms forward and upward to assist the legs.
- Don't collapse into a full squat position at the end of each hop.
- Allow the legs to flex to about a 1/4 squat position, no more.

Standing and Running Long Jump

The performer practices standing and running long jumps (from a short 3-stride run-up) using a takeoff

from the nonfavored leg. Because the triple jump is 3 jumps in succession, 1 of the jumps occurs from the nonfavored leg. This practice familiarizes the performer with this action.

Coaching Tips

- Drive powerfully with the jumping leg at takeoff.
- Lift the thigh of the leading leg to horizontal.
- Swing your arms forward and upward as strongly as possible at takeoff.

Combinations of Hops, Jumps, and Bounding Strides

The step (the second element in the triple jump) is really a bounding stride. Participants practice combinations of hops, jumps, and bounding strides, initiated from a standing start and then from a short controlled approach of 3 strides. The step is used in the following combinations:

- hop, hop, step;
- step, step, jump;
- hop, step, hop, jump; and
- hop, hop, step, step, jump.

Distance and Time Competition

Instruct students to practice the previous 4 sequences and award points for the greatest distance achieved. For the latter contest, require a minimum distance of all participants, determine combinations to be performed, and require all jumps to be performed from a standing start. A time competition forces the participant to drive low and forward as powerfully as possible with the legs and arms throughout all jumps.

Repetitive Bounding and Jumping Over Low Obstacles

Place mats short distances apart and use low obstacles, such as bamboo canes on traffic cones or elas-

Figure 9.5 Standing long jump

Figure 9.6 Combining hops and steps

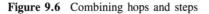

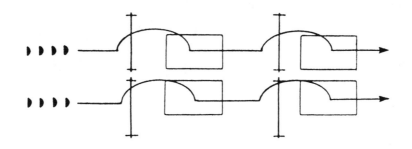

Figure 9.7 Repetitive bounding and jumping over low obstacles

tic crossbars. Students perform combinations of jumps. Increase distances between mats to make the athlete reach out with each jump. The low obstacles require a minimal height to be achieved with each jump.

Step 2: The Triple Jump

Learning the Sequence and Rhythm of the Triple Jump

On grass or mats, participants practice the sequence of jumps in the triple jump by hopping (left to left), stepping (left to right), and jumping (both feet land together). All sequences begin by the athlete's placing the left foot behind a line and attempting a triple jump. You provide a verbal count: "left, right, together." Then change the starting foot to accommodate those who wish to begin with the right foot.

Coaching Tips

- Try to make each of the three jumps in the hop, step, and jump equal in size.
- Take off into each of the three jumps with a powerful leg drive.
- Swing the thigh of the leading leg to horizontal at each takeoff and simultaneously swing your arms forward and upward.

Standing Triple Jump Into the Jumping Pit

Using starting positions that vary in distance from the side of the pit, athletes practice the triple jump to land in the sand. Participants attempt to "graduate" to the takeoff line, which is farthest from the pit. Each jumper should still attempt to make the hop, step, and jump more or less equidistant. Figure 9.10 shows the recommended ratios.

Coaching Tips

- Lift the thigh of the leading leg to horizontal on each of the three jumps.
- Swing your arms forward and upward as vigorously as possible on each of the three jumps.
- "Claw" back at the ground with the foot of your supporting leg at the end of each jump.
- Think of jumping long and low rather than up.

Triple Jump Using a Run-Up

Each participant attempts a triple jump using a run-up and jumping from a takeoff area. Place the takeoff area 5 to 8 meters from the sand pit. The selected distance will depend on age and ability. A run-up of 9 to 11 strides together with check marks is worked out in the same manner as in long jump (see chapter 8).

Figure 9.8 A triple jump from a standing start

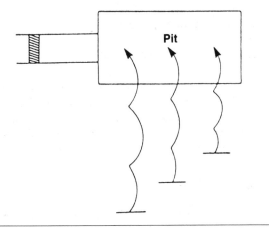

Figure 9.9 Standing triple jump into the pit

Coaching Tips

- Drive long and low at the takeoff. Concentrate on horizontal rather than vertical movement (i.e., don't hop high in the air).
- Aim for equal distances in each of the jumps.
- Listen to the rhythm of the footfalls during the triple jump; the cadence should be regular (''da—da—da'').
- Lift the thigh of the leading leg to horizontal at the midpoint of the hop and the step and for the takeoff in the jump. Aim for a wide stride position on each occasion.
- Land flat-footed at the end of the hop and step.
- Pull the body forward with the foot of your

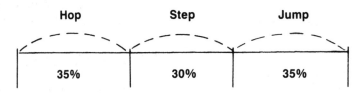

Figure 9.10 Length ratio for segments of the triple jump

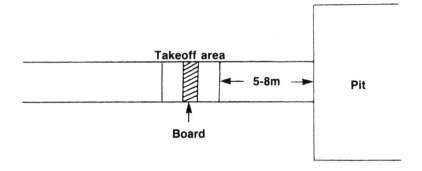

Figure 9.11 Triple jump takeoff area 5–8 m from pit

supporting leg using a clawing or pawing action at the end of the hop and the step.

Double Arm Action

Participants attempt double arm action during the three jumps as an alternative to the more natural alternating arm action (i.e., left leg forward, right arm forward). The double arm action is used by many elite jumpers and is easy enough for young athletes to attempt.

Figure 9.12 Double arm action

Coaching Tips

- At the takeoff from the hop and the step, swing both arms forward, sideways, and upward together, to a point where they are horizontal and parallel to the ground; this will help to lift your body forward and upward.
- Keep your arms flexed at the elbows (approximately 120 degrees).

Note: The following exercises are extremely demanding and are recommended only for mature and experienced athletes, not for novices. They are usually practiced in the off-season and only after an athlete's leg strength has been developed in other less demanding activities. Increase height and distance between obstacles in the same manner as with a weight-training schedule. Participants should become well accustomed to landing from low heights before trying to land and rebound from greater heights. All of the following examples are variations of rebound jumping.

Repetitive Bounding Over Obstacles Varying in Height and Distance

The performer bounds or strides from one foot to the other over various obstacles. Carefully select obstacles according to the maturity and ability of the athlete. You may choose one or two sections of a vaulting box, mats placed lengthwise or crosswise, elastic high jump "crossbars," or low hurdles. Whatever you choose, the athlete should be both challenged by and capable of leaping the obstacles.

Place the most challenging obstacles first. Place last easier obstacles that fatigued athletes can knock over without risking injury.

Coaching Tips

(Applicable to all types of rebound and depth jumping)

- Cushion the landing on the full foot, not on the ball of the foot or on the heel. (This action transfers the shock of landing through the bones to the joints of the body rather than to the muscles.)
- To absorb the shock of landing, partially flex at the knees and hips.
- Be sure to roll forward and push off the ball of the foot for the rebound.
- Initially practice from low heights of 15 to 30 centimeters (6 to 12 inches). Increase heights gradually.

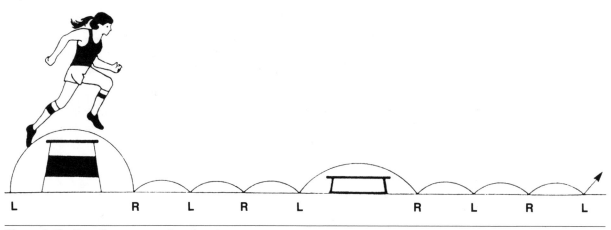

Figure 9.13 Bounding over varying obstacles

Combination Hopping and Bounding Over Obstacles

To increase the work load placed on the athlete, add repetitive hopping to bounding over high obstacles.

Rebound Jumping

The performer jumps down from one vaulting box onto a mat, immediately rebounding up onto the next box. Boxes are varied in height.

Figure 9.14 Hopping and bounding over obstacles

Figure 9.15 Rebound jumping

Repetitive Two-Leg Jumps Over a Series of Hurdles

This activity allows no momentary pause, as can occur on top of a vaulting box. Hurdles are varied in height.

Figure 9.16 Two-legged jumps over a series of hurdles

Two-Leg Jump Up Onto a Vaulting Box, Followed by a Single-Legged Landing and an Immediate Rebound

The athlete must have sufficient power to control the single-leg landing and then immediately drive up onto the next vaulting box. Elite athletes frequently increase the demand on the legs even further by wearing weight belts and weighted jackets! This level of power takes a long time to develop and is achieved only after years of hard training.

Figure 9.17 Jumping and rebounding

COMMON ERRORS AND CORRECTIONS

ERROR	REASONS	CORRECTIONS
The athlete uses stutter steps in the run-up. The run-up is irregular.	The athlete is unsure of the run-up. Check marks may be incorrect, and the athlete may be tense and anxious prior to jumping.	The athlete practices the run-up, assessing positioning of check marks on the run-up (see chapter 8).
The jumper uses too much backward lean at takeoff.	The penultimate and final strides are too long, and the athlete overemphasizes height in the hop. The leg is too straight during the takeoff, and the head falls back as the athlete (incorrectly) concentrates on height in the takeoff.	The athlete practices run-up and takeoff, aiming for a fast, flat takeoff. The takeoff leg is slightly flexed, the upper body erect, and the vision ahead. The athlete concentrates on a low, flat trajectory in the hop.

ERROR	REASONS	CORRECTIONS
The hop has too much height and distance. The jumper "collapses" at the end of the hop and has no momentum for the step and the jump.	The athlete leans backward at the takeoff. Strides prior to the takeoff are too long. The athlete overemphasizes the hop and forgets that two more jumps follow.	The athlete practices repetitive jumps, hops, and bounding strides with upright or slight forward lean at takeoff. The athlete practices hops and steps with the distances well defined by cones or markers.
The jumping leg is allowed to hang or drag during the hop.	The athlete relaxes the jumping leg after extension for the step.	The athlete practices sequential hopping, jumping, and bounding on grass or mats, emphasizing forward and upward drive with the thigh of the jumping leg.
The athlete performs the triple jump with stiff legs throughout.	The athlete does not flex the legs at the midpoint of the hop or the step or on landing at end of the hop and step.	Correct as for the previous error.
The athlete lands on the toes at the end of the hop or step and complains of painful landings at the end of the hop and step.	The athlete is reaching out with the toes for distance instead of with the heel followed by a flat footed landing.	Correct as for the previous 2 errors, emphasizing a heel–flat-footed landing throughout. The athlete should aim for a pawing or clawing action with the foot and should "drag" the ground backward with the supporting leg at the end of the hop and step.
The athlete's arm action is poor and haphazard during each of the 3 jumps.	The athlete is unsure of the technique.	Have the athlete repeat standing triple jumps, emphasizing strong upward arm swing at the takeoff of each of the 3 jumps. Decide on alternate or double arm action.
The step is extremely short, and there is no drive for distance.	The athlete has too much height and distance in the hop, and the jumping leg "collapses" at the end of the hop. The athlete is unable to drive forward with the leading leg in the step. Arm action is weak and ineffective.	The athlete practices repetitive jumps with emphasis on vigorous arm action and powerful leading-leg action (i.e., the thigh driven forward and upward to horizontal on each occasion). Assign hop and step practice over low obstacles and require specific distances.
After the hop and step the jump is weak and achieves poor distance.	The athlete loses momentum in the hop and the step, and speed throughout the hop and the step drops off dramatically. Errors in hop and step culminate in a poor jump.	The athlete practices sequential hops and steps on grass and mats, using a short run-up. Emphasize maintenance of horizontal speed throughout. Have the athlete practice long jumps from short run-ups, taking off from the nonfavored leg.

ASSESSMENT

1. Assess the following theoretical elements as taught during instructional sessions.

   a. Fundamental rules governing the triple jump.
   b. Good safety habits for use in the triple jump.
   c. Basic elements of triple-jump technique.
   d. Basic elements of triple-jump training.

2. Assess the performance of technique during the following stages of skill development.

   a. Repetitive bounding, hopping, and jumping.
   b. Various combinations of bounding, hopping, and jumping.
   c. Triple jump using a short run-up (3 to 5 strides).
   d. Triple jump using a full-length run-up.

Critical Features of Technique to Observe
During Assessment

   - Ability to use a run-up and 2 check marks.
   - Achieving a strong forward drive with a flat trajectory in the takeoff for the hop.
   - Driving the leading leg back and stretching out with the takeoff leg in the flight of the hop.
   - Pawing or clawing backward with the foot of the supporting leg in the landing at the end of the hop.
   - Driving forward and stretching out in a wide stride position in the step.
   - Driving upward with the arms to horizontal at the takeoff for hop, step, and jump.
   - Pawing or clawing backward with the foot of the supporting leg in the landing at the end of the step.
   - Swinging the thigh of the leading leg up and forward in the takeoff for the jump.
   - Reaching out with the legs well in front of the body for a good landing position at the end of the jump.
   - Achieving a distance ratio of 35 percent–30 percent–35 percent between the hop, step, and jump.

3. Hold graded competitions to help develop motivation and technique.

   a. Jumpers compete for distance from a standing start using a jump from a single-legged takeoff and then a jump from a double-legged takeoff.
   b. Jumpers compete for distance using these sequences: 3 bounding strides from a standing start, 3 hops from a standing start, 2 bounding strides and a jump taken from a standing start, and 2 hops and a jump taken from a standing start.
   c. Jumpers compete for distance from 3- and 5-stride run-ups using a selection from the sequences listed under *b*.
   d. Jumpers compete against each other and the stopwatch by jumping a series of hops, bounds, and jumps that you designate. Who can compete the series covering a specified distance or more in the shortest time?
   e. Jumpers compete for distance in a triple jump from 3- and 5-stride run-ups.
   f. Jumpers compete for distance in a triple jump from an extended run-up of 9 to 13 strides. Takeoffs can occur from a takeoff area rather than a takeoff board.
   g. Jumpers compete under full competitive conditions.

SUGGESTED PERFORMANCE STANDARDS (METERS)

MALE

Age	Satisfactory	Good	Excellent
11-12	7.0	7.5	8.5
13-14	8.0	8.5	10.0
15-16	8.5	9.5	11.0
17-19	9.1	10.5	11.5

FEMALE

Age	Satisfactory	Good	Excellent
11-12	6.9	7.3	8.3
13-14	7.5	8.1	9.2
15-16	7.9	8.8	10.0
17-19	8.7	9.7	10.3

CHAPTER
10

POLE VAULT

Pole vaulting was included in the first modern Olympic Games in 1896, and since that date the event has undergone dramatic changes. In the early years, vaulters used wooden poles and landed on grass, sand, or wood chips. Today's pole vaulter combines superior training with the modern technology of fiberglass poles, high-speed runways, and foam-rubber landing pits.

The fiberglass pole, in particular, has played a large part in the heights that have been achieved in pole vaulting. This pole has many advantages over the old aluminum pole. The fiberglass pole reduces the shock of takeoff and smooths the athlete's change in direction from horizontal to vertical. By flexing at takeoff, the pole allows the athlete to use a higher handhold. Plus, the energy stored at takeoff (by flexing) is returned to the vaulter when the pole straightens out.

A good pole vaulter is known for excellent sprinting speed, gymnastic ability, and fearlessness. In any instructional group, some members will not have these qualities; many will find it difficult to swing on a pole, much less lift their legs above the handhold. These students will be unable to complete all of the drills in this chapter. To allow for this, teach pole vaulting as a specialist event, not as a whole-class activity.

Short, light, highly flexible fiberglass training poles are excellent for introducing young athletes to pole vault. These poles are easy to carry and are preferable to aluminum poles because the athlete quickly learns to accept and use the flexion of the pole. You can teach the fundamentals of pole vault using rigid aluminum poles, but you will ultimately need to teach the athlete the technique required by the fiberglass pole, and the earlier this is done the better.

The finer aspects of pole vaulting take considerable time to learn well, and you must be aware of this fact when you teach the event. Young athletes cannot be expected to raise their grips on the pole and sprint down the run-up in one or two instructional periods. Although students can master the basics in a short period of time, a high handhold combined with a fast run-up is the result of repeated practice and dedication.

SAFETY SUGGESTIONS

Of all jumping events, pole vault has witnessed the most dramatic increase in heights attained. This increase is primarily due to the use of fiberglass poles. And more height requires more safety.

Landing Areas

An athlete using a fiberglass pole not only vaults high but flexes the pole considerably in the early part of the vault. Much of this flexion occurs while the athlete is suspended above or near the vaulting box. For the protection of the athlete, large landing pads, deep enough to cushion the vaulter's fall, have been designed with sections that fit around the pole-vault box. Do not use landing pads that fail to satisfy these requirements. For example, do not use high-jump landing pads, which are small and lack the additional sections needed to surround the pole-vault box. Nor should you fabricate pole-vault landing areas out of a series of stacked gymnastic crash pads. Even when these pads are tied together, an athlete could fall into the division between the mats.

The filling in landing pads deteriorates with time. Check the filling regularly and replace it where necessary, paying particular attention to the corner areas of the landing pads to make sure they give adequate support.

Excluding the front protection pads, the minimum size of a pole-vault pit is 5 meters by 5 meters. Although sand pits can be used for teaching some fundamental pole-vault skills, they should not be used for intermediate and advanced vaulting.

Crossbars

Rubber surgical tubing is an excellent substitute for the competitive crossbar. However, take care to ensure that pole-vault standards are weighted down at the base and that the elastic tubing stretches sufficiently so as not to pull the standards in toward the athlete during a landing.

Run-Ups

All run-ups should be well maintained, particularly at the takeoff area. Grass and artificial surfaces can be slippery for those not wearing spikes.

Poles

It is now possible to teach the fundamentals of pole vaulting using fiberglass poles specifically designed for training. These are much shorter than the competitive poles and because of their small cross-sectional diameters are easy for a young athlete to hold. The manufacturer will specify the body weight for which the pole is designed. The greater the variety of these poles that you have available, the easier it is to accommodate differences in body weights. Unfortunately, the expense of these poles frequently makes this prohibitive, and instructors still teach the fundamentals with cheaper but acceptable aluminum poles.

Tape each pole in the area where handholds occur. Tape, combined with resin and spray adhesives, assist in maintaining grip. Carefully check all poles for damage prior to each practice session, and do not allow students to leave fiberglass poles lying flat on grass areas and stadium infields, where poles can be punctured by spikes.

Uprights and Pole-Vault Box

High-jump uprights are adequate for use with novice pole vaulters. For more advanced vaulters, use regu-lation pole-vault uprights. You can fabricate a pole-vault box without much difficulty, but be sure that it is built strongly enough and that the sides and end are angled as specified to allow for the forward flexion of the pole. The box must be rigidly seated and set flush in the ground according to official specifications.

Characteristics of a Pole Vaulter

A good pole vaulter is usually a combination of a sprinter and a gymnast. The urge to "fly" high while hanging on a pole demands fearlessness and a type of character not unlike trapeze artists and circus stars. Besides having an excellent strength–weight ratio, an elite pole vaulter is extremely flexible and able to withstand the hyperextension that occurs in the back at the moment of takeoff when the body is hanging from the pole and being lifted upward. Young pole vaulters must develop this level of flexibility slowly and progressively.

Any class will contain those who will want to vault and those who are afraid of the event. Many with the desire to vault may not have the strength to hang and swing on the pole, much less lift the legs above the handhold. It is important that you recognize these individual differences and allow for them. Graded gymnastic skills will help develop the necessary power for those who wish to vault. Make other track and field events available for those who do not have the physical ability to vault. On no account should you browbeat members of the class into attempting this event if there is any doubt concerning their desire or physical abilities.

TECHNIQUE

There are five basic stages in pole-vaulting technique: the run-up, the plant, the takeoff, the rock back phase, and the bar clearance.

Grip, Carry, and Run-Up

A right-handed vaulter carries the pole on the right side of the body. The pole rests on the thumb and is gripped by the fingers of the left hand, which is just above waist height and approximately 1 foot in front of the hips. The right hand is rotated with the palm forward and presses downward, balancing the weight of the pole. The athlete begins with a fast, relaxed run-up and sprints at high speed immediately prior to the pole plant.

The Pole Plant

The plant begins on the third to last stride. The athlete pushes the pole forward and upward so that the right arm is extended above the head. The left arm provides forward pressure and causes the pole to flex.

The Takeoff

The body drives forward directly behind the pole. The athlete's body weight, hanging from the right arm, is combined with the forward thrust of the left arm to flex the pole.

The Rock Back Phase

Following the takeoff, the legs are flexed, the hips are raised, and the athlete rocks back on the pole. As the pole straightens, the arms pull and the body extends with the feet driven up close to the pole.

Action Over the Bar and Bar Clearance

A 1/2 rotation, coupled with flexion at the hips, rotates the athlete to a face-down position above the bar. The pole straightens out, helping to elevate the athlete. The athlete hyperextends his back and simultaneously pushes away from the pole. A relaxed fall onto the landing pads completes the vault (Figure 10.1).

TEACHING STEPS

STEP 1.	Lead-Ups
STEP 2.	Swing and 1/2 Rotation on the Pole
STEP 3.	Intermediate Pole-Vault Skills

Figure 10.1 Pole vault technique

Step 1: Lead-Ups

Pole vaulting requires a combination of sprinting, jumping, and gymnastic ability. To improve sprinting and jumping ability, see chapters 2, 7, 8, and 9. Gymnastic floor exercises and apparatus skills (low horizontal bar, parallel bars, rings, and ropes) develop power and coordination and relate directly to pole vaulting. The teaching progressions and safety techniques for the following gymnastic skills can be obtained from elementary and intermediate gymnastic manuals. Activities that emphasize pulling, pushing, and the development of abdominal strength are particularly good for pole vault.

Rope Climb

This activity develops upper body strength and simulates the pull on the pole. Figure 10.2 shows the rope climb without the use of the legs and feet. The same activity can be modified and made more difficult by holding the legs in a sitting *V* position or made easier by gripping the rope with the legs.

Figure 10.2   Rope climb

Swinging on a Rope and Lifting the Knees

This activity develops abdominal and upper body strength and also simulates the swing and ride on the pole.

Coaching Tips

- Combine the upward swing of the rope with the knee lift.
- Try to touch the rope as high as possible with your knees.

Figure 10.3   Swinging on a rope and lifting the knees

Swinging on a Rope With Partner Assistance

The performer runs, grabs the rope, and lifts the knees as high as possible. A partner provides assistance and more closely simulates the "feel" of elevation on the pole for the performer by pulling and straightening the rope. This activity develops upper body and abdominal strength.

Swinging on a Rope and Rotating Onto a Box Top

The performer runs, grabs the rope, and swings upward to turn onto a vaulting box top or a stack of crash pads. This activity simulates the elevation and rotation of the body on the pole and develops upper body and abdominal strength.

Coaching Tips

- Scissor your legs and turn to look back at the run-up for the rotation onto the box.
- If you fail to balance on the box top, hold onto the rope and swing back to the floor.

Pulling Up and Rotating on a Rope

The performer lies on the floor and simultaneously pulls up and rotates on the rope. This simulates the 1/2 rotation and upward drive on the pole and develops shoulder and arm strength.

Figure 10.4 Partner-assisted rope swinging

Figure 10.5 Rope swing onto a box top

Figure 10.6 Pulling up and rotating on a rope

Coaching Tips

- Pull hard and look back at the floor to help initiate the rotation.

Pullovers on the Horizontal Bar

This activity simulates the upward pull on the pole and also develops general upper body and abdominal strength. Initiating the action from a hang is considerably more difficult than from a jump off the floor. Use undergrip, overgrip, and mixed grip (left hand over and right hand under or vice-versa).

Figure 10.7 Pullovers on the horizontal bar

Coaching Tips

- Flex your legs and pull them up as close to the bar as possible.
- Drop your head back and pull vigorously with your arms.

Back Extension to Handstand

This gymnastic activity should be practiced initially with spotters. This skill simulates the upward drive on the pole for the bar clearance and develops good explosive extension in the arms and shoulders.

Coaching Tips

- Make sure your seat has rolled "over" and past your head before extending upward.
- Position your hands shoulder-width apart on each side of your head.
- Spotters should stand on each side of the performer and use a squeeze grip around the per-

Figure 10.8 Back extension to a handstand

former's knees. As the performer drives up into the handstand, assist by lifting his legs directly upward in a straight line above his hands.

Back Extension to Clear a Bar

The addition of an elastic crossbar makes the back extension more closely resemble the bar clearance in the pole vault. The crossbar also provides the performer with a target to clear. Begin by placing the bar at 30 centimeters (12 inches) and progressively raise it with each successful clearance. See the previous drill for teaching points to emphasize.

Figure 10.9 Back extension to clear a bar

Roundoff Along Single Sections of a Vaulting Box

The roundoff is a gymnastic skill that should initially be learned with the help of spotters. The use of single sections of vaulting boxes that increase in height simulates the 1/2 rotation and the final single-armed upward thrust that occurs during bar clearance.

Coaching Tips

- Practice this activity at ground level before trying it on box sections.

Figure 10.10 Roundoff along a vaulting box

- Turn the last hand placement and bring your legs together to assist in rotating your body.
- Your hips and legs must pass directly over your hands.
- Pull your stomach in and do not arch your back.

Underswing on a Low Horizontal Bar

This gymnastic activity should initially be practiced with the help of spotters. It develops upper body and abdominal strength and simulates the upward drive on the pole.

Figure 10.11 Underswing on a low horizontal bar

Coaching Tips

- Flex (pike) at the hips and bring your feet close to the bar for the underswing.
- Extend your body away from the bar for the dismount.

Underswing and 1/2 Turn Dismount on the Horizontal Bar

Performers should initially practice this activity on a low horizontal bar with assistance from spotters.

Figure 10.12 Underswing and 1/2 turn dismount on the horizontal bar

The activity simulates elevation on the pole together with rotation of the body over the bar and develops general upper body and abdominal strength.

Coaching Tips

- Perform the underswing and scissor your legs to initiate the rotation.
- Release your right hand when rotating to the left, and vice versa.
- Push away and release the bar for the dismount.

Dynamic Push-Ups to Clear a Low Obstacle

These explosive push-ups (press-ups) simulate the upward drive for bar clearance in pole vault. A block of sponge rubber is a safe obstacle to use in this activity.

Figure 10.13 Dynamic push-ups to clear a low obstacle

Coaching Tips

- Flex your arms only slightly, not all the way. Then extend them explosively.

Step 2: Swing and 1/2 Rotation on the Pole

Finding the Direction of Bend in a Fiberglass Pole

Each fiberglass pole "wants" to bend in one direction. Students must take this factor into account during vaulting. To find this direction, lift the pole at the grip end and allow the pole to rotate freely in the hand, with the tip of the pole on the ground. Another method is to allow the pole to roll while it is supported on a hurdle. Whatever the method, the pole will roll and hang in the same arc each time. Mark the lower part of this arc; when a right-handed vaulter runs down the run-up carrying the pole, the marked part of the pole should face the ground and be angled toward the right. When the pole is lifted, rotated, and planted in the box, the mark will face forward and to the left. The vaulter will swing up on the "inside" of the arc with the pole bending away from the vaulter toward the left.

Figure 10.14 Finding the direction of bend in a fiberglass pole

Swinging on the Pole From a Low Height

The performer stands on 2 sections of vaulting box and plants the pole in the sand at the takeoff end of a long-jump pit (or in the pole-vault box). A right-handed vaulter grips the pole at shoulder height with the left hand, keeping the right arm fully extended.

Coaching Tips

- Look to the left side of the pole and swing on the right.
- Push away with your feet from the vaulting box and swing as far out into the sand pit or landing pad as possible.

Variation

Lay ropes across the sand pit to form distance zones. Participants compete to reach the farthest zone they can with their feet.

Figure 10.15 Swinging on the pole from a low height

Experiencing the Flexion of the Pole and Swinging From Greater Height Into a Sandpit

Use all sections of the vaulting box to create a height that requires a high handhold and allows a novice to

Figure 10.16 Swinging into a sand pit

Figure 10.17   Swinging on the pole from a short run-up

experience the flexion of the fiberglass pole. The student plants the pole in the sand at the takeoff end of the long-jump pit (or in the pole-vault box).

Swinging on the Pole From a Short Run-Up

In this drill you hold the pole in the box ready for the athlete who runs up to grip and swing on the pole. Plant the pole in the sand at the takeoff end of the long-jump pit (or in the pole-vault box). Hold the pole at an angle so that each approaching jumper will grip it approximately 5 to 10 centimeters (2 to 4 inches) above vertical reach. Use a short unmeasured run-up for this drill. Each jumper runs to grip the pole and, with you assisting, swings through to land in the sand or on the pole-vault landing pad.

Coaching Tips

- Run slowly, grab the pole, and hang on.
- Don't try to lift up on the pole, just swing.

Finding Vertical Reach on the Pole

Vertical reach is the spot reached by the outstretched arm on a pole held vertically with the tip on the ground. Holding this position on the pole allows the novice to hang on the pole but be lifted a minimal distance from the ground.

Measuring a 5-Stride Run-Up

Each vaulter must have a measured approach, and a 5-stride run-up is adequate for novices. The run-up will differ for each individual. It can be measured in the following manner.

Figure 10.18   Finding vertical reach on the pole

Each vaulter stands beside a pole with 1 arm extended upward. A position 5 to 10 centimeters (2 to 4 inches) above where the hand touches the pole will become the upper handhold on the pole. The athlete grips this position on the pole with the right hand and places the tip of the pole in the pole-vault box (or the sand of the long-jump pit). The right arm is fully extended above the head and the lower hand (left) grips the pole at shoulder height. The athlete places the left foot directly below the upper handhold and, to simulate the takeoff, raises the right thigh. A partner marks the position of the left foot on the ground. Without carrying the pole, and beginning with the left foot, each individual runs back 5 strides, and a partner marks the 5th stride.

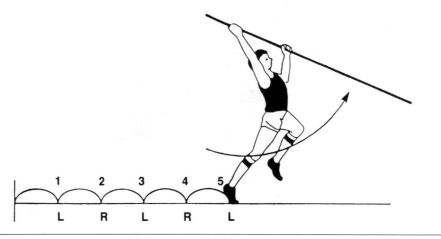

Figure 10.19 Five-stride run-up (right-handed)

Coaching Tips

- Start with your feet together and run back 5 even strides at moderate speed.
- Look forward as you run.

A 5-Stride Run-Up for a Right-Handed Vaulter

A right-handed vaulter begins the 5-stride run-up with the left foot. On the fifth stride, the left foot is beneath the upper handhold and the right thigh is driven up for the swing on the pole.

Coaching Tips

- If your left foot is ahead of its correct position after 5 strides, shift the start of the run-up back an equal amount.
- Do the reverse if the foot is to the rear of its correct position.

Figure 10.20 Run-up with pole in plant position

Run-Up With the Pole Held in Plant Position

To simplify the plant action for novices, the athlete runs up with the pole held above the head in the plant position. The pole remains in this position throughout the 5-stride run-up.

Coaching Tips

- Run directly behind the pole.
- Keep the pole in position with the tip just off the surface of the run-up.

Swinging in Straddle Position on the Pole

The athlete plants the pole in the sand at the takeoff end of the long-jump pit and swings on the pole with the legs straddled on either side. This practice teaches the performer to stay directly behind the pole.

Using a sand-pit as a substitute pole-vault box makes the plant action easier for the novice, because it demands less accuracy. The pole drives down into the sand, which acts as a pole-vault box, providing sufficient stability and support for this elementary drill.

Coaching Tips

- Hang on the pole with one leg on each side.
- Swing on the pole, and as the pole lowers toward the landing area, pull with your arms.

Swing and 1/2 Rotation on the Pole

The performer uses a 5-stride run-up, holding the pole above the head in the plant position. The athlete plants the pole in the sand at the takeoff end of the long-

Figure 10.21   Swinging in straddle position on the pole

Figure 10.22   Swing and 1/2 rotation

jump pit and, instead of straddling the pole (as in the previous drill), swings both legs together on the same side of the pole (right side for a right-handed vaulter). A 1/2 rotation completes the swing.

Coaching Tips

- Swing first, lift your legs, and then pull with your arms.
- Look back toward the takeoff and scissor your legs; your body will rotate.

Elementary Pole Vault— No Pole Carry

Using a 5-stride run-up, a swing, and a 1/2 rotation, the novice can attempt to clear an elastic crossbar set at head height. You hold the pole in the pole-vault box for each performer, so the novice can experience an elementary vault without having to carry the pole.

Step 3: Intermediate Pole-Vault Skills

Technique

Figure 10.23a illustrates the pole carry as seen from the side. The higher that the athlete holds on the pole, the greater the angle of pole carry.

Figure 10.23b illustrates the pole carry as seen from behind. The athlete carries the pole at the side of the body with the tip of the pole elevated to approximately shoulder height. A wide grip makes the pole easy to carry. For a right-handed vaulter, the pole rests on the thumb of the left hand, which is at waist height and ahead of the hips. The right hand is rotated palm forward and presses downward, balancing the weight of the pole.

Figure 10.23 Two views of the pole carry

Drills
Sprinting With the Pole

Participants run short sprints of 15 to 20 meters with the pole.

Coaching Tips

- Relax as you run.
- Avoid too much shoulder shrugging or pushing back and forth with the pole.

- Keep the tip of the pole pointing directly ahead; don't let it wander around.

Simulating the Pole Plant From a 5-Stride Run-Up

Athletes first practice this drill on grass. Athletes simulate the plant of the pole into the pole-vault box by pushing the tip of the pole along the ground. The athlete initially walks through the sequence then progressively increases the speed of action.

The sequence of a 5-stride run-up and pole plant is as follows.

- The performer starts with the feet together, holding the pole in carry position with the upper handhold at 5 to 10 centimeters (2 to 4 inches) above vertical reach position.
- On Stride 1 (left foot forward), the pole remains in carry position.
- On Stride 2 (right foot forward), the arms start to push the pole forward. The left arm is extended, and the right hand on the pole moves past the body.
- On Stride 3 (left foot forward), the athlete extends the left arm forward and uses the right hand to rotate and push the pole upward past the shoulder.
- On Stride 4 (right foot forward), the athlete extends the arms with the right hand directly above the head. The tip of the pole is almost touching the ground.
- On Stride 5, the athlete steps forward with the left foot, drives the right thigh upward, and hops on the left foot. (The hop simulates the jump of the takeoff.) The arms remain extended above the head, and the tip of the pole slides along the ground.

Instructors' Count: Left-right-left- right -left-hop
    Stride: 1 - 2 - 3 - 4 - 5

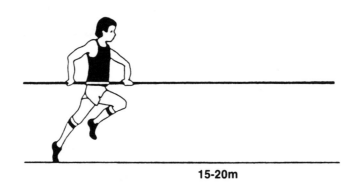

15-20m

Figure 10.24 Sprinting with the pole

Figure 10.25 Simulating the pole plant from a 5-stride run-up

Practicing the Pole Plant

Athletes can also practice the pole plant slowly and mechanically from a 3-stride run-up using benches put end to end to form an elevated approach. The extra height allows for the complete movement to be performed slowly and methodically and for a swing to be included at the end of the plant. The pole is planted into the sand of a long-jump pit.

Instructors' Count: Left-right-left-swing

Stride: 1 - 2 - 3

Combining the 5-Stride Run-Up and Plant

Each athlete measures a 5-stride run-up from the takeoff end of the long-jump pit. The sequence is as follows.

The athlete plants the pole in the sand (takeoff end of the long-jump pit) and holds the pole in the takeoff position with the right thigh raised and upper arm extended. The left foot is directly below the upper handhold. The right hand holds the pole 5 to 10 centimeters (2 to 4 inches) above vertical reach with the lower hand at shoulder height. A partner marks the position of the left foot.

The athlete turns around on the mark and places both feet together, holding the pole in the carry position. Beginning with the left foot, the athlete runs 5 strides, and a partner marks the 5th stride.

The athlete starts the 5-stride run-up with the feet together, taking the 1st stride with the left foot. The hopping action previously practiced on the grass now becomes a takeoff followed by an easy swing on the pole. The athlete makes no effort at this stage to elevate the legs. Assist at takeoff where necessary.

Figure 10.26 Practicing the pole plant using benches

Transferring a 5-Stride Run-Up and Pole Plant to the Pole-Vault Run-Up

The athlete repeats the same process as in the previous drill, using the pole-vault run-up and planting the pole in the box. At takeoff, the vaulter will raise the legs and swing to land on the pads in a sitting position.

Coaching Tips

- Drive the pole forward and upward during the last 2 strides of the pole plant.
- Stay directly behind the pole at takeoff.
- Extend your right arm.
- With your left arm, push forward into the pole.

Increasing the Length of the Run-Up and Using Check Marks

With practice, the athlete progressively raises the handhold and increases the run-up to 7 and 9 strides, and thereafter to 11 and 13 strides. Measure the longer run-ups in the same manner as for the 5-stride run-up. The longer run-ups will vary considerably for each individual. The length of the run-up will ultimately depend on how long the athlete takes to reach maximum speed. Use check marks on longer run-ups to ensure accuracy during the run-up. In Figure 10.27, the 1st and 5th strides have check marks. Frequently athletes will use a second check mark, which is often placed at the first stride of the run-up.

Learning to Bend the Pole

This practice teaches the athlete to coordinate the plant with actions that emphasize flexion of the pole. No takeoff occurs, and all actions are performed at high speed. The complete action is initially performed in 2 to 3 strides. The athlete drives the pole forward in the pole plant and drives his body weight toward the pole. The body weight moving forward is transferred into flexion of the pole by the pull of the upper arm and the push of the lower arm.

The athlete should be ready for the rebound of the pole after it is flexed, because it will drive the athlete back toward the run-up. This drill demands excellent

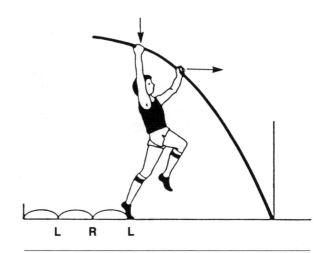

Figure 10.28 Bending the pole

timing and is extremely tiring. With practice, the athlete will be able to run up from beyond 2 to 3 strides, performing the plant and drive into the pole explosively.

Coaching Tips

- Get the pole above your head as fast as possible.
- Straighten the left arm.
- Be sure your left elbow and wrist are directly below the pole.
- Drive the right knee up toward the left hand.
- Be prepared for the rebound of the pole.

Emphasizing the "Rock-Back" Action After Takeoff

This practice requires the athlete to rock or roll backward after takeoff so that the back is parallel to the ground. Backward rotation of the body occurs at the shoulder axis. The hips and knees are flexed as the rock-back occurs, so they are ready for the drive up above the handhold.

To perform this drill, the athlete must have enough speed in the run-up to force the pole into a bend that is forward and across to the left side of the pit. Frequently, the athlete performs the rock-back practice dropping the legs after they have been driven upward and landing on his back on the landing pad.

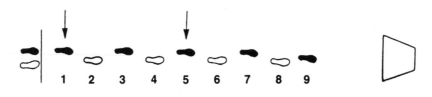

Figure 10.27 Lengthening the run-up and using check marks

Figure 10.29   The "rock-back" action

An elastic crossbar set at about 60 centimeters (2 feet) above the height of the upper handhold and with the standards placed the same distance to the rear of the box will give the vaulter a target for the feet.

Coaching Tips

- Hang from your upper arm and drop your shoulders back.
- Flex your legs and swing them upward, driving them toward the target (the elastic crossbar).

Elevating the Body Above the Handhold

After the rock-back, the pole will be bent to the left and the athlete's hips will rise above the lower handhold. As the pole straightens, the hips and feet must be driven upward with the left leg leading the way. The athlete pulls vigorously when the hips are as high as possible and when the pole begins to straighten. The pull will also initiate the 1/2 rotation to put the vaulter facedown for the bar clearance. The final push and release with the upper hand complete the vault.

An elastic rope 2 feet above the height of the upper handhold provides an adequate target. The standards are placed approximately 60 centimeters (2 feet) to the rear of the box.

Coaching Tips

- Keep your feet close to the pole during the upward pull.
- Remember to pull at the same time that the pole is straightening.

Figure 10.30   Elevating the body above the handhold

Practicing the Pull, Rotation, and Push on the Pole

The athlete can practice the pull, rotation, and push on the pole with the pole in the box. The action is performed as dynamically and vigorously as possible.

Coaching Tips

- Drop back against the pole to give it some flexion.
- As it rebounds, pull, rotate, and push as quickly and as dynamically as possible.

Bar Clearance

The bar clearance is one of the easier pole-vaulting actions, although the timing has to be precise. The athlete drives as forcefully as possible on the pole to complete the upward push. A vigorous hyperextension of the muscles of the back elevates the upper body.

Figure 10.31 Practicing pull, rotation, and push on the pole

Figure 10.32 Bar clearance

Coaching Tips

- Time the back-arch so that it occurs as the legs and trunk drop downward. This will help to rotate you away from the bar.

Raising the Handhold and Lengthening the Run-Up

As the athlete's confidence and ability increase, the run-up is progressively increased in length. Greater speed in the run-up allows for a higher handhold and more bend in the pole and also increases the time that the athlete has to maneuver on the pole. The 13- and 15-stride run-ups can easily produce 3.5- to 4-meter vaults.

COMMON ERRORS
AND CORRECTIONS

ELEMENTARY VAULT

(The athlete does not carry the pole; the instructor holds the pole in the box at the required takeoff angle.)

ERROR	REASONS	CORRECTIONS
The upper arm is bent during takeoff.	Grip is incorrectly positioned on the pole. The speed of the run-up and the body position below the pole at takeoff vary.	The athlete practices swinging on the pole with the upper arm extended, taking off from a vaulting box. Have the athlete remeasure the run-up and swing on the pole from a 5-stride run-up. Hold the pole ready in the takeoff position. The athlete should emphasize a fully extended upper arm.
The chest hits the pole during takeoff.	The left arm collapses and does not keep the body away from the pole. The pole does not flex.	Use a pole that the novice can bend easily. The athlete should hang with the right arm and push with the left.
The athlete takes off with the body too far to the side of the pole.	The athlete is afraid of swinging on the pole and raising the legs and is not directly to the rear of the pole at takeoff.	The athlete should work on "riding the broomstick"— swinging with one leg on each side of the pole. The athlete should be directly behind pole at takeoff.
Legs are not elevated during the swing.	The athlete is trying to raise the legs by pulling with the arms. The legs are raised without any flexion at the knees. The athlete may have poor abdominal strength.	The athlete should leave the upper arm extended and raise the legs by dropping the shoulders back and bending the legs at the knees. The athlete should practice abdominal exercises.
The swing and 1/2 rotation are not completed. The athlete performs a 1/4 rotation or none at all.	The legs are not raised at all, there's no pull and turn action from the arms, and the head is not turned back toward the run-up. The athlete may have poor abdominal and shoulder strength.	Instruct the athlete to practice the swing and 1/2 rotation on a rope, also the underswing dismount with 1/2 rotation on the low horizontal bar. The athlete should practice general upper body and abdominal exercises.

INTERMEDIATE POLE-VAULT SKILLS

(performed without instructor assistance)

ERROR	REASONS	CORRECTIONS
The run-up is inaccurate and varies each time. The athlete slows down during the run-up.	The athlete's ability to run with the pole is poor. The athlete is afraid of the takeoff and riding on the pole. Measurement of run-up and check marks is incorrect, and the run-up may be too long.	Have the athlete remeasure the run-up. The athlete should practice sprinting with the pole and should work to improve sprint endurance. To improve accuracy of the approach, have the athlete practice at lower heights from a shorter run-up.
The takeoff foot is not directly below the upper handhold at takeoff. The pole jerks in the athlete's hand at takeoff.	The run-up is poorly measured, or the speed of the run varies with each approach. Upper arm may not be extended at takeoff.	Have the athlete remeasure the run-up, making sure that speed used running back from the takeoff spot is same speed as the approach run. The athlete should work for smooth, regular acceleration in each run-up.
The takeoff foot is too far to one side at takeoff.	The athlete overemphasizes the swing to the side of the pole. The body is not directly behind the pole at takeoff.	Instruct the athlete to practice the pole plant from a short run-up. Place orientation marks on the ground to assist in foot positioning.
Legs and hips are poorly elevated after takeoff.	The athlete is afraid of dropping the shoulders back and lifting the legs and has insufficient abdominal power. There's no upward drive with the thigh of the leading leg at takeoff.	Assign power exercises for the upper body, arms, and abdomen as well as gymnastic, rope, and pole activities in which the lower body is lifted upward.
The athlete extends the body too early. The legs are driven toward the bar, not upward and parallel to the pole.	Timing of the extension of the body is incorrect. The athlete is hurrying the extension of the body instead of waiting for the completion of the swing. The shoulders do not drop backward.	Assign rock-back and extension activities using ropes and poles. Instruct the athlete to drive the feet up parallel to rope and pole. Provide verbal assistance on timing of extension.
The pole does not bend sufficiently, and no energy is stored in the pole.	The pole is too stiff for the weight and strength of the vaulter. The athlete's grip is too close or too low on the pole, and the lower arm is not extended and driven forward into the pole. Run-up speed prior to pole plant is too slow.	Check pole specifications relative to athlete's body weight. Check grip height and grip width. Have the athlete practice the plant and pole bend from a short run-up.
Vaulter and pole slow down and fail to reach a vertical position.	The vaulter runs too slowly during the run-up, and the grip is too high on the pole. The legs and hips are elevated too early.	Help the athlete improve sprinting ability with the pole. Check grip height and lower if necessary. Instruct the athlete to wait until the pole begins to straighten before driving upward. Provide verbal assistance on timing.

ERROR	REASONS	CORRECTIONS
The athlete has too little time to complete vault and knocks the bar off on the way up.	The grip is too low on the pole, and the legs and hips are elevated too late. Extension of the body above the handhold occurs too late. The athlete's center of gravity is not directly below the upper handhold at takeoff.	The athlete must raise the grip on the pole. Have the athlete practice the complete vault, working to correct the timing for the elevation and extension of the body above the handhold.
The athlete crosses the bar on his back and never achieves the facedown position over the bar. The athlete uses no rotation.	The athlete's feet are not close together or close to the pole during the upward pull. The legs and hips drop away from the pole.	Have the athlete practice with the rope and pole, pulling and rotating with the feet as close to the rope and pole as possible. Work to improve abdominal and upper body strength.

ASSESSMENT

1. Assess the following theoretical elements as taught during instructional sessions.

    a. Fundamental rules governing pole vault.
    b. Good safety habits for pole vault.
    c. Basic elements of pole-vault technique.
    d. Basic elements of training for pole vault.

2. Assess the performance of technique during the following stages of skill development.

    a. Vaulters run to swing on the pole, which you hold ready for them.
    b. Vaulters run to swing and perform a 1/2 turn on the pole while you hold it.
    c. Vaulters run up carrying the pole in plant position. They swing and perform a 1/2 turn on the pole.
    d. Vaulters perform the plant action with the pole, using a 5-stride approach on grass.
    e. Vaulters perform the run-up, pole carry (pole at the side of the body), plant, and swing. They don't elevate the hips and legs, and no 1/2 rotation is required.
    f. Vaulters perform a run-up, pole carry (pole at the side of the body), plant, swing, and elevation of the hips and legs. No 1/2 rotation is included.
    g. Vaulters use a short run-up, plant and flex the pole without taking off.
    h. Vaulters perform the complete vault from an extended run-up.

Critical Features of Technique to Observe During Assessment (Right-Handed Vaulter)

- Gripping and carrying the pole.
- Accelerating through the run-up.
- Pushing the pole forward and upward and taking off below an extended right arm.
- Flexing the pole from the forward push of the left arm, combined with the downward pull of the right.
- Flexing the legs and hips during the ride on the pole.
- Pulling with the arms and extending the body upward close to the pole as the pole straightens.
- Rotating 180 degrees and flexing at the hips to achieve a piked position above the bar.
- Hyperextending and pushing away from the pole for the release and landing.

3. Hold graded competitions to develop motivation and technique.

    a. Vaulters compete for height using an elementary swing and 1/2 rotation on the pole. (You assist with the pole at takeoff.)
    b. Vaulters compete for height using a run-up, swing, and 1/2 rotation on the pole. The vaulters carry the pole in plant position above the head during the run-up, and you assist with the pole at takeoff if necessary.
    c. Vaulters compete using full competitive conditions.

SUGGESTED PERFORMANCE STANDARDS (METERS)

	MALE		
Age	*Satisfactory*	*Good*	*Excellent*
11-12	1.5	1.9	2.4
13-14	1.9	2.4	2.7
15-16	2.2	2.6	2.9
17-19	2.6	2.9	3.2

CHAPTER

11

SHOT PUT

The shot put is contested as a separate event for males and females and also as part of the decathlon and heptathlon. Over the years, the event has come to be dominated by big, powerful athletes.

A major advance in the technique of the event occurred in the 1950s, when Parry O'Brien began his throw facing the rear of the ring. This method, known as the O'Brien technique or more commonly as the glide technique, is used by the majority of modern shotputters.

A technique gaining popularity is the rotary shot-put technique, which employs a discus-style rotation across the shot-put ring rather than the backward shift or glide that characterizes the O'Brien technique. Both glide and rotation have been equally successful in achieving long throws.

The rotary technique is more difficult to master than the glide technique, because the rotation has to be performed in the confines of the shot-put ring (2.135 meters or 7 feet in diameter) and because the rotary action makes the control of the shot more difficult.

First teach beginners the glide technique. Once the young athlete has worked seriously with this technique and can perform the footwork for rotational discus throws, the athlete can experiment with the rotary shot-put technique.

SAFETY SUGGESTIONS

Choose shot for practice that are appropriate to the strength and hand sizes of the participants. A large selection of shot that vary both in weight and size will help you achieve this objective. Shot can range from .5 kg (1.1 pounds) up to competitive weights (7.25 kg [16 lb] for men and 4 kg [8 lb 13 oz] for women).

From experience you should be able to assess whether a shot is too light or too heavy for the athlete using it. As a general rule, the shot should be heavy enough to require a "putting" (i.e., pushing) action but not light enough to allow the performer to throw it easily, like a ball!

A good warm-up of jogging, stretching, and light exercises is necessary prior to shot putting. In particular, the ligaments and muscles of the wrists and hands should be well prepared for the explosive actions that characterize this event. Even when the athlete uses correct technique, a poor warm-up can cause ligament and muscle injuries.

All shot must be safely stored and then carried to the throwing circles for each training session. Do not allow athletes to throw or play with the shot (or any throwing implements) during the time that the implements are being transported from one area to another.

Although the shot travels a far shorter distance than the discus, javelin, or hammer, it still demands rigorous safety regulations to which all involved must adhere. Most problems in shot put tend to occur from lack of communications between the thrower and whoever is (often unknowingly) in the line of flight. Shot-putters begin both the glide and rotational technique facing away from the direction of throw and so are momentarily blind to what is happening out in the throwing sector. When athletes are practicing, those waiting to throw should act as spotters or observers for the athlete in the ring about to throw. The observers make sure that no one has moved into the throwing sector and that officials have finished measuring and have moved out of the line of flight.

During competition as well as during training, all spectators and those waiting to throw should stand at least 3 to 4 meters (10 to 14 feet) to the immediate rear of the ring. Experienced officials will stand close to the ring in order to check for foot violations, but their proximity to the ring is based on a firm understanding of the particular characteristics of the event.

The rotary technique of throwing has added another dimension to the shot put and has increased the need for vigilance by those conducting the event. Adopted from the discus throw, the rotary shot-put technique causes considerably more control problems than the glide technique, particularly for those who are trying this method of throwing for the first time. Because of the rotation and the centrifugal pull of the shot, the trajectory and line of flight can frequently be outside of the throwing sector, and it is not infrequent for beginners to ''lose'' the shot at the midpoint of the rotation across the ring. This is one reason why it is recommended that only mature athletes practice the rotary technique, and only under instructor supervision. The glide technique is far easier to perform than the rotary technique and has a high rate of success in producing long throws. For the highest level of safety when the rotary technique is being practiced, nonthrowers should stand at least 4 meters to the left rear of a right-handed thrower and 4 meters to the right rear of a left-handed thrower.

TECHNIQUE—GLIDE

The glide technique has not fundamentally changed since its invention in the 1950s. Although bigger and more powerful athletes have dramatically increased distances, the main elements of technique remain essentially the same.

Preparation

The athlete stands at the rear of the ring with his or her back toward the direction of the throw. The weight is on the right leg (for a right-handed thrower), and the vision is to the rear. The athlete cradles the shot under the chin and raises the left arm.

Glide

The athlete flexes the right leg and lowers the upper body in preparation for the backward shift (glide) across the ring. The athlete kicks the left leg backward, and simultaneously the right leg drives the athlete toward the center of the ring. The upper body stays in its lowered position. At the end of the glide, the athlete pulls the right leg in under the body and

places the left foot in position at the front of the circle. At the end of the glide, the upper body is still inclined toward the rear of the ring.

The Put

The athlete initiates the put with a rotary drive of the right leg toward the direction of throw. The hips rotate, the chest is pushed forward, and the body lifts upward. The right side of the body rotates forward around an extended left leg, and an extension of the throwing arm and fingers completes the put (Figure 11.1). After the shot has left the hand, the legs reverse positions to stop the athlete from fouling at the front of the ring. The action is called a *reverse*.

TECHNIQUE—ROTARY

The rotary technique is a discus-style rotation that occurs prior to the final putting action of the shot. The technique uses discus-thrower footwork in the first 2/3 of the throw. The final putting action resembles that used in the glide technique.

The athlete stands in a shoulder-width stance at the rear of the ring with his or her back toward the direction of throw. The athlete cradles the shot in the neck. The legs are slightly flexed, and the vision and free arm are directed toward the rear.

Rotation

The athlete rotates in discus style by pivoting on the balls of both feet toward the direction of throw. Continuing to pivot on the left foot, the athlete then drives across the ring. The putting position that occurs at the end of the rotation is similar to the glide technique (Figure 11.2). The right leg is flexed and the left leg stretched out to the front of the shot-put ring. The upper body is flexed at the hips toward the rear of the ring.

The Put

Both legs rotate and extend upward, driving the hips and chest toward the direction of throw. The put is completed by an extension of the arms and fingers. After the shot has left the hand, athletes frequently perform a reverse in the same manner as the glide technique to stop the athlete from fouling the throw at the front of the ring.

Figure 11.1 Glide technique

Figure 11.2 Rotary technique

TEACHING STEPS

STEP 1.	Lead-Ups
STEP 2.	Shot Put From a Standing Position
STEP 3.	Shot Put Using the Glide Technique
STEP 4.	Shot Put Using the Rotary Technique

Step 1: Lead-Ups

Preparatory activities for shot putting can begin with all forms of throwing using soccer balls, basketballs, or light medicine balls. Initially, throwing is two-handed (e.g., from behind the head, between the legs, and around the side of the body). Then require one-handed or two-handed throwing in a "pushing" or "putting" fashion, which simulates the action required in shot putting.

A Push-Throw With a Medicine Ball

Students throw medicine balls against the wall using a pushing or putting action. The throwers catch the balls on the rebound.

Coaching Tips

- Push forward into the throw with your body, making sure your legs are extended.
- Keep your chest high and your head up.

Figure 11.3 Push-throw with a medicine ball

- Extend your arms as vigorously as possible and be sure to push with your fingers.

Push-Throws in Pairs

Pairs face each other and use one- and two-handed push passes with a medicine ball.

Figure 11.4 Push-throw in pairs

Coaching Tips

- If you are throwing with your right arm, be sure to step forward 1 long stride (before you throw) with the left foot. This will give you a good throwing stance.
- Keep your elbow of the throwing arm at shoulder level; don't let it drop down to the side of the body.
- Keep your chest up and extend your legs as you throw.

Putting the Medicine Ball for Distance

Individuals put the medicine ball for distance. Distance lines are marked on the ground.

Coaching Tips

- Try to make your throwing action as long as possible. Push from as far back to as far forward as possible.
- Drive up onto your toes and push forward with your body. Use your whole body in the throw, not just your arms.
- To obtain the longest distance, a trajectory of about 40 to 43 degrees above horizontal is necessary. Release the medicine ball so that your arms are fully extended in front of you and just above head height.

Putting a Medicine Ball for Height and Distance

This practice emphasizes both height and distance. Surgical tubing is suspended between 2 high-jump or pole-vault standards 2 to 3 meters (7 to 10 feet) above the ground. If the student can throw the medicine ball over the crossbar, the thrower takes 2 paces back. Who ends up the farthest away from the standards? (Be sure that the elastic will stretch sufficiently when hit. It is also a good idea to weight down the bases of the high-jump or pole-vault standards.)

Coaching Tips

- This lead-up will test whether you are achieving the best trajectory.
- Remember to extend your legs and lift your chest upward as you throw.
- Use the big muscles of the legs, back, and chest before using the arms, not afterwards.

Passing Relay

Students push-pass a medicine ball in zigzag fashion from one end of a team to the other. Which team is

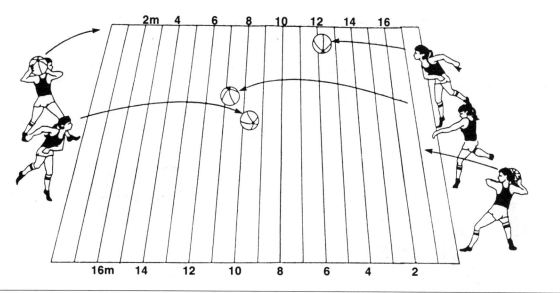

Figure 11.5 Putting a medicine ball for distance

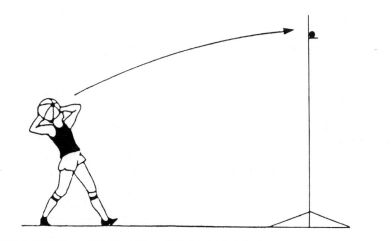

Figure 11.6 Putting a medicine ball for height and distance

quickest in passing the medicine ball? Make sure that the medicine ball is light enough to catch easily.

Coaching Tips

- Be alert and ready to catch the ball.
- Reach out to catch the ball and absorb its momen-

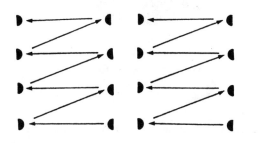

Figure 11.7 Passing relay

tum by drawing your arms and body back the moment your hands contact the ball.
- Throw the ball accurately and with the correct amount of force so that your partner can catch the ball easily.
- Whoever drops the medicine ball has to pick it up, so be accurate when you throw.

Step 2: Shot Put From a Standing Position

Technique

The athlete begins a standing put facing away from the direction of throw, keeping the vision to the rear, and cradling the shot under the chin. The athlete flexes the right leg and reaches back with the left leg into the putting stance, lowering the upper body at the hips. The shoulders at this point remain square to the rear. The athlete drives upward and rotates toward the direction of the throw by extending the legs and thrusting the hips and chest forward. A powerful thrust of the throwing arm and the vigorous snap of the fingers complete the putting action (Figure 11.8).

Figure 11.8   Shot put from a standing position

Drills

The Correct Handhold for Cradling the Shot

Each participant raises and lowers the shot from the shoulder to full arm's length several times. This develops a feel for the manner in which the shot rests between the fingers and the thumb.

Figure 11.9   Cradling the shot

Coaching Tips

- Hold the shot between your fingers and thumb; don't let the shot drop into your palm. If you can only hold the shot in your palm, the shot is too heavy and you need to use a lighter one.
- Raise and lower your arm slowly. This will give you a feel for the support given to the shot by the combined action of the thumb and the fingers.

Standing Put—Initial Stance Facing the Direction of Throw

Participants stand facing the direction of throw and holding the shot in the correct hand position. The thrower steps forward with the left foot (right-handed thrower) and then puts the shot.

Figure 11.10   Standing put facing throwing direction

Coaching Tips

- Keep the elbow of the throwing arm high (at shoulder height) during the put.
- Begin the putting action by moving your body forward. Move the hips forward and keep your chest high and square (at right angles) to the direction of throw.
- Extend your legs and be sure to put the shot from your fingers (not from your palm).
- Finish the putting action with the throwing arm extended in front of your body and with your hand raised to just above head level.

Standing Put—Shoulders Rotate 90 Degrees From the Direction of Throw

The thrower steps toward the direction of the throw with the left leg (right-handed thrower), rotating the

Figure 11.11   Standing put with 90-degree shoulder rotation

shoulders 90 degrees to the right (i.e., away from the direction of throw). The put begins with the right leg extending and driving the hips and the chest toward the direction of throw. The extension of the arm and the thrust of the fingers complete the putting action.

Coaching Tips

- Be sure to begin the putting action by extending your legs.
- After your legs are extended, turn your hips and chest toward the direction of the throw before using the throwing arm.
- Be sure to keep the elbow of the throwing arm at shoulder level. Do not let it drop downward, otherwise the shot can bend the fingers backward. Think of the putting action as a bench press in the weight room!
- Finish the put with a thrusting action from the fingers toward the direction of the throw.

Standing Put—Initial Stance Facing the Direction of Throw

The performer begins facing the direction of the throw with the feet together, then takes 1 pace forward (slightly wider than shoulder width) with the left leg. This provides the correct foot positioning for the final throwing stance. The thrower then rotates 180 degrees on the balls of the feet and faces directly away from the direction of the throw, shifting the body weight back over the right foot. From this position the athlete simultaneously lifts upward, turning the hips and chest toward the direction of throw. The put is completed with a strong extension of the throwing arm.

Coaching Tips

- Lift upward with your legs and back and simultaneously rotate toward the direction of the throw.
- Don't be in a hurry to use the throwing arm; wait

until your body has lifted up and rotated toward the direction of the throw.

- Try to keep the sequence in the correct order: Legs extend and rotate simultaneously, followed by the hips and chest, and finally the throwing arm extends.
- Keep the elbow of the throwing arm at shoulder level throughout.

Standing Put—Initial Stance 180 Degrees From the Direction of Throw

This is the complete action of the standing put. The thrower begins facing 180 degrees from the direction of throw (i.e., facing the rear of the shot-put ring). There are 2 acceptable methods for performing the standing put: The athlete begins with both feet already positioned in the putting stance (as in Figure 11.13); or the athlete begins with both feet together, then initiates the standing put with the left foot reaching back into the putting stance.

For a right-handed thrower the standing put occurs in the following sequence. The athlete begins by lowering the upper body downward and flexing the right leg to approximately a 1/4 squat position. The right leg rotates and extends upward, forcing the hips around and toward the direction of throw. The chest

Figure 11.13 Standing put with feet positioned in the putting stance

Figure 11.12 180-degree rotation followed by standing put

is thrust forward by the action of the hips, and both legs extend fully. The extension of the throwing arm completes the standing put.

When the left foot is positioned in the putting stance, the foot must be "offset" correctly in the manner illustrated in Figure 11.14. The reasons for this are explained in the next drill.

The Putting Stance

The foot positions used in the putting stance allow the body to rotate and move forward toward the direction of the throw. For a right-handed thrower facing the rear of the ring, the left foot is placed approximately 1 foot width to the thrower's right of a line indicating the direction of throw. If the left foot is positioned to the left, it will block the thrower's efforts to drive forward into the throw. The distance between right foot and left foot in the putting stance is slightly more than shoulder width.

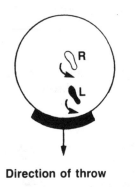

Direction of throw

Figure 11.14 Putting stance

Step 3: Shot Put Using the Glide Technique

Learning the Glide With Partner Assistance

A partner holds the performer's hands, making sure that the performer's upper body remains low and the shoulders are "square" or facing directly to the rear. As the performer glides backward, the partner moves in the same direction, making sure at the same time that the performer's upper body stays low throughout. The thrower concentrates on the following actions, which are performed simultaneously. One action is a low backward thrust of the left leg, with the left foot landing in the correct throwing position each time (i.e., offset to the right; see Figure 11.14). Another

Figure 11.15 The glide with partner assistance

important action is a backward drive with the right leg, which after extension is flexed and immediately pulled in directly below the upper body. The right foot and knee should also rotate approximately 45 degrees toward the direction of throw. The performer must be sure that the right and left legs perform their separate actions almost simultaneously. Both feet should land in the putting stance at the same time.

Repetitive Glide Practice Without Partner Assistance (No Shot Used)

The performer assumes an initial stance similar to the standing put position. After lowering the upper body and flexing the right leg, the performer drives backward for each glide.

The athlete should concentrate on each glide individually, making sure it is completely correct. This drill should not become a series of aimless backward hops.

Figure 11.16 The glide without partner assistance

Coaching Tips

- The backward gliding action is not an upward jump. Don't raise your back or jump up in the air.
- Keep your feet close to the ground throughout.
- After extending the right leg, pull it in so that it ends up in a flexed position directly below the upper body. (If this is not done, the right leg will be unable to provide power for the throw.)

Glide and Shot Put Using a Short Glide and Light Shot

The initial stance in this drill is the same as for the standing put. A short glide allows the thrower to concentrate on the rhythm of both glide and put. In this way the performer is not concerned about the distance that must be covered in a normal glide.

Figure 11.17 Using a short glide

Coaching Tips

- Keep your upper body low until the glide is complete; then lift into the putting action, not before.
- Extend and flex the right leg so that it is pulled in directly below your upper body at the end of the glide. Don't leave the right leg "behind" you, otherwise you'll land with both legs extended and with no leg power available.

Glide and Shot Put Using a Full-Size Glide

This is the complete putting action using the glide technique (see Figure 11.1). The rhythm of glide and put must be smooth, not jerky. A controlled glide takes the athlete from the back of the ring to a putting stance in the center. A full-size glide requires the athlete to shift backward approximately 60 centimeters (2 feet). The glide is then followed by an explosive putting action. The momentum of the body driving the shot toward the direction of throw and the vigorous extension of the legs should force the athlete to step forward with the right leg and so perform the reverse.

Coaching Tips

- A longer glide will demand more effort from the right leg. Think of the action as a push and a pull-in with your right leg.
- Thrust your left leg backward to its position in the putting stance the same time that you extend your right leg.
- Remember to stay low until both feet are in position.
- Thrust forward into the throw as powerfully as possible, and perform the reverse only after the shot has left your hand.

The Reverse

Athletes use the reverse to keep from falling out of the front of the ring and fouling the throw. Figure 11.18 shows the athlete bringing the rear leg forward against the stopboard for the reverse.

Figure 11.18 The reverse

Coaching Tips

- Make sure your hips and chest move forward beyond the left foot before initiating the reverse.
- Don't get into the habit of performing the reverse without extending your legs fully and driving your body well forward into the throw.

Step 4: Shot Put Using the Rotary Technique

The rotational technique uses a discus-style rotation across the shot-put ring in place of a glide (Figure 11.19). Once the athlete has completed the rotation, all else in the throw is basically the same as with the glide technique. However, the addition of the rotary action causes control problems that do not exist in the glide technique, problems due to the centrifugal force generated in the rotation. Quite simply, the shot "wants" to fly out sideways, and the athlete must generate the additional force to hold the shot in position. The timing required in the rotary technique is also critical, because the athlete must be able to change, at the right instant, a rotary action into an essentially linear action. Athletes who have not

Figure 11.19 The rotary technique

mastered the rotary technique will find that they may throw the shot out of the sector (right-handed throwers tend to throw the shot outside of the sector on the right side); lose control of the shot during the rotation across the ring; or land in a poor (narrow) throwing stance at the end of the rotation, (usually caused by using a ''discus-size'' rotation across the shot-put ring, which is 37 centimeters, or 14.5 inches, smaller than a discus ring).

It is strongly recommended that you teach only the glide technique as a class activity. The rotational technique should be taught to advanced throwers only as an alternative and experimental method after they have mastered the glide technique.

Participants Learn the Discus Rotation

Teach the rotary action used in the discus throw to all participants attempting the rotary shot-put technique (see chapter 12).

Simulating the Position of the Shot During the Rotary Technique

With the throwing hand held at the neck, but without using the shot, the athlete practices the rotary technique in the shot-put ring.

Coaching Tips

- Be sure to make the rotation at the back of the ring tight enough to allow sufficient room in the front of the ring for a wide throwing stance.
- Concentrate on rotation only in the rear half of the ring. A linear (nonrotary) thrust in the direction of the throw must predominate after both

feet have landed in their final positions at the front of the ring.
- Put your left arm out to the side during the rotation to help maintain balance.

A Rotary Shot Put Using a Light Shot

Choose a shot that is 1 to 2 kilograms (approximately 2 to 4 pounds) lighter than the shot used by the performer in the glide technique. The athlete rotates slowly into the putting stance (Figure 11.19), using the outward swing of the left arm to help initiate rotation from the rear of the ring. The athlete must hold the shot firmly in the neck. Once the rotation has been completed, the final part of the put is performed in essentially the same way as with the glide technique.

Coaching Tips

- Squat down at the rear of the ring as though sitting on a stool.
- Look forward and pivot on the balls of both feet to initiate the rotation.
- Keep pivoting on the balls of your feet until facing the direction of throw.
- Continue the pivot on the left foot, meanwhile bringing the right leg around to be positioned in the center of the ring.
- Land with the toes of the right foot pointing out toward the right side of the ring.
- Shift the left leg as quickly as possible into its position in the final putting stance.
- Try to keep your body weight to the rear of the ring, so that when you land in the putting stance, your upper body will be over a flexed right leg.
- Throughout the rotation, hold the shot tightly against your neck and keep the elbow of the throwing arm at shoulder level throughout.
- Complete the putting action with a linear thrust at the shot. This action is similar to that used in the glide technique.

Rotary Shot Put Using a Competitive Weight Shot

The thrower selects a shot that is the correct weight for his or her competitive age level and attempts the rotary shot put, slowly at first. Control over the shot during the rotation (or a good throwing position at the end of the rotation) must not be forfeited for increased rotary speed at the back of the ring.

COMMON ERRORS
AND CORRECTIONS

STANDING PUT

ERROR	REASONS	CORRECTIONS
The performer has no thrust from the fingers during the put.	Handhold is incorrect; the shot is put from the palm of the hand.	The athlete should support the shot with the pads of the fingers and thumb. Have the athlete practice standing puts, emphasizing extension of arm and thrust of fingers (use underweight shots). Or, the athlete can practice the action of the hand and fingers without the shot.
The shot is thrown rather than put. The novice complains of the shot "bending" the fingers backward during the put.	The shot is not cradled under the chin. The elbow of the throwing arm drops below the shoulder in the putting stance.	Correct the handhold and the position of the shot in the neck. The athlete must hold the elbow high, keeping the thumb of the throwing hand down and the little finger uppermost. Have the athlete practice the standing put after these factors are corrected.
The athlete's seat goes backward as the shot is thrust forward.	There's no extension and thrust from the legs, and the hips are not driven forward. The left foot is in the wrong position in the putting stance, and the left leg blocks the athlete's rotation toward the direction of the put.	Have the athlete practice the standing put, emphasizing leg thrust and hip movement toward the direction of throw. The left foot in the putting stance must be offset in the manner shown in Figure 11.14.
The left side of the body "collapses" during the final phase of the put.	No extension or "resistance" is provided by the left leg and the left side of the body during the put. Vision is not toward the direction of the throw.	Have the athlete practice the standing put, emphasizing upward thrust of the left leg and left side of the body. The chest should rotate toward the direction of throw around the axis of the left side of the body.
The shot is put with the body sideways to the direction of the throw. The shot is released over the top of the head.	There's no rotary drive from the right leg, and the hips are not turning toward the direction of the put. The rear leg is not extending toward the direction of put and the left foot is incorrectly positioned.	The left foot must be in the correct position in the throwing stance. The athlete should practice (without shot) the positioning of the left foot, followed immediately by the lift and extension of the legs, chest, and throwing arm. The athlete can then practice this action using light shot.

ERROR	REASONS	CORRECTIONS
The shot has no height, released with a low trajectory.	The athlete does not extend the body upward during the put. Both the throwing arm and line of vision are too low.	The athlete should practice a standing put over a high jump bar set high enough to emphasize extended legs, lifted chest, and forward vision.
The sequence and timing of actions are incorrect (i.e., the throwing arm performs its thrust on the shot prior to the thrust of the legs and chest).	The athlete is too eager to throw and has poor understanding of sequence and timing of actions.	Have the athlete practice a standing put without the shot, then a standing put without extending the arm from the neck. The athlete can practice using the action of legs and chest alone to drive the shot forward.

GLIDE TECHNIQUE

ERROR	REASONS	CORRECTIONS
The athlete swings the left leg back and forth in pendular fashion before initiating the glide.	The athlete relies on the swing of the left leg to help shift the body across the ring and uses insufficient drive from the right leg. The left leg should be thrust backward.	Have the athlete practice repetitive glides using correct leg action.
The athlete jumps upward instead of gliding low and close to the ground, and the left leg is kicked high in air at the start of the glide.	The drive from the right leg is upward instead of backward and across the ring. The left leg is swung upward instead of thrust backward at the start of the glide.	Have the athlete practice glides without shot, emphasizing powerful backward thrust of the left leg followed by a similar drive from the right leg.
The athlete is upright at the end of the glide; body weight is not over the rear (right) leg at the end of the glide.	The upper body is raised at the start of or during the glide, then the athlete falls backward during the glide. The right leg is not pulled in under the body at the end of the glide.	The athlete should practice glides while maintaining low upper body position, making sure both feet hit the ground at the same time with the body weight over the right leg throughout.
The athlete turns prematurely toward the direction of the throw.	The left foot is incorrectly placed. The athlete rotates at start and during the glide, turning the head and shoulders prematurely toward the direction the throw.	Have the athlete practice the glide, keeping the vision to the rear throughout. Mark on the ground the final foot positioning at the end of the glide. The left arm should extend and point to the rear throughout the glide.
The athlete's hips move backward as the throwing arm and shot are driven forward.	The athlete's weight remains over the rear foot during the final phase of the put. The athlete does not extend the right leg or move the hips and chest toward the direction of the throw.	The athlete should practice the standing put, emphasizing upward lift and forward motion of the body over the left foot while keeping the body moving forward toward the direction of the throw.

ERROR	REASONS	CORRECTIONS
The athlete extends the throwing arm in the putting action before the legs, hips, and chest drive forward into the put.	The athlete is overeager to complete the throw. Timing and sequence of actions are incorrect.	Have the athlete practice action of the standing put, emphasizing action of legs, hips, and chest. The athlete should practice with and without shot.
The athlete performs the reverse before the shot leaves the hand.	The athlete is afraid of making a foul put and is not moving the body weight toward the direction of the put. The athlete extends the left side of the body too soon.	Instruct the athlete to practice the standing put without a reverse. The athlete should push forward beyond the left foot position during the put and delay the extension of the left leg and left side of body.

ROTARY TECHNIQUE

ERROR	REASONS	CORRECTIONS
The athlete uses too much rotation and has no linear thrust on the shot. The athlete loses control of the shot, and the shot lands outside of the sector. The hips ''open'' up (i.e., rotate too far) by the time the throwing stance is achieved.	Rotation continues too long. The athlete fails to achieve a strong throwing stance.	Have the athlete practice rotation and putting action without a shot, then slowly with a light weight shot, emphasizing a good throwing position. Slow down the rotation.
The thrower is upright before assuming the throwing stance and achieves no power in the throw.	The upper body is elevated and legs are fully extended at back and in the middle of the ring. The athlete lifts upward when performing the rotation.	The athlete must practice keeping low during rotation, lifting upward only out of the final putting position.
Rotation across the ring is not toward the direction of the throw.	The time spent rotating at the back of the ring is either too long or too short.	Use lines on the ground and a rhythm count to assist with directional control.
The athlete loses control of the shot, which flies away from the neck before the final putting action is complete.	The throwing hand is not holding the shot firmly enough in the neck. Timing of the final thrust is incorrect, and rotation across the ring is too fast.	Instruct the athlete to practice slow rotational puts, waiting until the throwing position is fully assumed before initiating final thrust on the shot.

ASSESSMENT

1. Assess the following theoretical elements as taught during instructional sessions.

   a. Fundamental rules governing shot put.
   b. Good safety habits for use in shot put.
   c. Basic elements of shot-put technique.
   d. Basic elements of training for the shot put.

2. Assess the performance of technique during the following stages of skill development.

   a. Standing put initiated with the athlete's side to the direction of throw.
   b. Standing put initiated with the athlete's back to the direction of throw.
   c. The glide action across the shot put ring without release of the shot.

d. The complete glide technique and putting action.

e. The rotational technique performed without a shot.

f. The complete rotational technique and putting action.

Critical Features of Technique to Observe During Assessment

Glide Technique

- Gripping the shot in the hand and cradling it under the chin.
- Flexing the right leg and driving back across the ring.
- Holding the upper body in a lowered position and kicking the left leg back to its position in the throwing stance.
- Pulling the right leg directly under the upper body at the end of the glide.
- Holding the shoulders square to the rear of the ring and maintaining the backward lean of the upper body through the completion of the glide.
- Initiating the drive toward the direction of the throw with the right leg, followed by the hips.
- Thrusting the chest out and straightening the legs toward the direction of the throw.
- Extending the throwing arm and fingers at about 40 degrees from horizontal to complete the throw (put).
- Bringing the right leg forward in front of the left for the reverse.

Rotary Technique

- Gripping the shot in the hand and cradling it under the chin.

- Turning the shoulders and shot fully to the right prior to rotating across the shot-put ring.
- Squatting and rotating on the balls of both feet toward the direction of the throw.
- "Running" across the ring so that the legs rotate ahead of the shoulders.
- Landing in a wide throwing stance with the body weight well back over a flexed right leg.
- Offsetting the left foot correctly in the throwing stance.
- Initiating the final throwing (putting) action with a spiraling extension of the legs.
- Driving the hips upward and forward toward the direction of the throw, following with the chest, and lastly extending the throwing arm.
- Bringing the right foot forward in front of the left for the reverse.

3. Hold graded competitions to help develop motivation and technique.

a. Throwers compete for distance using a standing throw, which they initiate with their backs to the direction of the throw. Select shot according to age, size, and gender.

b. Throwers compete for distance using the glide technique. Select shot according to age, size, and gender.

c. Throwers compete for distance using the rotational technique. Select shot according to age, size, and gender.

SUGGESTED PERFORMANCE STANDARDS (METERS)

MALE

Weight of Shot (kg)	3	4	5	3	4	5	3	4	5
Age	*Satisfactory*			*Good*			*Excellent*		
11-12	6.5	5.5	—	8.0	7.0	—	9.0	7.5	—
13-14	—	6.5	5.5	—	8.0	7.0	—	8.6	7.6
15-16	—	7.5	6.5	—	9.0	8.0	—	9.7	8.7
17-19	—	8.5	7.5	—	10.0	9.0	—	10.8	9.8

FEMALE

Weight of Shot (kg)	3	4	3	4	3	4
Age	*Satisfactory*		*Good*		*Excellent*	
11-12	5.5	4.5	7.0	6.0	8.0	6.5
13-14	6.0	5.0	7.0	6.0	8.0	7.0
15-16	7.0	6.0	8.0	7.0	9.0	8.0
17-19	8.0	7.0	9.0	8.0	10.0	9.0

CHAPTER

12

DISCUS

The discus throw is included in the Olympic Games as an individual event for males and females. It is part of the decathlon (men) but is not included in the heptathlon (females).

The tremendous increase in distances thrown by modern athletes has resulted from improvements in technique employed by athletes who have also spent years in weight training specifically related to the event. Today, athletes use a common technique of throwing, and little variation is seen from one thrower to the next.

The modern thrower begins the throw facing to the rear of the 2.5-meter (8-foot–2-1/2-inch) ring. Using approximately 1-3/4 rotations, the athlete is able (counting windup) to accelerate the discus through two full rotations during the throw. Some athletes have attempted to add an additional hammer-style spin to the 1-3/4 rotation across the ring, but this has proved to be ineffective because it gives no additional acceleration to the discus.

Of all throwing implements, the discus most resembles an airfoil. Spin is essential for stability during flight, and a head wind gives lift to the discus and assists in producing the longest throws.

For a right-handed thrower, a quartering wind of about 10 to 15 miles per hour approaching the thrower from the left front produces the most favorable conditions for the longest throws. Under these conditions, the wind combines with the aerodynamic shape of the discus to give it lift. The rules of the event allow records to be set in any wind conditions.

SAFETY SUGGESTIONS

The discus event can be hazardous because of its rotary method of throwing. Novices experience difficulty in gripping and releasing the discus, and their directional accuracy is poor.

This chapter's recommendations for teaching progressions and the use of substitutes for the competitive implements will eliminate much of the risk, but you must still develop and continuously reinforce good safety habits.

As with other throwing equipment, you should regularly check all discuses to see that they are in good order. The metal rim must be smooth and without nicks or burrs. Substitute equipment that you use for training purposes must also be safe and designed to withstand repeated use.

Discuses should be stored safely and carried in an orderly fashion to the throwing area. Do not allow youngsters to throw, bowl, or play with the discuses in any way while they are being transported. In wet conditions, provide towels for wiping off the rim and the surface of the discus.

A concrete pad is the best type of throwing surface; avoid wet grass, which can be slippery when wet.

The organizational format used when the discus is rolled or tossed directly forward is different from that used when standing and rotational throws are practiced. For rolling or tossing the discus, station participants along a line, 3 to 4 meters (10 to 13 feet) apart. On command, all release the discuses together, and all retrieve together. Do not allow students to roll, bowl, or throw discuses back to the throwing area. Those who are late in performing are ordered not to throw, and must wait until allowed to do so. It's best to station yourself centrally and to the rear so that you can see all throwers and they are within earshot of commands. Those waiting their turn also stand to the rear.

Participants use a slinging action in the discus event for both standing and rotational throws. The centrifugal nature of this action causes greater problems with directional control than occur in events like the javelin or the shot put (with the glide technique). Because of the slinging method of throwing, the safest arrangement for practicing standing and rotational throws is to position those waiting their turn well to the rear (5 to 6 meters, or 16 to 20 feet) of the thrower, preferably to the left rear if the thrower is right-handed and vice versa for a left-handed thrower. Participants then step forward individually to throw.

Specific Characteristics of the Discus Throw

Experienced officials know that a discus can be difficult to see edge-on and that it will skip and bounce, particularly on wet grass. Allowances are also made for the wind shifting the flight path of a discus and causing throws to land outside of the throwing sector. Knowledgeable officials usually know the capabilities of throwers and are prepared for exceptional throws. They keep other athletes well clear of the throwing

sector, particularly those who are exhausted and less likely to be aware of what is happening around them. Brightly colored netting set beyond the outer limits of the sector is an excellent safety device for trapping bouncing discuses. Netting also stops athletes and spectators from wandering into the throwing area.

TECHNIQUE

The object of modern discus technique is to simulate a rotary cracking of a whip, with the whip (i.e., the discus arm) swung around the side of the body. The discus thrower runs across the ring, twisting the legs and hips ahead of the upper body as though winding up a coiled spring. Once the athlete has arrived in the throwing stance he or she unwinds the spring and cracks the whip. The tip of the whip is the throwing hand holding the discus (Figure 12.1).

Grip and Windup

The athlete holds the discus by the pads of the fingertips, the thumb resting against the side of the discus. Centrifugal force generated during the athlete's rotation across the ring holds the discus in the hand. The thrower begins in a shoulder-width stance facing away from the direction of throw; vision is directly ahead. The thrower rotates the shoulders and discus arm as far as possible to the right (right-handed thrower). The athlete's body weight shifts momentarily over the right foot. The legs are slightly flexed.

Figure 12.1 Modern discus technique

Rotation

The athlete's body weight pivots around the left foot as the athlete rotates on the balls of the feet toward the direction of the throw. The discus trails behind the body. The athlete runs across the ring with the legs rotating ahead of the shoulders and discus arm and places both feet in the throwing stance as quickly as possible.

Throw and Reverse

When the feet are in the throwing stance, the athlete powerfully extends the legs and drives the hips forward toward the direction of the throw. The hips are followed by the chest and finally the throwing arm, which simulates the action of a whip. When releasing the discus, the athlete arrests the forward movement of the body by reversing the feet, bringing the rear (right) leg forward against the inner edge of the rim of the circle.

TEACHING STEPS

STEP 1.	Lead-Ups
STEP 2.	Standing Throw Using a Discus Substitute
STEP 3.	Rotational Throw Using a Discus Substitute
STEP 4.	Standing Throw With the Discus
STEP 5.	Rotational Throw With the Discus

Step 1: Lead-Ups

The use of a small rubber ring (quoit) or hula hoop as a substitute for the discus eliminates handhold problems that a novice commonly experiences with the discus. The young athlete grips the ring normally and then concentrates on other parts of the throw, such as the footwork. Once the athlete learns the footwork, practice then begins with the discus itself.

These substitutes are useful because they

- are safe to use and can be thrown both indoors and outdoors;
- are easy to grip and light enough to be held at arm's length;
- have a certain amount of drag that forces the throwing arm into a good trailing position; and
- cannot be thrown far, which means that novices can repeat throws more often.

Slinging a Small Rubber Ring

Each participant steps forward and slings a small rubber ring, keeping the throwing arm straight throughout and swinging it around the body just below shoulder level. A right-handed thrower steps forward into the throw with the left foot, extending the legs powerfully and driving the hips and chest forward into the throw.

Coaching Tips

- As you swing your arm back, step forward with your left foot into the throwing stance.
- Thrust your hips and chest well forward ahead of the throwing arm.

Figure 12.2 Slinging a rubber ring

• Keep the throwing arm below shoulder level, and release the ring ahead of your body and at eye level.

Accuracy Competition With Small Hoops

Set up a pole-vault standard to use as a target. Individuals or teams compete against each other for points, which are awarded for hitting or dropping the hoop on the standard. The slinging action used earlier is repeated in this lead-up activity. Combining height and distance requirements teaches the performer to lift the body upward into the throw.

Slinging a Volleyball, Basketball, or Light Medicine Ball for Distance

Use any slinging activity with volleyballs, basketballs, or light medicine balls as an introduction activity for the discus throw. Particularly beneficial are two-handed slinging activities, which teach the twist or windup of the shoulders relative to the hips. Throwers use various throwing positions (e.g., standing, sitting, or kneeling).

Coaching Tips

• Concentrate on thrusting your chest forward into the throw ahead of the arms and the ball.
• Extend your legs vigorously toward the direction of throw when you use the standing throw.

Step 2: Standing Throw Using a Discus Substitute

Standing Throw Initiated With the Side to the Direction of Throw

A right-handed thrower stands side-on to the direction of the throw (i.e., with the left shoulder toward the direction of the throw). The feet are shoulder-width apart with the left foot offset correctly in the throwing stance. (The offset position allows the athlete to drive the body fully into the throw. Any other

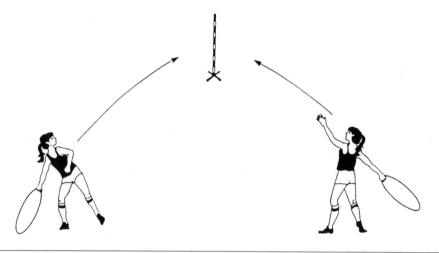

Figure 12.3 Accuracy competition with hoops

Figure 12.4 Slinging a ball from a sitting position

Figure 12.5 Standing throw with the side to the direction of the throw: whole view (a) and foot position only (b)

stance effectively blocks this action. This is also true for the shot put and the javelin.)

The athlete swings the hoop (and shoulders) back and around to the right side of the body and rotates on the balls of the feet toward the right, shifting the body weight over the right leg. The standing throw begins with the hips turning vigorously toward the direction of throw. The hips lead the chest and throwing arm, and the body drives upward and forward.

Coaching Tips

- Swing your throwing arm back as far as possible to the right and rotate your shoulders as far as you can in the same direction. This will generate a windup or muscular stretch that you will use to pull on the discus.
- Start the standing throw by turning your knees toward the direction of the throw and extending your legs.
- Thrust your hips and chest forward before your throwing arm swings around.
- Keep the throwing arm just below shoulder level, and release the hoop in front of your body, just below eye level.

The Step-Back Standing Throw

The performer begins with the back toward the direction of throw. As the performer rotates the hoop and shoulders to the right for the windup, he or she simultaneously places the left foot back in the throwing stance. The thrower's body weight remains to the rear over a flexed right leg during this action.

The rotation of the knees drives the hips and chest toward the direction of throw, and the throwing arm is subsequently dragged around by the action of the chest. The arm completes the throw with a whiplike action, releasing the hoop as far ahead of the body as possible.

Coaching Tips

- Keep your weight over a flexed right leg as you shift the left foot back into position.
- Be sure to step back into the correct offset position with your left foot.
- Initiate the throwing (slinging) action from "the ground up" (i.e., rotate the knees toward the direction of throw, followed by the hips, chest, and finally the throwing arm).

Figure 12.6 The step-back standing throw

Figure 12.7 Rotational throw with discus substitute

Step 3: Rotational Throw Using a Discus Substitute

A rotary throw using a substitute for the discus (i.e., a rubber ring or small hoop) requires the same footwork and body actions as a throw with the competitive implement (Figure 12.7).

Rotational Throw Initiated Facing the Direction of the Throw

Mark foot positions on the ground to guide the athlete through the rotary steps of this drill. The athlete begins facing the direction of the throw with the left foot placed one step forward. The athlete gently swings the throwing arm (and the implement) back

as far to the right as possible for the windup and then holds the arm in this position.

The thrower begins by pivoting on the left foot and rotating forward and around onto the right foot. The right foot is positioned one pace forward with the heel now pointing toward the direction of the throw. The thrower's weight remains to the rear. The remaining part of the throw is a repetition of the step-back standing throw, taught previously (see Figure 12.6).

Coaching Tips

- Step directly back into the correct throwing position with your left foot. Don't swing the foot out and around into position, because this takes too long. (For the correct foot positions in the throwing stance see Figure 12.5b).

Figure 12.8 Rotational throw initiated facing the direction of the throw

- Initiate the throwing action by rotating your knees toward the direction of the throw.
- Follow the rotation of the knees by turning your hips and chest toward the direction of the throw.
- Last, bring the throwing arm around just below shoulder height to complete the throw.

Rotational Throw Initiated With the Side to the Direction of the Throw

Mark foot positions on the ground to guide the athlete through the rotation. The athlete begins with the left side of the body toward the direction of the throw. This adds a further 90 degrees of rotation to the previous drill. The hoop is gently swung around as far as possible to the right for the windup and remains in this position. The athlete pivots on the left foot and steps forward and around on to the right foot, continuing to pivot until the heel of the right foot points toward the direction of throw. The remaining part of the throw is a repetition of the step-back standing throw.

Coaching Tips

- Always keep your weight back toward the rear of the circle (i.e., don't shift it forward) as you pivot and step forward to position the right foot.
- Continue to keep your weight to the rear as you thrust your left leg back into the throwing stance. This will put you into a powerful throwing stance in which your right leg is partially flexed and your upper body is tilted toward the back of the circle. From this position you can now drive up and rotate around into the throw.

Rotational Throw Initiated With the Back to the Direction of the Throw

Mark foot positions on the ground to guide the athlete through the rotation. The athlete begins with the back toward the direction of the throw, adding yet another 90 degrees of rotation to the previous drill. The hoop is gently swung back as far as possible to the right for the windup and is held in this position. The athlete begins to rotate, shifting the body weight over the left foot, and pivots on the balls of both feet until the left foot points toward the direction of the throw. The athlete continues the pivoting motion while bringing the right foot around and placing it down with the heel pointing toward the direction of the throw. The remaining part of the throw is a repetition of the step-back standing throw.

Coaching Tips

- This drill simulates the competitive discus throw.
- Flex your knees slightly and "sit" as though squatting on a stool during the rotation at the back of the ring.
- Pivot on the balls of both feet until you face the direction of the throw.
- Continue to pivot, placing your right foot 1 pace ahead with the heel facing the direction of the throw.
- Keep your body weight to the rear.
- Step back with your left leg into the throwing stance (body weight still to the rear of the circle).
- Make sure the left foot is offset correctly in the throwing stance.
- Drive around into the throw, working from the ground up (i.e., extend and rotate the legs, followed by the hips, chest, and finally the throwing arm).

Rotational Throw in the Discus Circle (Initiated With the Back to the Direction of the Throw)

Mark foot positions in the discus ring, and have athletes repeat the action of the previous drill. Using this drill, the athletes will become accustomed to rotating

Figure 12.9 Rotational throw initiated with the side to the direction of the throw

Figure 12.10 Rotational throw initiated with the back to the direction of the throw

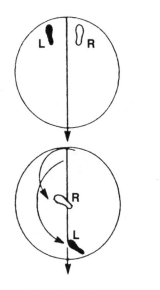

Figure 12.11 Foot positions in the discus circle

within the discus ring. The athlete begins in a shoulder-width stance, straddling the line of throw.

Coaching Tips

- Swing the hoop as far to the right as possible, and maintain this position throughout the rotation across the ring.
- Shift your weight over your right foot as you swing the hoop to the right.

- Enter the rotation by shifting your weight back over the left foot.
- Pivot on the balls of your feet until the left foot points toward the direction of the throw.
- Step around the left foot with the right, placing the right foot in the center of the ring (heel toward the direction of throw).
- Place the left foot approximately 6 inches from the front rim of the discus ring, offset to the thrower's right.
- Complete the forward rotary drive of your body into the throw, as before.

Step 4: Standing Throw With the Discus

Technique

The athlete stands with the back toward the direction of the throw. The athlete swings the discus back to the right, and steps back with the left foot, keeping the body weight over a flexed right leg.

After the left foot is in position the athlete vigorously rotates the hips toward the direction of throw. The hips are followed by the chest and the throwing arm, which is swung around the body just below shoulder level. The squeeze of the hand on the discus gives it a clockwise rotation (right-handed thrower). The index finger of the throwing hand is last to contact the discus (Figure 12.12).

Figure 12.12 Technique for the standing throw

Drills
Gripping the Discus

The athlete holds the discus on the pads of the fingers, resting the thumb against the side of the discus and flexing the hand slightly inward at the wrist. Some variation in grip can occur (e.g., the index and second finger can be placed close together rather than spread apart.)

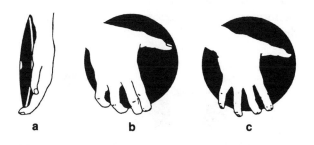

Figure 12.13 Three views of gripping the discus

Coaching Tips

- As your throwing arm hangs beside your body, the discus will rest on the last pads of your fingers (i.e., nearest the fingertips).
- Your thumb does not hook around the edge of the discus but rests against the side of the discus.

Swinging the Discus

Participants swing the discus lightly forward and back at the side of the body (i.e., 20 degrees either side of perpendicular) with the arm acting as a pendulum. This provides a feel for the pressure of the discus against the pads of the fingers. The discus is not released in this practice.

Coaching Tips

- Use your left hand to help control the discus at the apex of the forward swing. Squeeze the discus

Figure 12.14 Swinging the discus

between the left and right hands at the top of the swing.

Learning to Spin the Discus

This drill teaches the spin that is given to the discus when it is released from a rotary throw. Place participants 3 to 4 meters (10 to 13 feet) apart along a line. Each thrower steps forward with 1 foot (right-handed throwers with the left foot). Each participant swings a discus forward and backward beside the body and then gently tosses it forward and up in the air so that it hits the ground 3 to 4 meters (10 to 13 feet) ahead of the performer. A squeezing action initiated from little finger through to the index will cause the discus to roll out of the hand and rotate with a clockwise movement during flight. Participants throw at the same time or in sequence according to the command of the instructor. See Figure 12.15b for a view from above of a right-handed thrower imparting spin to the discus.

Coaching Tips

- Squeeze the discus out of your hand like a bar of soap, starting with the back of your hand and completing the action with your index finger.
- The index finger is the last finger to be in contact with the rim of the discus, not the little finger!

Figure 12.15 Spinning the discus

Bowling the Discus

Participants bowl the discus along the ground a distance of 5 meters (16 to 17 feet). The discus rolls off the index finger in a clockwise direction. On a flat surface the discus should roll directly ahead.

Figure 12.16 Bowling the discus

Coaching Tips

- Right-handed throwers step forward with your left feet.
- Swing the discus back gently and then bend forward and release it with your hand almost touching the ground.
- Squeeze the discus out of your hand, pulling your fingertips toward your palm in sequence from the little finger to the index. Perform this action quickly and vigorously.

Standing Throw With the Discus (Initiated With the Side to the Direction of the Throw)

The initial attempt at this type of standing throw using the competitive implement must be performed with minimum effort and with little to no windup (backswing). A right-handed thrower begins in a shoulder-width stance with the left side toward the direction of throw and the left foot offset to the left in the throwing stance. The performer swings the right arm and the discus loosely back and forth around the body with the discus at hip level (no higher) and no more than 30 centimeters (1 foot) away from the side of the body during the swing. When the discus has swung back and around the body as far as possible, the performer rotates on the balls of the feet toward the direction of throw, pushing the hips and chest ahead of the discus arm. The performer throws the discus only 3 to 5 meters (approximately 10 to 16 feet). In subsequent attempts with this type of standing throw, the performer will use more windup and throw greater distances.

Figure 12.17 Standing throw with the discus

Coaching Tips

- Start the throw by turning on the balls of your feet and pushing your chest and hips toward the direction of throw immediately after you swing the discus back for the windup.
- Don't try swinging the discus a long way out from your body. We will try this action later.
- As your throwing arm swings toward the direction of throw, your throwing hand will be above the discus with the thumb leading.
- Don't be tempted to turn your hand sideways to the direction of throw or turn your hand palm up so it is underneath the discus.

- Squeeze the discus out of your hand.
- The index finger is in contact with the rim of the discus last of all.

Step-Back Standing Throw With the Discus

The athlete begins in a shoulder-width stance with the back toward the direction of throw, loosely swinging the right arm and discus back and forth. Using a strong backswing with the discus, the performer immediately places the left foot backward into the throwing stance, keeping the body weight over the right leg as the left is thrust back into position. Legs, hips, and chest then drive around and forward into the throw. The throwing hand is on top of the discus with the thumb leading. With the exception of gripping the discus, all actions replicate those performed earlier with the rubber ring or hoop.

Figure 12.18 Step-back standing throw with the discus

Coaching Tips

- Don't try to swing the discus far out from your body. Keep the discus at hip level and about 30 centimeters (12 inches) from your body.

- Try to make your body move ahead of your throwing arm.
- Thrust the legs, hips, and chest toward the direction of the throw.
- The pull on the discus arm is the last action that you perform.

Step 5: Rotational Throw With the Discus

See technique description and Figure 12.1

Rotary Discus Throw Initiated Facing the Direction of the Throw

Although this drill was performed earlier with a rubber ring or hoop, the use of the discus will present some control problems. Students can overcome these in the following manner.

The performer swings the discus back gently for the windup with the discus kept low (at hip level) and 30 centimeters (12 inches) from the body. When the discus can be swung back no further, the athlete immediately rotates into the throw. Carrying the discus low coupled with immediately starting the rotation will stop the discus from falling out of the throwing hand.

The performer swings the discus back at hip level and then presses it against the seat, holding the discus in a pseudo windup position. This allows the novice to rotate more slowly and concentrate on the correct footwork.

Coaching Tips

- Trail the discus behind your body throughout the rotation. When the rotation is complete, drive your body forward into the throw ahead of your throwing arm.
- Keep your throwing hand on top of the discus,

Figure 12.19 Rotary discus throw initiated facing the direction of the throw

and remember that the index finger touches the discus last of all.

Rotary Discus Throw Initiated With the Side to the Direction of the Throw

The thrower begins with the left side of the body toward the direction of the throw, using the same methods as used previously for controlling the discus.

The footwork replicates the rotary throw initiated with the side to the direction of throw when using a substitute for the discus.

Coaching Tips

• Try to keep the complete throw flowing and continuous, which will help you keep the discus under control. The more fluid the motion, the

Figure 12.20 Rotary discus throw initiated with the side to the direction of the throw

Figure 12.21 Rotary discus throw initiated with the back to the direction of the throw

easier it is to hold the discus in the correct position.

Rotary Discus Throw Initiated With the Back to the Direction of the Throw

This is the complete rotational discus throw. The athlete begins with the back toward the direction of the throw, then either swings the discus back low and close to the hip, using rotational speed to hold it in position, or swings the discus back and holds it on his or her seat during the rotation across the ring. The footwork replicates the same action practiced earlier using a substitute for the discus.

Coaching Tips

- Keep the discus arm trailing to the rear of your body during the rotation across the ring.
- Try to increase the speed of rotation and run into the throwing stance with the discus trailing behind.
- Work on getting both feet into the throwing stance almost simultaneously.
- The instant your feet land in the throwing stance, thrust forward into the throw with your hips by turning your knees as fast as possible toward the direction of the throw. Think "knees, hips, chest, arm, discus" to help you remember the sequence.
- Make the right side of your body and the discus arm rotate around the left side of your body and the left leg. Imagine the left side of your body as the axle of a wheel.
- Once your throwing arm swings forward and releases the discus, bring your right leg forward for the reverse.

Variations in Starting Position at the Back of the Discus Ring

Many athletes begin their throws with a stance in which the feet straddle the line of direction of the

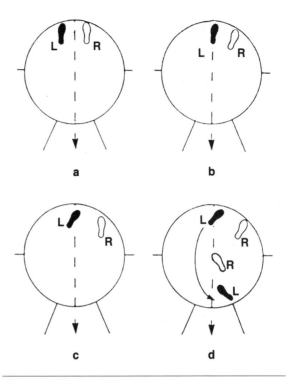

Figure 12.22 Four variations in discus starting position

throw. Others shift the starting position farther to the right (right-handed throwers), attempting to add more rotary pull to the discus at the back of the ring. Members of the group experiment with each starting position.

Coaching Tips

- The farther you shift your starting position to the right, the longer you must pivot on the balls of both feet at the beginning of the rotation across the ring. Pivot, don't fall backward, across the ring.

COMMON ERRORS AND CORRECTIONS

STEP-BACK STANDING THROW

ERROR	REASONS	CORRECTIONS
The novice steps back with the wrong leg.	The athlete is unsure of the correct action.	Right-handed throwers step back with the left leg, not the right. The athlete should practice the correct actions without the implement.

ERROR	REASONS	CORRECTIONS
As the athlete steps back into the throwing stance the body weight is shifted the same direction.	The athlete is too eager to throw with the arm. The athlete lifts the upper body or falls backward into the throwing stance.	The body weight must stay over the right leg as the athlete steps backward into the throwing stance, and the right leg must remain partially flexed until the left leg is in position. The throwing sequence is hips, chest, and arm.
The athlete turns prematurely toward the direction of the throw as the left foot is placed into the throwing stance.	The hips rotate prematurely toward the direction of the throw.	Instruct the athlete to practice the step-back action of the left leg with seat toward the direction of the throw. The athlete should begin the rotation of the hips toward the direction of throw only after the left foot is in position on the ground.
The left leg blocks the thrower from turning fully toward the direction of throw.	The left foot is not offset correctly during the step back into the throwing stance. The left foot is too far to the left.	The athlete should practice shifting the left foot back into the correct throwing position without using the discus.
As the throwing arm and chest move forward into the throw, the hips and seat move backward.	There's no leg or hip action during the throw, and the chest drops forward during the throw.	Instruct the athlete to practice pushing the hips forward and elevating the chest during the throw. The left foot must be offset correctly in the throwing stance.
During the release the body falls to the left or right.	Foot positioning is incorrect, and the body weight does not shift toward the direction of throw. The throwing arm is above shoulder level during the release, and the head and shoulders are dropped to the opposite side.	Mark correct foot positions on the ground. Have the athlete practice stepping back into the correct foot positions, driving the body ahead of the discus toward the direction of throw.
The athlete releases the implement with the throwing hand close to the hip.	The throwing arm is too low.	The throwing arm must be swung around the body just below horizontal (or the line of the shoulder). The athlete should practice this action without the implement.
The discus has no spin but flutters in flight.	The discus is not squeezed out of the hand; the fingers release the discus simultaneously. The palm is toward the direction of throw.	Have the athlete practice bowling the discus. The athlete should also practice standing throws, with the back of hand uppermost and the thumb leading. The discus must be squeezed out of the hand beginning from the little finger, with the index finger touching the rim of the discus last.

ERROR	REASONS	CORRECTIONS
The athlete releases the discus out of the back of the hand.	The performer is unsure of the hand action to be used when releasing the discus. The throwing arm is flexed at the elbow immediately prior to release.	Have the athlete practice bowling and tossing the discus forward, keeping the throwing arm extended. The thumb should lead the throwing hand and the index finger touch the discus last of all. The athlete should practice easy standing throws with the discus.

ROTARY DISCUS THROW

ERROR	REASONS	CORRECTIONS
The discus does not trail behind the body during the rotation across the ring.	The discus is not held back at the end of the backswing.	Instruct the athlete to practice rotary throws with the discus held on the seat. The athlete should also practice the rotation without the discus or using a light substitute for the discus.
The athlete "dives" or falls backward across the ring.	The athlete's vision is not horizontal, and the left foot does not pivot toward the direction of throw at the start of the rotation at the back of the ring. There's no flexion in the knees.	The vision must be up and forward, and the head and left knee must lead into the rotation across the ring. The athlete should practice the footwork using a discus substitute. The athlete should sit and pivot as though squatting on a stool.
Rotation across the ring is not toward the direction of the throw.	The athlete uses too much or too little rotation at the back of ring. The athlete's weight does not move across the ring, and the line of vision is incorrect.	The athlete should practice rotational throws without the discus or with a substitute discus. The athlete should concentrate on legwork and direction of rotation across the ring.
When the athlete is in the throwing stance, the athlete's body weight is prematurely over the front (left) leg.	The upper body continues to move toward the direction of the throw during rotation. The athlete's weight does not stay over the flexed right leg as the left leg is pushed back into the throwing position.	Instruct the athlete to practice the step-back standing throw, emphasizing body weight over the right leg as the left steps back. Repeat with slow rotational throws.
When in the throwing stance, the athlete has no windup and is unable to pull on the discus. The athlete is unable to use the power of the hips and chest on the discus. The discus is swung ahead of the thrower.	The athlete does not hold the discus back during rotation, and the legs and hips do not rotate ahead of the shoulders and throwing arm. The left leg is swung around to its position at the front of the ring instead of driven straight back into the throwing stance.	The athlete should work on step-back standing throw, emphasizing straight backward thrust of the left leg. Using a discus substitute, the athlete practices running the legs around ahead of the shoulders, placing the feet into throwing position simultaneously.

ASSESSMENT

1. Assess the following theoretical elements as taught during instructional sessions.

   a. Fundamental rules governing discus throw.
   b. Good safety habits for the discus throw.
   c. Basic elements of discus-throw technique.
   d. Basic elements of training for the discus throw.

2. Assess the performance of technique during the following stages of skill development.

The thrower uses either a substitute for the discus (rubber ring or hoop) or the competitive implement.

   a. Standing throw initiated with the side to the direction of the throw.
   b. Step-back standing throw initiated with the back to the direction of the throw.
   c. Rotational throw initiated facing the direction of the throw.
   d. Rotational throw initiated with the side to the direction of the throw.
   e. Rotational throw initiated with the back to the direction of the throw.

Critical Features of Technique to Observe During Assessment

Rotational Throw (Right-Handed Thrower)

- Gripping the discus correctly.
- Winding up the shoulders and discus arm to the rear of the body prior to rotation across the ring.
- Squatting down and shifting the body weight over the left foot while initiating the pivot and rotation across the ring.
- Allowing the shoulders and discus arm to trail to the rear as the legs "run" across the ring to the throwing stance.
- Landing in the throwing stance with the body weight over a partially flexed right leg.
- Extending the right leg and rotating the hips forward toward the direction of the throw.
- Extending both legs and thrusting the chest out toward the direction of the throw.
- Pulling the discus arm around the body just below the line of the shoulder.
- Releasing the discus off the index finger and establishing a clockwise spin on the discus.
- Bringing the right leg forward in front of the left for the reverse to complete the throw.

3. Hold graded competitions to help develop motivation and technique.

   a. Throwers compete for distance using a substitute for the discus or using the competitive implement. Require a specific type of standing throw.
   b. Throwers compete for distance using a substitute for the discus or using the competitive implement. Require a specific type of rotational throw (i.e., facing the direction of throw or with the side or back to the direction of throw).

SUGGESTED PERFORMANCE STANDARDS (METERS)

MALE

Age	Weight of discus (kg)	Satisfactory	Good	Excellent
11-12	1 kg	10	15	20
13-14		15	20	25
15-16		20	25	30
15-16	Weight of discus (kg) 1.5 kg	15	20	25
17-19		25	30	35
17-19	Weight of discus (kg) 2 kg	20	25	30

FEMALE

Age	Weight of discus (kg)	Satisfactory	Good	Excellent
11-12	1 kg	10	14	18
13-14		14	18	22
15-16		18	22	26
17-19		20	24	28

CHAPTER

13

JAVELIN

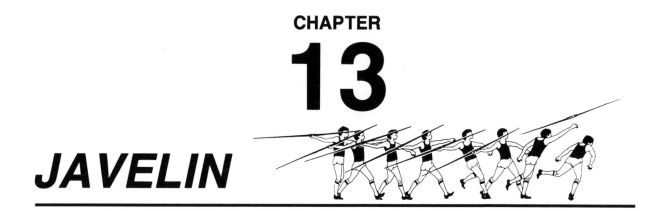

Javelin throwing has been in the Olympic Games since 1908 as an individual event for men and women; it is now also part of the decathlon and heptathlon competitions.

Two developments have affected the conduct of competitive javelin throwing. The first was an attempt to use a discus-style rotation to throw. Although this method produced great distances, it was subsequently banned, and the rules now prohibit the athlete from turning the back toward the direction of throw. In effect this law has entrenched the traditional style of javelin throwing.

The second development resulted from the tremendous increase in distances (over 100 meters) thrown by men. Worried rules makers subsequently changed the configuration of the javelin, substantially reducing the distances thrown with the men's implement. No such changes have been made in the women's event.

SAFETY SUGGESTIONS

Weighted balls are frequently used in javelin training. The weight must be sufficient to produce some drag on the throwing arm, but not so much that it causes injury. Try tennis balls that have been cut open, filled with lead shot, and bound with tape. Weighted leather "bean-bags" filled with lead shot are also useful, particularly because they do not bounce or roll after being thrown.

If you ever have a question about safety, substitute ball throwing using javelin-style run-up and javelin throwing technique for throwing the competitive implement.

Both ends of the javelin can cause injury. Conse-

quently, javelins must always be stored safely and carried in an upright position only. Young athletes must not be allowed to play with javelins or to treat them casually while they are being transported. When not in use, javelins must be stuck in the ground in an upright position, never left in the ground at an angle.

Prior to throwing, athletes need a thorough and careful warm-up. This should include specific stretching and flexibility activities for the shoulders, hips, and back that prepare the young athlete for the explosive actions characteristic of javelin throwing. Avoid repetitive practices and competitive situations until the athlete is well conditioned and physically ready for the demands of the event. Javelin throwing places considerable stress on the back, shoulders, and elbow, particularly if the javelin is thrown incorrectly around the side of the body. Although the javelin-throwing action is comfortable when a ball is used, the drag produced by the javelin when it is thrown around the side of the body affects mostly the elbow and shoulder and is liable to cause chronic injuries.

When javelins are being thrown, you should rigorously supervise all throwing until safety habits become second nature and participants are deemed responsible enough to throw on their own.

During class instruction, position javelin throwers at least 3 meters apart along a line, making sure all are within earshot of commands. You stand in a central position to the rear of the throwers. Those waiting to throw stand well to the rear so that no one is struck by the tail of the javelin when the thrower extends the arm back to throw.

All participants should throw at the same time or throw in sequence, according to your command. On command, all students retrieve the javelins together and carry them back in upright positions to the throwing area. Care must be exercised when several javelins are stuck in the ground near each other; a javelin vigorously pulled out of the ground can injure someone who is standing to the rear. The javelin should be "levered upward" rather than pulled backward. However, if the javelin is stuck deep, levering might break the tip. Throwers should first place a hand over the rear end (to avoid hitting anyone) and then carefully pull the javelin out backward.

Throwers must never throw back toward their partners. Also be ready for the participant who is late in following a command to throw; tell this person not to throw but to wait until the next round.

Make sure that groups involved in other events are well beyond the throwing area. Allow for wind blowing a javelin off course, for throws landing outside of the designated area, and even for exceptional throws!

Wet conditions demand particular care. Run-ups on grass can be slippery unless students use spikes. Allow sufficient distance for the skidding of javelins on wet grass.

In competitive situations, the meet organizer should provide a throwing area that conforms to the official specifications for the event. Officials should be fully qualified and well aware of the idiosyncrasies of the event. The javelin area, like other throwing areas, should be clearly marked and roped off well outside of the required 29-degree throwing sector.

Only experienced officials stand close to or in line with the flight path of a javelin. Javelins viewed head-on are very difficult to see, and their speed of flight is highly deceptive. Landing flat, they may also bounce in a fashion similar to a discus. Officials with less experience should stand well to the side of the line of flight and then run out to mark the point of landing.

Officials must also keep other athletes well clear of the throwing sector, particularly those who are exhausted and less likely to be aware of what is happening around them.

The technique of javelin throwing is the most natural action of the 4 throwing events, and youngsters who naturally throw a ball well usually have little difficulty grasping javelin fundamentals. Throwing softballs and baseballs is a good introductory activity for javelin throwing, although you must remember that ball throwing must be adapted to the specifics of javelin technique, and not vice versa.

TECHNIQUE

Modern javelin throwing shows little variation in technique from one athlete to the next. Some throwers rotate the javelin arm forward, downward, and then extend it back prior to throwing. Others extend the throwing arm directly back without any forward motion at all.

Another variation occurs in the number of crossover (or impulse) steps that are used. Some throwers use one, others two. Beyond these differences, the main elements of the throw are the same for all throwers.

Run-Up

The athlete faces the direction of the throw with the shoulders and hips square to the front. The javelin points toward the direction of the throw as the athlete accelerates down the run-up. The athlete takes the javelin back to a full arm's length with the tip of the javelin raised to the trajectory angle. The shoulders rotate 90 degrees to the right (right-handed thrower), and the hips remain facing the direction of throw.

Cross-Step, Crossover, or Impulse Step

The right leg reaches across and in front of the left leg. This helps to move the lower body ahead of the torso, tilting the body and taking the shoulders and javelin arm as far back as possible.

Throwing Position

The left leg steps out into a wide throwing stance with the heel contacting the ground prior to the rest of the foot. The hips rotate to the right so that the left hip is toward the direction of throw. The rear leg (right) is partially flexed at the knee and turned out to the side. The body is tilted backward and the javelin arm is fully extended.

The Throw

The right knee rotates vigorously toward the direction of throw and forces the hips in the same direction. The hips are followed by the chest, which the athlete forces forward so that the body resembles a bow. The javelin arm now acts like the end of a whip that is pulled forward at tremendous speed above the shoulder. The body drives up and over a straight left leg, and the javelin is released in front of the thrower's head.

Figure 13.1 Javelin technique

Reverse

After the javelin is released the thrower continues to move forward bringing the right leg forward and placing it in front of the left. This action arrests any further motion and stops the athlete from fouling the throw (Figure 13.1).

TEACHING STEPS

STEP 1.	Lead-Ups
STEP 2.	A 3-Stride Throw With a Ball Using Javelin Technique
STEP 3.	A Standing Throw With a Javelin
STEP 4.	A Javelin Throw Using a Run-Up

Step 1: Lead-Ups

The following lead-up activities all involve throwing. They culminate with modified ball-throwing activities that are based on javelin-throwing technique.

Team Competition

Two teams stand on lines 20 meters apart, with a basketball placed on the ground equidistant from both teams. Each team throws volleyballs at the basketball, attempting to drive it over their opponents' line. Allow one-handed and two-handed throws from above the head only.

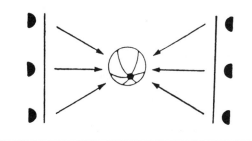

Figure 13.2 Team ball throwing competition

Accuracy Competition

Basketballs are placed on a box top and must be knocked off by group members throwing tennis balls or softballs. Throwing distances are appropriate for

Figure 13.3 Accuracy competition

the ages of the participants. All participants throw the same direction.

Two-Handed Throw With a Basketball

While sitting, the athlete uses both hands to throw a basketball from behind the head. This activity forces the thrower to lean back and pull the basketball vigorously over the head and helps the thrower to experience the stretch-pull action of the muscles of the chest and shoulders.

Figure 13.4 Two-handed throw with a basketball

Coaching Tips

- Reach back as far as possible behind your head with the basketball.
- Without overbalancing backward, let your elbows drop back as far as possible.
- Pull the ball forward and throw it as far as possible.
- Flex your arms at the elbows and lead the pulling action with your elbows.
- Extend the throwing action as far in front of your head as possible.

Two-Handed Basketball Throw From a Kneeling Position

This activity is similar to the previous drill except that the thrower is in a kneeling position. This drill simulates the pull of the javelin over the thrower's head.

Figure 13.5 Two-handed basketball throw from a kneeling position

Coaching Tips

- Tilt back to a position that you can comfortably control.
- Pull the ball forward as vigorously as possible.
- Contract your stomach muscles to help pull your chest forward.

Two-Handed Throw from a Standing Position

Each participant begins in a standing position with the feet together. The participant takes one stride (left foot forward for a right-handed thrower) and immediately performs a two-handed throw over the head. This practice simulates the thrower's forward body movement and the pull of the javelin over the head.

Figure 13.6 Two-handed throw from a standing position

Coaching Tips

- Step out into a wide throwing stance.
- When you throw, make sure that you move your body forward and past your front foot (left for right-handed throwers).
- Make the throwing action last for as long as possible. Pull from as far back as you can and drive the ball forward as far beyond the front foot as possible.

Running Two-Handed Throw

Add to the previous drill a short 2- to 3-stride run-up to simulate the approach of the javelin throw in the run-up. This practice is also similar to a soccer throw-in.

Coaching Tips

- The addition of the 2- to 3-stride run-up will let you lean back farther as you shift into the throwing stance.
- Step forward in the run-up quickly, then lean

Figure 13.7 Running two-handed throw

back a little more as you shift into the throwing stance.

Two-Legged Jump and Throw

This practice is quite difficult and demands good coordination and quick explosive muscle actions. It simulates the pull on the javelin and in doing so strengthens the abdominal muscles. Novices should begin with a small jump and a push-throw from above the head. The action then progressively builds so that each performer jumps higher and throws the ball from behind the head rather than pushing it from in front.

Figure 13.9 Lift, turn, and throw

formed slowly until the required actions are well learned. Thereafter, it can be made more vigorous and explosive.

Coaching Tips

- A right-handed thrower will turn the hips to the front by rotating the knees first in the same direction.
- Imagine a corkscrew action, with your knees turning to the front followed by your hips, chest, and arms.
- Practice the action slowly to begin with, and don't concern yourself with distance.
- As the action becomes more fluid, increase the distances.

Figure 13.8 Two-legged jump and throw

Coaching Tips

- First practice the action without the ball.
- Think of jumping and then contracting the abdominals to pull the shoulders forward.

Lift, Turn, and Throw

A lift, turn, and throw simulates the hip rotation that occurs in the javelin throw. This drill should be per-

Step 2: Three-Stride Throw With a Ball Using Javelin Technique

Technique

The thrower stands facing the direction of the throw with the feet together. The shoulders are turned 90 degrees, with the left shoulder toward the direction of the throw and the right shoulder back. The athlete extends the left arm in the direction of throw and the throwing arm to the rear. The ball (tennis ball or baseball) is gripped in the right hand with the palm uppermost.

The left foot steps one stride forward, and the shoulders remain rotated with the throwing arm fully extended to the rear. The right foot steps across and ahead of the left foot, and the body leans backward (the cross-step or impulse step). The throwing arm remains fully extended to the rear, palm uppermost. Next, the left foot steps forward into the throwing stance, with the heel placed down first. The thrower's body weight begins to shift forward.

To begin the throw, the hips and chest rotate toward the direction of the throw and, thrusting the chest forward, the athlete pulls the throwing arm forward with the hand passing above the shoulder. The throwing arm flexes, and the elbow leads the throwing hand in the throw. The left leg and left side of the body straighten, and the right side of the body moves forward and rotates around the left side. The athlete releases the ball above and in front of the head. After the ball is released, the right leg steps in front of the left to arrest further forward motion (Figure 13.10).

Drills

Reaching Back to Throw

Place several tennis balls or baseballs (4 to 5) on a box top to the rear of the thrower. The thrower stands in a wide stance (slightly wider than shoulder width). The thrower reaches back, grasps a ball, turns to the front, and completes a standing throw.

The balls must be placed far enough back to ensure that the thrower reaches well back with a straight arm, shifting the body weight well over the right foot and partially flexing the right leg.

As a variation, a partner offers balls individually

Figure 13.11 Reaching back to throw

on an open palm to the thrower. The thrower must be forced to reach well back to get each ball.

Coaching Tips

- Once you grasp the ball, turn your right knee (right-handed thrower) vigorously in the direction of the throw, forcing your hips toward the direction of the throw.
- Your hips will pull your chest around.
- Your chest will then pull your throwing arm; be sure that your arm flexes and your elbow leads your hand in the throwing action.
- Release the ball well ahead of you and above shoulder level.
- Concentrate on the action of each throw individually; don't rush.

Throwing at Targets

Suspend hoops from soccer goalposts or draw circular targets on a wall. Students throw tennis balls at the targets from various distances. All throwers throw the same direction, and each begins the throw with the body weight well to the rear and with the throwing arm extended. The targets force throwers to throw both forward and upward. You can award scores for accuracy.

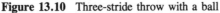

Figure 13.10 Three-stride throw with a ball

Figure 13.12 Throwing at targets

Coaching Tips

- Reach well back with an extended throwing arm, and make sure your weight is well over the rear leg.
- Move your weight forward and rotate your right knee (right-handed thrower) toward the direction of the throw.
- Finish the throw with your body extended upward, and step with your right foot 1 more pace ahead of the left foot. This action will make sure that your body moves forward into the throw.

Practicing the 3-Stride Throw

Participants practice the 3-stride throw using the technique explained previously (Figure 13.10). A right-handed thrower begins a 3-stride throw with the throwing arm fully extended and takes the 1st stride with the left foot. All actions are initially performed slowly and mechanically so that they are fully understood.

Coaching Tips

- Keep your throwing arm extended as you walk forward into the 3-stride throw.
- Tilt your body backward as your right leg steps forward in the cross-step (right-handed thrower).
- Step out into a wide throwing stance with the heel of your left foot.
- Initiate the throwing action from the ground up in the following sequence: right knee, followed by hips, then chest, and finally the throwing arm.
- Keep your body moving forward all the time.
- Release the ball well ahead of your body at an angle of 30 to 40 degrees above horizontal.

Increasing the 3-Stride Throw to a 5-Stride Throw

The performer adds 2 additional strides at the start of the 3-stride throwing sequence, making it a 5-stride throw. The thrower walks through the sequence with the throwing arm extended.

A right-handed thrower begins the 5-stride throw in the same manner as the 3-stride throw (i.e., taking the 1st stride with the left foot). The thrower keeps the throwing arm extended throughout the approach and turns the shoulders 90 degrees away from the direction of the throw until the actual throwing action occurs. A 5-stride throw is as follows:

Sequence: Left-right-left-right-left-throw

                 (cross-

                 step)

Stride: 1 - 2 - 3 - 4 - 5

    1   2   3   4   5

Figure 13.13 The 5-stride throw

The cross-step (impulse step) occurs on the penultimate stride, and the throw occurs after the last stride has been completed.

Coaching Tips

- Remember that this drill is similar to the 3-stride throw. The only difference is the addition of 2 strides in the approach.
- Be sure to keep the palm of the throwing hand uppermost and the throwing arm extended so that it is parallel to the line of throw.
- Turn your shoulders 90 degrees so that your right shoulder is directly to the rear, but walk through the approach with your hips facing the direction of throw.

Extending the Throwing Arm During the Approach

This drill teaches the thrower to extend the throwing arm during the approach. Participants repeatedly rotate their shoulders 90 degrees and extend their throwing arms as they jog. The ball is not thrown.

Coaching Tips

- Rotate your shoulders a full 90 degrees so that your left shoulder is forward and your right

Figure 13.14 Extending the throwing arm

shoulder is back. Then bring your shoulders square to the front, and repeat the complete action again.
- Extend your throwing arm each time so that it is parallel to the direction of throw and directly to the rear of your body.

A 3-Stride Walk and Throw With the Throwing Arm Extended on the First Stride

The thrower begins with the throwing arm flexed and the ball held at chest height in front of the body. On the 1st stride, the thrower rotates the shoulders 90 degrees from the direction of throw and extends the throwing arm. The remaining portion of the 3-stride throw is performed as before.

Coaching Tips

- Be sure to turn your shoulders a full 90 degrees, no less! Keep your hips facing the front until you complete the cross-step.
- Extend your left arm and point it toward the direction of the throw. This will keep your left shoulder in front and your right shoulder to the rear.

A 5-Stride Walk and Throw With the Throwing Arm Extended on the First Stride

The performer adds 2 strides to the 3-stride walk and throw, extending the throwing arm during the 1st stride, as before. The throwing arm stays extended until the throwing action itself is performed. Once the athlete extends the arm, he or she performs the remaining part of the 5-stride walk and throw as before. Stress the same coaching points as in the previous drill. Once the 5-stride walk and throw has been learned well, the speed of approach can increase from a walk to a jog.

Figure 13.15 Extending the throwing arm on the first stride of a 3-stride approach

Figure 13.16   Extending the throwing arm on a 5-stride walk and throw

Step 3: Standing Throw With the Javelin

Technique

The performer places the left foot forward in a wide throwing stance, keeping the throwing arm fully extended, palm uppermost, tip of javelin at eye level, and vision forward. The left shoulder and left arm are forward and the left arm points in the direction of the throw.

The right knee rotates in the direction of the throw, forcing the hips and chest in the same direction. The left arm swings to the left to help pull the chest forward. The athlete pulls the javelin over the shoulder. The throwing arm flexes at the elbow. The left leg and left side of the body extend upward.

The sequence of actions is fast and explosive. Beginners initially practice slowly, thereafter increasing the speed of movement.

After the javelin has left the hand, the forward movement of the body will cause the thrower to step forward with the right leg ahead of the left. This action is used to arrest further forward motion (Figure 13.17).

Drills
Learning to Grip the Javelin

Members of the group try 3 javelin grips, each of which is described here. Of all the methods of grasping the javelin, Grip A is most commonly used and is the one you will probably want to teach. Grip B is often called the Finnish grip and is moderately popular. Grip C is used least.

Figure 13.17   Standing javelin throw

GRIP A	**GRIP B**	**GRIP C**
Index-Finger Grip	**Second-Finger Grip**	**V Grip**
The index finger grips the javelin shaft to the rear of the binding. The thumb lies along the side of the binding. The javelin lies in the center of the palm of the hand and is gripped by the fingers of the hand.	The second finger grips the shaft of the javelin to the rear of the binding. The index finger is extended along the shaft of the javelin, and the thumb lies along the side of the binding. The javelin lies in palm of the hand and is gripped by the fingers of the hand.	The shaft of the javelin is gripped in the *V* formed by the index and 2nd fingers. This grip is immediately to the rear of the binding. The thumb lies along the side of the binding. The javelin lies in the palm of the hand and is gripped by the fingers of the hand.

- The index finger (for the index-finger grip) wraps to the rear of the binding, and the thumb lies along the side of the binding.
- The remaining fingers of the hand wrap around the binding.

Figure 13.18 Three methods of gripping the javelin

Securing the Grip on the Javelin

The participant sticks the javelin in the ground and slides the throwing hand down the javelin from the tail to the grip.

Coaching Tips

- Each javelin must lie along the ''lifeline'' in the palm of the hand.

Throwing the Javelin Forward Into the Ground

Once the athlete secures the grip, and beginning with a flexed throwing arm, the athlete slowly takes the javelin back to arm's length. The palm of the throwing hand is uppermost. Stepping forward with the left leg (right-handed throwers), each participant throws the javelin down into the ground 3 to 4 meters (10 to 13 feet) directly in front.

Figure 13.20 Throwing the javelin into the ground

Coaching Tips

- Keep the point of the javelin just below eye level and directed down at the ground.
- Pull on the javelin as though pulling a rope past your ear.
- Flex your throwing arm at the elbow as you pull the javelin forward.

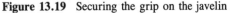

Figure 13.19 Securing the grip on the javelin

- Pull your throwing arm forward, keeping the elbow of the throwing arm close to the javelin and well ahead of the throwing hand.

Preparation for Standing Throws

Participants work in pairs without throwing or releasing the javelin. The partner stands to the rear of the thrower, holds the tail of the javelin, and provides gentle but mobile resistance. Beginning in a throwing stance with the javelin arm fully extended, the thrower practices rotating the right knee, hips, and chest "under" the javelin and toward the direction of the throw, producing the "bow" position that the body passes through during the throw. Led by the elbow of the throwing arm, the thrower pulls the javelin forward over the head. The partner holding the tip of the javelin moves forward, still providing gentle resistance. *Note*: The javelin is not released or thrown in this drill.

Figure 13.21   Partner practice

Coaching Tips

- Aim for smooth, nonjerky actions, beginning with the rotation of the right knee, hips, and chest under the javelin.
- Keep the elbow of your throwing arm close to the javelin throughout.
- Perform the action slowly and precisely at first.

The Standing Throw With the Javelin

The athlete throws the javelin from a wide stance with the throwing arm fully extended to the rear (Figure 13.17). Participants no longer throw down at the ground, but perform 8- to 10-meter (25- to 30-foot) throws.

Coaching Tips

- Begin the throw by rotating your hips and chest toward the direction of the throw. Remember to

initiate the hip rotation by the forward movement of the right knee.
- Keep the palm of your throwing hand uppermost.
- Pull the javelin forward, with your elbow leading the hand, and release the javelin above and in front of your head.

Step 4: Javelin Throw Using a Run-Up

Technique

The thrower faces the direction of the throw, holding the javelin in the carry position. The body is square to the direction of throw, the throwing arm is flexed at the elbow, and the palm of the throwing hand is uppermost.

The athlete steps forward with the left foot and begins to take the javelin back to arm's length. By the second step, the thrower has extended the javelin arm and rotated the shoulders 90 degrees from the direction of the throw. The hips are still square to the direction of throw. On the third step, taken with the left foot, some backward lean is apparent (5 to 10 degrees).

The cross-step and the fifth step occur in quick succession. The cross-step will put the thrower into a backward lean with the right knee slightly flexed and turned outward. The shoulders remain rotated 90 degrees with the left shoulder toward the direction of throw. With the fifth stride, the left leg steps out into a wide throwing stance with the heel of the left foot contacting the ground first. Once the athlete is in the throwing stance, he or she rotates the right knee vigorously to the front, pushing the hips and chest toward the direction of the throw. The body resembles a bow with the javelin being pulled whiplike over the shoulder. The body rises up, forward, and over an extended left leg. A sixth stride occurs when the athlete performs the reverse, bringing the right leg in front of the left in order to arrest any further movement forward (Figure 13.22).

Drills
Extension of the Javelin Arm

The athlete practices extending the javelin arm directly backward, initially at a walk, then at a jog, and then at sprinting speed.

Coaching Tips

- Hold the javelin just in front of your head and parallel to the direction you will be running.

Figure 13.22 Javelin throw using a 5-stride run-up

Figure 13.23 Extension of the javelin arm

- Keep your body square to the front, your shoulders relaxed.
- Rotate your shoulders and take the javelin back to arm's length.
- Keep the palm of the throwing hand uppermost.
- Look to the front and keep your hips square to the line of the run-up.
- Keep the tip of the javelin at eye level when you extend the throwing arm.

A 3-Stride Javelin Throw at Walking Speed—Throwing Arm Extended on the First Stride

The performer extends the javelin arm directly backward on the 1st stride of the approach, keeping the javelin parallel with the direction of the throw. As the right foot steps forward into the cross-step, the upper body tilts backward slightly. The left foot steps well out into the throwing stance.

Once the athlete is in the throwing stance, the right knee pushes the hips and chest toward the direction of the throw. This action must occur before the thrower pulls the javelin arm forward over the shoulder.

A 3-Stride Javelin Throw With the Throwing Arm Extended Throughout the Run-Up

When the approach speed approximates a fast run, the performer must try to shift both feet into the throwing stance as quickly as possible. This fast shift of the feet can be practiced using a 3-stride approach. With this approach, the performer should try to use a rhythm pattern in which both feet land in the throwing stance almost simultaneously. Immediately when the feet have landed, the thrower must concentrate on driving the hips and chest toward the direction of throw *before* pulling forward on the javelin with the arm.

Coaching Tips

- Listen to the sound of your feet landing, and try to make them land simultaneously in the throwing stance (1 footfall rather than 2).

Figure 13.24 Extending the arm on the first stride of a 3-stride javelin throw

- Drive your hips and chest into the throw as soon as your feet land.
- Keep your body moving forward.

A 5-Stride Javelin Throw With the Throwing Arm Extended Throughout the Approach

A 5-stride throw at walking speed will add 2 more strides to the start of the 3-stride throw. The athlete begins with the javelin arm extended. The sequence of actions is schematically laid out as follows, with the 6th stride occurring as the reverse.

Sequence:	Stride:
left	1
right	2
left	3
right (cross-step)	4
left (throwing stance)	5
throw	
right (reverse)	6

A 5-Stride Javelin Throw With the Throwing Arm Extended During the First 2 Strides

The thrower starts the approach with the javelin held in the carry position (Figure 13.22). The thrower then takes the javelin directly back to an extended arm position during the first and second strides of the approach, which is practiced at walking speed.

Coaching Tips

- Keep the javelin parallel to the direction of the throw as you extend your throwing arm.
- Keep the tip of the javelin just below eye level.
- Aim for a fast shift with both legs into the throwing stance.
- As soon as you place your left leg down in the throwing stance, "strike" forward with your right knee, then hips, and chest toward the direction of throw.
- Brace your left leg and the left side of your body.
- Make the right side of your body move forward, upward, and around the "post" formed by the left leg and the left side of the body.

Increasing the Approach to 9 to 11 Strides

Add additional strides to the approach. For beginners, a 9- to 11-stride approach is recommended. Elite athletes frequently use a 25- to 30-meter (80- to 100-foot) approach, in which 10 to 15 strides are devoted to a smooth acceleration into the throwing stance. Elite athletes also use one or two check marks, the most

Figure 13.25 Five-stride javelin throw

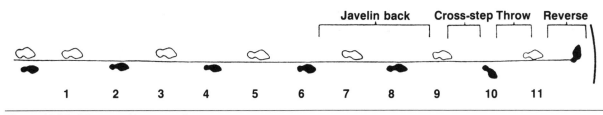

Figure 13.26 Eleven-stride approach

important of which is commonly placed at the 5th stride prior to throwing. Thus the most important phase of throwing is accurately positioned. The recommended teaching sequence for increasing the size of the run-up is as follows:

1. The athlete repeats the 5-stride throw, extending the javelin arm during the first and second strides. The athlete begins with a walking approach, counting out the strides, then attempts the same actions using a slow jog.
2. Add 4 strides for a 9-stride throw. The athlete begins with a walking approach, using a verbal count and check marks to indicate where to extend the javelin arm and where to enter the throwing stance.
3. Add 2 more strides for an 11-stride throw. The

athlete increases the speed of the approach and adjusts check marks accordingly. Using javelin-thrower's spikes will help the thrower obtain a good backward body lean without fear of slipping.

Coaching Tips

- Drive your right foot forward into the cross-step and tilt your body backward.
- With the heel of your left foot, step out long and low into the throwing stance.
- Drive your hips and chest ahead of the throwing arm.
- Think of your body as the handle of a whip and the javelin as the tip of the whip; strike forward with the handle and "crack" the whip.

COMMON ERRORS AND CORRECTIONS

3-AND 5-STRIDE THROW WITH A BALL

ERROR	REASONS	CORRECTIONS
The ball is not taken back to arm's length prior to the throw.	The athlete is overeager to throw, and the timing of the throw is incorrect.	The athlete practices standing throws and 3- and 5-stride throws at walking speed, emphasizing the full extension of the throwing arm.
There is no backward body lean prior to entering throwing stance. The thrower is upright throughout the throwing sequence.	The thrower is using only the arm during the throwing action and is too eager to throw.	The thrower practices the 3-stride throw, emphasizing backward lean as the right leg steps across for the cross-step.
During the crossover, the right foot steps to the rear of the left foot instead of in front of it.	The athlete is unfamiliar with the crossover action of the right leg in the cross-step.	Have the athlete slow down the action and practice a 1-stride throw beginning with the right leg forward and across the left. The athlete marks foot positions on the ground and walks through 3- and 5-stride throws.
The wrong leg is forward in the throwing stance.	The sequence of actions is too hurried. Stutter steps in the approach confuse the thrower.	The athlete practices standing throws with the correct foot placed forward, then progressively adds additional strides to the approach.

ERROR	REASONS	CORRECTIONS
The thrower falls toward the left during the throwing action (right-handed thrower).	The left side does not extend upward during the throw. The left leg collapses rather than extends, the hips move backward during the throw, and the head and left shoulder drop to the left during the throw.	The athlete practices standing throws, keeping the left foot forward and lifting the body forward, up, and over a braced left leg during the throw.
The ball is "put" in shot-put style rather than thrown like a javelin.	The thrower has poor timing and has difficulty coordinating the actions of the throwing arm.	Instruct the athlete to practice standing throws, moving the arm slowly through the throwing action. A partner guides the motion from the rear by controlling the movement of the thrower's hand and elbow. The elbow must lead the throwing hand in the throwing sequence.
The athlete throws the ball around the side of the body. The throwing hand passes below shoulder level.	Although this is a comfortable and adequate method for throwing a ball, it is not the correct way to throw the javelin, because the throwing arm is not pulled forward above the shoulder.	Correct as for the previous error. The thrower must apply javelin technique to ball-throwing action. The throwing hand must pass above the shoulder. The athlete practices the required action slowly with a partner guiding the motion of the throwing arm.
The athlete does not extend the throwing arm in a direct line to the rear, but rather swings the arm back around the body from right to left (for right-handed thrower).	The right leg does not step directly forward in the cross-step but out to the right side of the body. The shoulders rotate more than 90 degrees in relation to the direction of the throw.	The athlete practices reaching back and throwing a ball placed directly to the rear or held directly to the rear by a partner. The athlete walks slowly through a 3-stride throw, extending the throwing arm directly to the rear and parallel to the direction of throw.
The thrower rotates sideways during the approach, using a crablike approach.	The thrower overemphasizes the crossover action of the cross-step in the approach and is unsure of the required motions at each phase of the approach.	The athlete must rotate the shoulders so the right shoulder and throwing arm are directly to the rear and should keep the hips square to the direction of throw until entering the cross-step.
The athlete throws the ball from ahead of the body like a dart.	The sequence of throwing actions is slow and mechanical. The throwing action is unfamiliar.	The athlete practices the sequence of hip, chest, and arm action in a standing position as a partner guides the throwing arm through the correct path. The athlete then practices alone slowly, speeding up actions until they are fluid and coordinated.

STANDING THROW WITH THE JAVELIN

ERROR	REASONS	CORRECTIONS
The athlete holds the javelin in the center of the binding and uses a "fist grip" on the javelin, rotating the palm of the hand inward.	The athlete does not know the correct grip or hand position.	Have the athlete stick the javelin pointfirst in the ground and slide the hand down to gain the correct grip. The index or 2nd finger should be to the rear of the binding and the javelin should lie along the "lifeline" in the palm.
The point of the javelin is not in line with the direction of throw.	The hand does not grip the javelin forcibly enough, and the javelin is allowed to swing around. The hand may be turned inward, and the palm may not be upward. The shoulders are not rotated a full 90 degrees when the javelin arm is extended.	The athlete practices keeping the tip of the javelin at eye level and under the chin. The palm of the hand must be uppermost, with the fingers pointing to the rear. The shoulders must be turned so that the left shoulder is directly to the front. The athlete must grip the javelin in the whole of the hand, not just with the fingertips and thumb.
The athlete throws the javelin around the side of the body, and the tail of the javelin hits the thrower's back.	The athlete does not bring the throwing hand forward over the shoulder and past the ear. There is poor hip and chest rotation toward the direction of the throw.	Have the athlete practice slow-motion throwing action (without release) with a partner guiding the motion. The athlete should emphasize the correct arm action with hip and chest rotation leading the sequence of action.
The athlete uses an extreme angle of release. The javelin stalls in flight and hits the ground tail first.	The tip of the javelin is too high. The throwing hand rotates at the wrist and allows the tip of the javelin to lift. The throwing arm is angled down far too low. The tail of the javelin is dragging on the ground.	The athlete should practice a slow-motion throwing action with partner assistance. Have the athlete work on standing throws, keeping the tip of the javelin at eye level.
The athlete throws the javelin with the wrong leg forward.	The athlete is unsure of the correct throwing stance.	Instruct the athlete to practice a standing throw using a numbered sequence of actions: for example, 1—extend throwing arm, 2—step forward with the left foot, and 3—throw.
The body has no arch or bow position during the throwing action. The seat moves backward as the upper body and throwing arm move forward.	The hips and chest do not rotate and drive forward ahead of the arm during the throw. The throwing arm is used too soon.	The athlete should emphasize driving the hips and chest forward into the throw prior to the "strike" of the throwing arm. The athlete must keep body moving forward.

ERROR	REASONS	CORRECTIONS
The athlete throws the javelin with the weight over the rear foot. The javelin lands tail first.	Body weight does not shift forward during the throw. The athlete uses insufficient hip and chest rotation and drive toward the direction of throw.	The athlete should over emphasize the reverse (i.e., stepping forward with the right leg after throwing with the weight moving forward over the left). The athlete should empha- size shifting the body weight forward during the throwing action.
The athlete throws the javelin with a straight arm throughout the throwing action.	The throwing arm does not flex at the elbow, and the elbow does not lead the throwing hand as it pulls on the javelin.	Instruct a partner to practice with the thrower, the partner guiding the thrower's hand and arm through correct actions. They repeat this practice with the partner guiding the javelin.

JAVELIN THROW USING A 9- TO 11-STRIDE RUN-UP

ERROR	REASONS	CORRECTIONS
The run-up is not in line with the direction of the throw. A right-handed thrower "drifts" to the right side of the run-up or begins to shuffle sideways.	The athlete anticipates entry into the throwing stance. The hips turn to the side too early, so that the thrower approaches sideways in "crab" fashion.	The athlete practices rotating the shoulders and taking the throwing arm back while the hips remain square to the di- rection of the throw. Athletes' flexibility should allow them to rotate their shoulders to a 90° angle from their hips. Draw lines along the length of the run-up to help keep the ap- proach straight.
The athlete hits the ground with the tail of the javelin during the cross-step.	The angle of carry is incorrect, and the extension of the throwing arm is not flat enough. The palm of the javelin hand may not be uppermost. The athlete may be kicking the right leg upward during the cross-step.	Correct the athlete's angle of carry; the athlete must maintain this angle when the throwing arm is extended. The athlete should practice driving the right leg low and forward rather than upward in the cross-step.
The thrower falls to the left during the throw (right-handed thrower).	The thrower's head drops toward the left during the throw, and the left side of the body collapses toward the left during the throw.	Have the athlete practice 3- and 5-stride throws, keeping the left shoulder "high" and vision toward the direction of the throw. The athlete must brace the left side of the body and drive the right side of the body up and around the left.
The athlete places the right foot at right angles to the direction of throw in the cross-step (i.e., pointing directly to the right in the cross-step).	The athlete may be running up to throw with the body side- ways to the direction of the throw. The athlete rotates the hips too far (and too early) prior to assuming the throwing stance.	Instruct the athlete to practice 3- and 5-stride throws with the right foot crossed over and positioned with the toes pointing 30 to 40 degrees to the right of the direction of the throw.

202 Fundamentals of Track and Field

ERROR	REASONS	CORRECTIONS
The athlete performs a series of shuffle steps in the run-up. The right leg is placed to the rear of the left leg instead of in front.	The thrower is unsure of the correct leg actions prior to the entry into the throwing stance.	The athlete should practice 3- and 5-stride throws at walking speed with the javelin extended throughout, concentrating on the leg action and footwork.
There is no forward drive during the throwing action.	The athlete's head is dropped forward, and the stride with the left leg into the throwing stance may be too big. As the shoulders move forward, the seat moves backward.	The athlete must keep the vision toward the direction of the throw and correct the stride length of the left leg in the throwing stance. The athlete can also practice 3- and 5-stride throws with emphasis on stepping forward onto the right foot for the reverse after the throw.
The athlete runs up much too fast and is unable to assume a good throwing position.	The athlete feels that run-up speed is a dominant factor in the throw and has poor knowledge of the importance of body position in the throwing stance.	Have the athlete practice walking and jogging throws from 3 to 5 strides, emphasizing correct throwing position. A partner gives verbal count to provide a cadence for the approach. The athlete must slow down the approach and aim for body lean in the cross-step.
The athlete slows down too much during the run-up.	The athlete is unsure of the run-up and feels that it serves no real purpose. The athlete anticipates the throw and is unable to transfer the speed of the run-up into the throw.	Have the athlete practice acceleration into optimal throwing position after taking the throwing arm back. Speed of the run-up must complement the ability to enter the throwing position.

ASSESSMENT

1. Assess the following theoretical elements as taught during instructional sessions.

   a. Fundamental rules governing the javelin throw.
   b. Good safety habits for use in the javelin throw.
   c. Basic elements of javelin-throw technique.
   d. Basic elements of training for the javelin throw.

2. Assess the performance of technique during the following stages of skill development.

   a. A standing throw with a ball using javelin-throw technique.
   b. A throw with a ball initiated from a 3- and 5-stride approach and using javelin-throw technique.
   c. A standing throw with a javelin.
   d. A javelin throw initiated from a 3- and 5-stride approach.
   e. A javelin throw initiated from an extended 9- to 11-stride run-up.

Critical Features of Technique to Observe During Assessment

- Running up with the javelin (or substitute), withdrawing the throwing arm, and rotating the shoulders 90 degrees to the direction of the throw.
- Stepping across the body in the cross-step and tilting the upper body backward.
- Stepping out into a wide throwing stance.
- Rotating the right knee and hips toward the direction of the throw ahead of the chest and the throwing arm.
- Thrusting the hips and chest forward so the body resembles a bow.

- Driving the body forward and up over a straight supporting leg.
- Pulling the javelin directly toward the line of throw, leading with the elbow, and releasing the javelin above the shoulder.
- Bringing the rear foot forward for the reverse.

3. Hold graded competitions to help develop motivation and technique.

   a. The athlete throws a ball from a standing position using javelin-throw technique.
   b. The athlete throws a ball from 3- and 5-stride approaches using javelin-throw technique.
   c. The athlete throws a ball from a 9- to 11-stride run-up, using javelin-throw technique.
   d. Athletes compete for distance throwing a javelin from a standing position.
   e. Athletes compete for distance throwing a javelin from 3- and 5-stride run-ups.
   f. Athletes compete for distance throwing a javelin from an extended run-up. Use full competitive conditions.

SUGGESTED PERFORMANCE STANDARDS (METERS)

MALE

Age	Javelin weight (g)	600	800	600	800	600	800
		Satisfactory		Good		Excellent	
11-12		15	12	20	15	24	22
13-14		18	15	24	20	30	25
15-16		20	18	28	25	34	30
17-19		26	22	34	30	40	36

FEMALE

Age	Javelin weight (g)	400	600	400	600	400	600
		Satisfactory		Good		Excellent	
11-12		16	14	18	16	20	18
13-14		19	16	24	20	26	24
15-16		22	18	26	22	30	26
17-19		23	20	28	25	34	30

14

HAMMER

The hammer throw was first contested in the Olympic Games in 1900 and since then has become one of the traditional field events for males. At track meets it is frequently contested by females as well, and it is likely that the hammer throw will soon join shot put, discus, and javelin in the Olympics as a throwing event for women.

The hammer throw is considered one of the most technical and complex of throwing events and unique in that the athlete repeats similar movements more than once (i.e., through 3 or 4 turns). Used correctly, the turns successively increase the velocity of the hammer; however, if errors are committed, they are progressively magnified from 1 turn to the next.

Although athletes claim it to be one of the most satisfying of throwing events, hammer throwing suffers from being confined to relative obscurity on waste tracts of land. To a large degree, this "rejection" stems from the fact that the event can be dangerous and requires the most rigorous of safety precautions. In addition, the impact of the hammer with the ground is such that the area cannot safely be used for other activities (except throwing events).

In recent years Soviet athletes have revolutionized the technique of hammer throwing, changing the footwork and the plane that the hammer follows. For the beginner, however, the traditional technique is more than adequate. After gaining some experience, the athlete can attempt the more advanced technique.

You can teach the fundamentals of hammer throwing with a variety of training implements. Athletes can use 3-to 4-foot broom handles or wooden poles for simulating the extension of the hammer while concentrating on the footwork. A basketball or medicine ball in a net with a handle attachment is also an excellent training implement. Using this equipment, the athlete can safely practice preliminary swings, turns, and the delivery (release) of the hammer both indoors and outdoors.

SAFETY SUGGESTIONS

The hammer throw is a rotary event that exerts tremendous centrifugal force on the thrower. This force increases and must be counteracted at all times as the athlete accelerates the hammer. Because the athlete is accelerating the implement far longer than in other throwing events, minor errors committed early in the swings and turns become major errors later in the throw. Frequently beginners (and sometimes even elite throwers) lose control and release the hammer in the wrong direction. Because of these control problems, a safety cage surrounding the thrower is absolutely essential for the protection of those watching, coaching, and officiating. The cage should be built to the required standards and regularly inspected and repaired.

All hammers should be safely stored and carried in an orderly manner to the throwing areas. Don't allow young athletes to play with throwing implements or treat them casually while they are being transported.

Prior to each throwing session, closely examine each hammer, checking the hammer pivot (in the head of the hammer), the wire, and the handle; replace worn parts immediately. This inspection must also include training equipment that is substituted for the actual hammer.

It's best to practice this event in an area that is only used for throwing events. When hammers are thrown within a stadium infield, the damaged turf must be carefully trod back into position so the ground is level.

A multipurpose concrete pad can be laid in which the smaller hammer and shot circles are painted inside a larger discus circle. This allows throwers to practice in sequence from within the same protective cage.

The following safety suggestions are recommended for training sessions in which participants throw the hammer or substitutes for the hammer.

- You (or other qualified personnel) supervise all throwing sessions (training and competition).
- Allow no group throwing; athletes throw one at a time.
- Require those waiting their turn to stand well behind the hammer cage in line with the "low point" of the hammer's arc.
- Be sure participants carry hammers back to the throwing circles. Under no circumstances are hammers ever thrown back.
- You, along with the athlete, check the throwing area to make sure it is clear before any throw is attempted.
- Take particular care in wet conditions. Footing must be adequate for throwing.
- Be sure that substitute equipment used for training purposes is safe and designed to withstand repeated use.
- Require the thrower to use a glove protecting the inner hand. Make several gloves of different sizes (right- and left-handed) available for practice sessions.

TECHNIQUE

Modern hammer throwers use 2 or 3 preliminary swings and 3 or 4 turns to rotate across the hammer ring. If the athlete is able to apply continuous acceleration to the hammer and can fit 4 heel-toe rotations in the 2.13 meter (7 foot) ring then 4 turns can be used. The following description and illustrations show the main elements of a hammer throw using 3 turns.

Initial Stance

A right-handed thrower grips the hammer handle with the left hand and wraps the right hand over the top of the left hand. The thrower stands at the rear of the ring, back toward the direction of the throw and feet approximately shoulder-width apart.

Preliminary Swings

The athlete places the hammer on the ground to the right rear and rotates the shoulders to the right so that a straight line exists between the hammer head and the athlete's left shoulder. To begin the preliminary swings, a right-handed thrower pulls the hammer upward toward the left. When the hammer has rotated as far to the left as possible, the thrower drops his or her head under the arms and accelerates the hammer in its arc from left to right. The arc has a high point to the left rear of the thrower and a low point to the right front of the thrower. The high point is progressively raised to the final trajectory angle as the athlete rotates through each turn.

As the hammer rotates, the thrower counteracts the pull of the hammer by shifting the hips in the opposing direction. Each full rotation of the hammer around the body performed prior to the athlete's entering the turns is called a preliminary swing, or simply a swing.

The Turns

When the head of the hammer reaches its lowest point in the last preliminary swing, the thrower "fixes" the arms and hammer in front of the body and rotates into the first turn. The left foot is rotated 180 degrees on the heel toward the direction of throw, and the right foot rotates 180 degrees on the toe. The athlete rolls (or rocks) along the outer edge on the left foot at the midpoint of the turn and performs another 180 degrees of rotation on the ball of the left foot. The athlete then picks up the right foot, brings it fully around, and places it on the ground parallel to the left. This completes 1 turn.

Elite athletes will perform 3 or 4 turns, although beginners frequently compete in hammer competitions using only 1 or 2 turns.

For each turn, the athlete attempts to rotate the legs (and hips) as quickly as possible ahead of the torso (and hammer). With both feet on the ground, the athlete is able to accelerate the hammer. With each turn the high point of the hammer is raised toward its final angle of release.

As the hammer rotates faster, centrifugal force increases, which the athlete counteracts by flexing the legs and "sitting back" during each turn. In this way the athlete maintains balance and at the same time achieves maximum radius from the axis of rotation out to the hammer head.

The athlete keeps the right foot low to the ground rather than (incorrectly) "pumping" the leg up and "stamping" the foot down with each turn. The correct action gets the right foot around and down to the ground as fast as possible.

The Delivery (Release)

After placing the right foot down at the end of the third (or fourth) turn, the athlete pulls on the hammer in an upward spiral by lifting the chest and extending the legs and the back. The athlete's pull on the hammer occurs when the hammer is in front of the body and passing through the low point of its arc. When the hammer is released, the athlete is fully extended with the left shoulder toward the direction of throw.

The Reverse

After releasing the hammer, the thrower concentrates on staying in the ring and not fouling the throw. This can be done by rotating on the right foot and bringing the left foot around and back to the rear. This thrower may also flex both legs and lower the center of gravity back and away from the forward edge of the ring (Figure 14.1).

TEACHING STEPS

STEP 1. Lead-Ups
STEP 2. Hammer Swings
STEP 3. Hammer Turns
STEP 4. Combining Hammer Swings, Turns, and Delivery (Release)

Step 1: Lead-Ups

All two-handed slinging and swinging throws are good lead-up activities for the hammer. These simulate the

Swings

Turns

Delivery

Figure 14.1 Hammer throw technique

delivery (final throwing action and release) in the hammer throw.

Two-Handed Throws With the Medicine Ball

The athlete throws a medicine ball in two-handed fashion for height. This activity resembles the upward thrust of the hammer thrower's body during the delivery (release) of the hammer.

Figure 14.2 Two-handed medicine ball throw

Coaching Tips

- Extend your legs and lift up onto your toes.
- Throw your head back and lift your torso.
- Use both arms to throw the ball as high as possible.

Two-Handed Overhead Throw With a Medicine Ball

An overhead throw for distance emphasizes not only the upward thrust of the body but also the backward lean required in the delivery of the hammer. Participants can compete for distance and height in this activity.

Coaching Tips

- Use your legs and back as powerfully as possible to drive the ball backward and upward as far as possible.
- Lift up high onto your toes.

Two-Handed Overhead Throw With the Medicine Ball Against a Wall

Participants throw the medicine ball in overhead fashion against the wall and then quickly rotate to

Figure 14.3 Two-handed overhead throw

Figure 14.4 Two-handed overhead throw against a wall

catch it on the rebound. This activity combines an extension of the body with quick reactions and rotation of the body.

Coaching Tips

- As soon as you throw the ball backward against the wall, pivot on the balls of both feet for a 1/2 rotation to catch the ball again. This pivoting action is used both in the hammer turns and in the delivery of the hammer.

Two-Handed Slinging of a Medicine Ball Over the Shoulder

This lead-up drill emphasizes the upward rotary lift of the body during the delivery of the hammer. The legs and body extend upward and the extended arms sling the medicine ball over the shoulder. The two-handed slinging action simulates the two-handed motion used in the hammer throw. Participants can compete in this activity for distance.

Figure 14.5 Slinging a medicine ball over the shoulder

Coaching Tips

- Extend your legs and back simultaneously and pivot on the balls of your feet toward the direction of throw.
- Release the ball high over your left shoulder (right-handed thrower).

Step 2: Hammer Swings

Technique

The athlete grips the hammer handle with the left hand inside the right (right-handed thrower). The swings begin with the hammer laid back on the ground to the right rear. The athlete rotates the shoulders to the right and fully extends the left arm, forming a straight line with the hammer wire. The legs are flexed.

The athlete begins by pulling the hammer upward to the left so that the plane of the hammer has a high point to the left rear. When the hammer has rotated as far to the left as possible, the athlete rotates the shoulders quickly toward the right, shifts the body weight in the same direction, and pulls the hammer down to its low point on the right side. This completes 1 swing. The athlete repeats the sequence for

1 or 2 more swings, increasing the hammer's speed each time.

When the hammer passes in front of the right foot in the final swing, the athlete shifts the body weight above the left foot in preparation for entry into the turns (Figure 14.6).

Drills
Hammer Swings Using a Pole

Introduce the hammer swings with the use of a 3- to 4-foot broom handle or pole. The left hand grips the near end of the pole, and the right hand grips the pole just beyond the left. Both arms are extended.

Coaching Tips

- Make sure your arms are extended in front of your body.
- Flex your legs slightly and look forward.
- Swing the pole as far to the left as possible, and at the same time move your hips to the right.
- Swing the pole upward on your left side so that the arc of swing has a high point to the left rear and a low point to the right front of your body.
- When the pole is swung as far to the left as possible, drop your head underneath your arms and rotate your chest and shoulders to meet the pole on the right.

Hammer Swings Using a Basketball in a Net

A basketball or light medicine ball in a net with a string extension is an excellent substitute for the competitive hammer. Swings that are practiced with this equipment will be much faster than those performed with a pole. It is very important to establish the correct body positions first, using the slower actions of

Figure 14.6 Hammer swing technique

Figure 14.7 Hammer swings with a pole

Figure 14.8 Hammer swings with a ball in a net

the pole. Participants can then work on the swings using the following sequence: (a) with both hands gripping the net handle, (b) with the left hand only gripping the net handle.

Coaching Tips

- Stand in a shoulder-width stance.
- Place the ball (in the net) on the ground to the right rear.
- A straight line should extend from your left shoulder down the string extension to the ball itself.
- Drag the ball upward to the left by extending the legs and body and pulling with the shoulders. This initiates the first of the swings.
- As soon as you have swung the ball as far to the left as possible, duck your head under your hands and the string and turn to meet the ball again on the right side.
- Throughout the swings, think of the ball and net as an extension of your arms and shoulders.

- Avoid bending your arms when the ball is in front of your body.

Hammer Swings and Delivery (Release) Using a Basketball in a Net

The athlete adds a delivery (release) to 2 to 3 hammer swings using a basketball in a net.

Coaching Tips

- Perform 2 or 3 swings, setting the high point of the ball's arc over your left shoulder.
- Shift your hips to the right when the ball rotates to the left.
- Begin the final pull on the ball for the delivery 2 to 3 swings when the ball is at its low point in front of your body.
- Extend your legs and back vigorously and throw your head back.
- Pivot on the balls of your feet toward the direction

Figure 14.9 Hammer swings and delivery using a ball in a net

of throw, and release the ball over your left shoulder.

The Grip on the Hammer Handle

Throwers become accustomed to the grip on the hammer handle. A right-handed thrower (who will release the hammer over the left shoulder) wears a protective glove on the left hand. The left hand grips the hammer handle, and the right hand is wrapped over the left. The reverse arrangement occurs for left-handed throwers.

Figure 14.10 Gripping the hammer

Coaching Tips

- When you grip the hammer, avoid making a tight fist with your hands.
- Form a long "hook" with the fingers of both hands and use this hook to grip the handle of the hammer.

Hammer Swings and Delivery (Release) Using a Light Hammer

Throwers practice hammer swings and delivery using a hammer that is approximately 1/2 of the competitive weight for their age range; in most cases a 4-kilogram (8.8 pound) hammer is adequate. The hammer is placed on the ground to the right rear of the thrower, who tows it into the first swing in the same manner as with the ball in the net. The high point of the hammer's arc is to the left rear of the thrower, whose

Figure 14.11 Hammer swings and delivery using a light hammer

hips are shifted to the right to counterbalance the pull of the hammer. When the hammer is to the left, the athlete shifts the hips to the right, and vice versa. With each swing, the high point of the hammer is raised in preparation for the delivery.

The delivery is performed through an upward extension of the legs and back. The athlete pivots on the balls of the feet toward the direction of throw and releases the hammer over the left shoulder. Throwers practicing this drill can compete against each other for distance.

Coaching Tips

- Keep the high point of the arc to the left rear of your body.
- Fully extend your arms when the hammer is in front of you.
- Drive up with your legs and chest in the delivery.
- Keep your arms extended during the delivery.

Step 3: Hammer Turns

Technique

After completing 2 or 3 swings, the athlete enters the turns with the hammer "fixed" in front of the body, the arms extended, and vision toward the hammer. The athlete (right-handed thrower) begins the 1st turn with rotation on the heel of the left foot (180 degrees) and the ball of the right foot (180 degrees). The right knee is turned inward to the rear of the left knee during the rotation to the left.

The athlete rolls along the side of the left foot and then rotates 180 degrees on the toe of the left foot, simultaneously lifting the right foot off the ground and bringing it fully around so that the body rotates 360 degrees. As the athlete enters each of the turns, the hammer is raised on the left side and lowered on

the right. This establishes a high point and low point in the arc that the hammer follows and also sets the angle of trajectory for the hammer when it is released.

With each turn the athlete attempts to rotate the lower body ahead of the upper body. By doing this, the athlete "winds up the body" like a coil spring. Because the feet are on the ground ahead of the torso in each turn, the unwinding of the spring progressively accelerates the hammer (Figure 14.12).

Drills
Rotation With the Arms Extended

Participants rotate on the spot with the arms outstretched in front. No implement is used and no specific footwork is demanded.

Variation

The athlete performs the same action, gripping the end of the 3- to 4-foot pole.

Coaching Tips

- Squat down, look forward, and extend your arms, holding them out horizontally in front of your body.

Figure 14.13 Rotation on the spot with the arms extended

Turns

Figure 14.12 Hammer turn technique

- Don't worry about footwork; shuffle around in a circle, turning on the same spot.

Footwork for Hammer Turns

Throwers practice the footwork used in hammer turns. Figure 14.14 shows the footwork of 1 complete turn. Each performer concentrates on this footwork, holding the arms outstretched but using no implement.

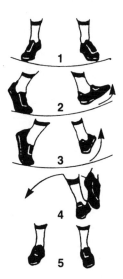

Figure 14.14 Footwork for hammer turns

Practicing a Sequence of Hammer Turns

Draw 2 parallel lines shoulder-width apart on the ground to assist the performer in the alignment of the feet during the turns. The athlete performs 1, 2, and then 3 turns in sequence.

Coaching Tips

- Squat down and look forward
- Pivot a full 180 degrees on the heel of your left foot and the toe of your right foot.
- Press the knee of the right leg in behind the left leg.
- Keep your legs close together.
- Pivot 180 degrees on the toe of the left foot, simultaneously picking up the right foot to rotate around and complete the turn.
- Don't swing your right leg out wide. Keep the legs close together.
- Make sure that your feet line up parallel at the end of each turn.
- Look forward throughout the whole action.

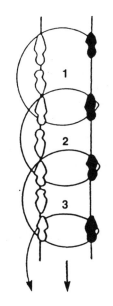

Figure 14.15 A sequence of hammer turns

Hammer Turns Using a 3- to 4-Foot Pole

Athletes perform the same action as in the previous drill, but using the 3- to 4-foot pole. Each performer squats down and holds the pole at arm's length and directly ahead of the body throughout each turn.

Coaching Tips

- Look forward and keep your arms fully extended.
- Don't raise or lower the pole during the turns.
- Concentrate on completing each 180-degree turn and ending up with both feet on the parallel lines.

Hammer Turns Using a Basketball in a Net

Each thrower uses a basketball in a net instead of the 3- to 4-foot pole. The performer passes the ball around the body to give it some initial rotary momentum, then enters the 1st turn holding the basketball in the net in extended position in front of the body. Providing that the 1st turn is completed correctly, the performer then moves immediately into the second turn.

Turns using a basketball in a net will be much faster than with a pole. If the athlete gets confused and performs the footwork incorrectly, the slower movements with the pole should be practiced again.

Coaching Tips

- Complete each turn so that your feet land on the parallel lines.

- Maintain a balanced squatting position throughout.
- Look forward.
- Concentrate on completing a full 180-degree rotation on the left heel, and then repeat it on the ball of the left foot.
- Keep your arms extended and the implement directly in front of your body.
- Make the first 180 degrees of the turn slow and precise, then finish the last 180 degrees of the turn quickly.
- Keep your knees close together during the turn.

Adding a High and Low Point to the Turns

In order to release a hammer at the correct angle of trajectory (called a high point), the performer must correctly angle the arc of the hammer during the turns. An elite athlete will progressively increase the angle through each turn. A right-handed thrower will lift the hammer high to the left rear and low to the right rear of the body. A novice can practice this action with the arms extended, holding a basketball or volleyball between the hands. An alternative is to use the 3- to 4-foot pole.

The athlete raises the ball or pole upward to a high point to the left rear during the first half of the turn, then lowers it to a low point to the right front during the second half of the turn.

Figure 14.16 High and low points of the hammer turns

Coaching Tips

- Keep your arms fully extended during the turns.
- Raise your arms for the high point as you complete the first 180-degree rotation on the heel of your left foot. Lower your arms for the low point when the final 180 degrees is completed.
- Keep your legs flexed and knees together during the turns, and squat down (as though sitting on a stool) and look forward to maintain balance.

Combinations of Swings and Turns

Put swings and turns together in various combinations to familiarize the athlete with the transition from swings to turns. This practice stresses the importance of the shift of body weight to the left for the entry into each turn and also the shift of the hips to counteract the pull of the hammer during the swings. Use a light hammer for this drill. Examples of combinations of swings and turns are (a) 2 swings followed by 1 turn; (b) 2 swings followed by 2 turns; (c) 2 swings, 1 turn, 2 swings; (d) 1 swing, 1 turn, 1 swing, 1 turn; and 2 swings, 2 turns, 2 swings, 2 turns.

Coaching Tips

- Establish a high point and a low point during the swings, and maintain these positions through the turns.
- Shift your weight over the left foot in the transition from swings to turns.
- Keep your knees close together in each turn.
- Keep your left foot in contact with the ground, and shift your right foot through the last half of each turn as fast as possible.
- Keep the implement "fixed" at arm's length in front of your body during the turns.
- Shift your hips away from the hammer in the swings, and squat down and lean away from the hammer in the turns.

Step 4: Combining Hammer Swings, Turns, and Delivery

The Complete Throw

The complete throw combines preliminary swings, followed by 1, 2, or 3 turns, and finally the delivery or release (Figure 14.1). Participants slowly practice this action using the 3- to 4-foot pole, then practice faster using a basketball in a net or a lightweight hammer. Thereafter, the athlete practices with progressively heavier hammers until working up to the competitive-weight hammer.

A typical practice sequence is as follows: (a) 2 or 3 swings, followed by 1 turn and the delivery; (b) 2 or 3 swings, followed by 2 turns and the delivery; and (c) 2 or 3 swings, followed by 3 turns and the delivery.

Coaching Tips

- Don't rush; perform the swings fairly slowly and increase speed in the turns and delivery action.
- Be sure to keep your arms extended and the hammer in front of your body.

- Try to bring your right leg around your body as fast as possible to complete each turn.
- Make sure your feet line up parallel to the direction of throw at the end of each turn.

Delivery and Reverse

The delivery (i.e., the actual release of the hammer) at the end of 3 turns demands extremely fast actions and precise timing. The rotation of the legs and hips in the third turn must occur at great speed so that both feet are on the ground well ahead of the upper body (and hammer). In this way, the athlete can exert tremendous pull on the hammer.

The pull on the hammer begins when the hammer head passes in front of the body. The athlete rotates on the balls of the feet toward the direction of throw, lifting the chest up and extending the legs and back. The action simulates an upward spiral. The athlete's body is fully extended when the hammer is released over the left shoulder.

The athlete avoids a foul throw by performing a reverse, withdrawing the left leg from the rim of the hammer circle and flexing or rotating on the right foot.

Figure 14.17 The delivery and reverse

Coaching Tips

- Begin the throw slowly and accelerate from swings to turns to the final release.
- Make the acceleration smooth throughout.
- Start with the plane of the hammer fairly flat, then successively raise the high point in each turn.
- Straighten your back and extend your legs as powerfully as possible in the delivery. Spiral upward toward the direction of throw.
- Throw your head back and deliver the hammer over your left shoulder.

Practicing the Reverse

The athlete practices the reverse (or recovery after releasing the hammer) at any time that the hammer is released.

Coaching Tips

- Complete the delivery, release the hammer, and then consciously pull your left foot back from the inside edge of the rim of the circle.
- Flex your right leg and lower your weight backward.

Alternative Technique for Performing the Reverse

In an alternate technique used to prevent fouling, the athlete continues to rotate on the balls of the feet after releasing the hammer and rotates back toward the center of the circle.

Coaching Tips

- After you release the hammer, rotate another 1/2 turn on the balls of the feet so that you face the direction of throw.
- Flex your legs simultaneously to lower your weight backward toward the center of the ring.

COMMON ERRORS
AND CORRECTIONS

HAMMER SWINGS

ERROR	REASONS	CORRECTIONS
The athlete bends the arms in the swings.	The thrower is fighting the hammer. The thrower fears loss of balance and uses no leg flexion. The athlete lowers the head and bends forward.	The thrower should allow the hammer to ''hang'' as an extension from the shoulders and should flex the legs and squat as though sitting on a stool. Instruct the athlete to practice one-handed, and two-handed swings, stretching the arms out in front of the body during the swings.
The athlete loses balance during swings.	The athlete uses no leg flexion and looks downward. There is no shift of the hips in opposition to the pull of the hammer. The arms may be flexed when the hammer is in front of the body.	Instruct the athlete to practice the swings slowly using a pole. The athlete should also practice ''sitting'' and shifting the body weight in opposition to the movement of the hammer. The faster the swings, the more emphatic the hip shift.
No high or low point occurs during the swings. Or, the low and high points are in the wrong position.	The athlete does not take the hammer to the left as far as possible during the swings. The arc of the hammer is not elevated to the left side of the body.	Have the athlete practice establishing the correct plane of the hammer using a pole and then a basketball in a net or a lightweight hammer. The athlete should sweep the implement upward to the left with each swing.
The athlete swings the arms and hammer like a windmill or propeller in front of the body. The hammer does not rotate to the rear of the thrower during the swings.	The thrower stands too erect and is afraid of swinging the hammer to the rear of the body and losing balance. The arms are flexed, and the hammer is not swept far enough to the left and rear during each swing.	The athlete should squat down, look forward, and sweep or ''tow'' the hammer upward to the left. The athlete must also shift the hips to the right and rotate the shoulders to the right as the hammer moves from left rear to right rear. The athlete should work to flatten the plane followed by the hammer (still keeping the high point on the left side of the body).

HAMMER SWINGS AND TURNS

ERROR	REASONS	CORRECTIONS
The thrower lands heavily on the right foot at the end of each turn.	The athlete's body tilts toward the right. The body weight is not shifted over the left foot during the transition from swing to turn.	The athlete must consciously shift the body weight to the left and over the left foot when entering the turns. The athlete should practice the turns without the hammer and then with a pole. The right leg action must be fast with both knees tight together during the turns. The athlete must avoid falling to the right as the right foot is placed on the ground at the end of each turn.
The thrower loses balance, particularly during the second and third turns.	The thrower does not counteract the increasing pull of the hammer by leaning away from the hammer. The legs are not flexed, and the arms may be flexed or the vision directed downward.	Instruct the athlete to practice the turns, progressively increasing speed. The athlete must "hang" on the hammer with "long arms," flex the legs, squat, and shift the hips away from the hammer to maintain balance as the rotational speed increases.
The hammer and thrower appear to rotate as a block. The legs do not shift ahead under the upper body during each turn.	The movement of the hips below the torso is slow. The knees are not pressed together during the turns, and the non-supporting leg is allowed to swing outward during the turns.	The athlete must rotate the right leg around in each turn as fast as possible. Have the athlete practice rotating the legs and hips ahead of the torso without the hammer. Then the athlete can use the hammer substitutes and finally the hammer.
The thrower is unable to make the transition from swings to turns. The thrower attempts to perform a swing while entering the first turn.	The thrower does not hold or "fix" the hammer at arm's length in front of the body when entering the turns.	Instruct the athletes to practice swings plus 1 turn using a pole. At the end of the second swing, the athlete holds the pole at arm's length in front of body and performs a turn. The athlete can work with a basketball in a net or with a lightweight short-wire hammer.
The thrower rotates on the spot or travels sideways during the turns. There is no movement across the ring in the direction of the throw.	The heel-toe pivot is poorly performed. The thrower may be pivoting continuously on the toe of the left foot.	Have the athlete practice the turns without the hammer, accentuating heel–toe action with each turn. The athlete should pivot on the heel of the left foot 180 degrees and then rock over the side of the foot to the ball of the foot to repeat the next 180 degrees. Use parallel lines to help establish correct footwork.

ERROR	REASONS	CORRECTIONS
The plane of the hammer is incorrect—either too flat or too high. The hammer hits the ground.	The upper body is tight, not relaxed. The angle of the arms at the shoulders is varied and not held constant.	Have the athlete practice turns slowly using a 4-foot pole to establish the correct angle of the arms. The athlete should progressively raise the hammer's plane in each turn to the correct angle for the delivery of the hammer.

HAMMER DELIVERY FOLLOWING 3 OR 4 TURNS

ERROR	REASONS	CORRECTIONS
The athlete flexes the arms during the delivery.	The athlete feels that by flexing the arms, he or she will direct more pull to the hammer. The legs are extended too early.	The pull on the hammer comes from a powerful extension of the legs and back. The athlete must think of ''long'' arms and ''loose,'' relaxed shoulders and must maintain flexion in the legs during the turn. The athlete should practice the correct action slowly using a pole.
The athlete loses balance and falls over during the delivery.	The athlete does not shift the body weight over the left foot during delivery. The pull during the delivery is not directed down the length of the hammer wire to the head of the hammer. The timing of the pull is incorrect.	The athlete should shift the body weight over the left foot during the delivery. The pull on the hammer occurs when the hammer head passes in front of the body. The athlete then extends the legs and back and rotates toward the direction of throw. The athlete should practice the timing using hammer substitutes.
The athlete does not generate any power in the delivery.	The legs and back are already extended prior to the delivery. The plane of the hammer may be too flat immediately prior to the delivery. The timing of pull on the hammer in the delivery is incorrect.	Have the athlete practice the swings and delivery action with no turns and without the implement. The athlete must raise the high point progressively through the turns and emphasize throwing the head back and extending the legs and back in the delivery. The upward thrust of the body should pull directly along the wire of the hammer, not at an angle.
The hammer head hits the ground during the delivery.	The upper body drops forward during the final turn and during the delivery. The high point of the hammer is too high in the last turn, or the high and low points are in the wrong positions.	The athlete should work on the correct action using a pole. The athlete lowers the high point a little but maintains the high point over the left shoulder. The athlete must flex the legs and keep the upper body perpendicular.

ERROR	REASONS	CORRECTIONS
The thrower is "thrown" or pulled out of the ring during the delivery.	The thrower initiates the delivery with far too much backward upper body lean. The timing of the extension of the legs and the position of the hammer head during the pull of the delivery are incorrect.	Have the athlete practice swings and delivery using 1 turn. The athlete pulls on the hammer by extending the legs when the hammer passes in front of the right foot. The athlete then extends the body in an upward spiral and performs the reverse immediately after the hammer is released.
The hammer flies out of the sector boundary (right-handed thrower).	The movement of the right foot into position for the delivery is too slow.	Have the athlete speed up rotation of the right leg and placement of the right foot, keeping the knees close together in the turns. Using a pole, the athlete can practice rotating the hips and legs around and ahead of the shoulders and hammer.

ASSESSMENT

1. Assess the following theoretical elements as taught during instructional sessions.

    a. Fundamental rules governing hammer throw.
    b. Good safety habits for hammer throw.
    c. Basic elements of hammer-throw technique.
    d. Basic elements of training for the hammer throw.

2. Assess the performance of technique during the following stages of skill development.

    For all the following, use either a substitute for the hammer or a lightweight hammer.

    a. Hammer swings.
    b. Hammer swings and delivery.
    c. Hammer turns performed along two parallel lines.
    d. Combinations of swings and turns performed along 2 parallel lines. Examples are 1 swing, 1 turn, 1 swing, 1 turn; 1 swing, 2 turns; or 2 swings, 2 turns, 2 swings, 2 turns.
    e. Hammer swings (2 or 3) and delivery (release).
    f. Hammer swings (2 or 3), turns (1, 2, or 3), and delivery (release).

Critical Features to Observe During Assessment

- Gripping the hammer handle correctly.
- Extending the arms in front of the body and achieving a high point to the left rear (right-handed thrower) during preliminary swings.
- Dropping the head and shoulders under the hammer and shifting the hips in the opposing direction to the hammer during the preliminary swings.
- Holding the hammer with extended arms in front of the body for each of the hammer swings.
- Performing the 180-degree rotations on the heel and toe during the hammer swings.
- Lowering the center of gravity by sitting as though on a stool during the entry to each of the turns.
- Raising the hammer to achieve a high point to the left in each of the turns.
- Counteracting the pull of the hammer in each turn by shifting the body weight in the opposing direction.
- Pulling the legs in close together for each of the turns.
- Performing an upward spiraling extension of the body in the delivery (release) of the hammer.
- Rotating on the toes and shifting the body weight back into the ring for the reverse after releasing the hammer.

3. Hold graded competitions to help develop motivation and technique.

   a. Throwers compete for distance using 2 or 3 swings and delivery (release).

   b. Throwers compete for distance using 2 or 3 swings; 1, 2, 3, or 4 turns; and delivery (release). You specify the number of turns.

SUGGESTED PERFORMANCE STANDARDS (METERS)

MALE

Age	Hammer weight (kg)	Satisfactory	Good	Excellent
13-14	4.0	15	20	25
15-16	4.0	20	25	30
	5.4	15	20	25
17-19	5.4	25	30	35

FEMALE

Age	Hammer weight (kg)	Satisfactory	Good	Excellent
15-16	3.0	20	25	30
17-19	4.0	25	30	35

SUGGESTED READINGS

Anderson, R. (1980). *Stretching*. Bolinas, CA: Shelter.

Baert, J-P. (1980). *The throws* (Canadian Track and Field Association, Level II Theory and Training). Vanier, ON: Canadian Track and Field Association.

Ballesteros, J.M., & Alvarez, J. (1979). *Track and field: A basic coaching manual*. London: International Amateur Athletic Federation.

Bauersfeld, K-H., & Schmolinsky, G. (1983). *Track and field: Textbook for coaches and sport teachers* (I. Mode, Trans.). East Berlin: Sportverlag.

Bompa, T.O. (1983). *Theory and methodology of training: The key to athletic training*. Dubuque, IA: W.C. Brown.

Bowerman, W.J., & Freeman, W.H. (1990). *Training for track and field*. Champaign, IL: Leisure Press.

Canadian Track and Field Association. (1975). *Elementary coaching manual* (Canadian Track and Field Association, Level I Theory and Training). Vanier, ON: Author.

Chu, D.A., & Signier, R. (1986). *Plyometrics for fitness and peak performance*. New York: Doubleday.

Costello, F. (1984). *Bounding to the top*. Los Altos, CA: TAFNews.

Dick, F.W. (1980). *Sports training principles*. London: Lepus.

Doherty, K. (1985). *Track and field omnibook* (4th ed.). Los Altos, CA: TAFNews.

Drowatzky, J.N. (1984). *Legal issues in sport and physical education management*. Champaign, IL: Stipes.

Fleck, S.J., & Kraemer, W.J. (1987). *Designing resistance training programs*. Champaign, IL: Human Kinetics.

Freeman, W.H. (1989). *Peak when it counts: Periodization for American track and field*. Los Altos, CA: TAFNews.

Gambetta, V. (1989). *TAC/USA track and field coaching manual* (2nd ed.). Champaign, IL: Leisure Press.

Gambetta, V. (1987, Fall). Principles of plyometric training. *Track Technique*, pp. 3099-3102.

Harre, D. (Ed.) (1982). *Principles of sports training* (English language edition). East Berlin: Sportverlag.

British Amateur Athletic Board. (1989). *How to teach the jumps-throws-track events*. Surrey, England: Author/Amateur Athletic Association.

International Amateur Athletic Federation. (1989). *I.A.A.F. official handbook*. London: Author.

International Amateur Athletic Federation. (1989). *I.A.A.F. scoring tables for men's track and field events*. London: Author.

International Amateur Athletic Federation. (1989). *I.A.A.F. scoring tables for women's track and field events*. London: Author.

International Amateur Athletic Federation. (1989). *Designs for 400 meter track and field terrain (4 designs)*. London: Author.

International Amateur Athletic Federation. (1989). *Track and field athletics—A basic coaching manual (development program book No. 1)*. London: Author.

International Amateur Athletic Federation. (1989). *Athletics officiating—A practical guide (development program book No. 2)*. London: Author.

Jacoby, E. (1983). *Applied techniques in track and field*. Champaign, IL: Leisure Press.

Mach, G. (1980). *Sprints and hurdles* (Canadian Track and Field Association, Level II Theory and Training). Vanier, ON: Canadian Track and Field Association.

Nygaard, G., & Boone, T. (1985). *Coaches guide to sport law*. Champaign, IL: Human Kinetics.

Pearl, W., & Moran, G.T. (1986). *Getting stronger*. Bolinas, CA: Shelter.

Powell, J. (1987). *Track and field—Fundamentals for teacher and coach* (4th ed.). Champaign, IL: Stipes.

Radcliffe, J.C., & Farentinos, R.C. (1985). *Plyometrics: Explosive power training* (2nd ed.). Champaign, IL: Human Kinetics.

Reid, P. (1982). *The jumps* (Canadian Track and Field Association, Level II Theory and Training). Vanier, ON: Canadian Track and Field Association.

Rosen, M., & Rosen, K. (1988). *Track: Championship running*. New York: Sports Illustrated.

Walker, L.T. (1984). *Track and field: A guide for the serious coach and athlete.* Chicago: Athletic Institute.

Walker, L.T. (1989). *Track and field: For men and women.* Chicago: Athletic Institute.